Organized
Crime
& Democratic
Governability

Pitt Latin American Series

Billie R. DeWalt, General Editor

Organized Crime

& Democratic

Governability

Mexico and the U.S.–
Mexican Borderlands

Edited by John Bailey
and Roy Godson

University of Pittsburgh Press

The chapter by Stanley A. Pimental was first published in *Trends in Organized Crime*, Volume 4, Number 3, Spring 1999. Copyright © National Strategy Information Center, 1999.

10 9 8 7 6 5 4 3 2 1

Library of Congress Cataloging–in–Publication Data

Organized crime and democratic governability : Mexico and the U.S.-Mexican borderlands / edited by John Bailey and Roy Godson.
    p. cm. — (Pitt Latin American series)
    Includes bibliographical references and index.
    ISBN 0-8229-4146-5 (cloth) — ISBN 0-8229-5758-2 (paper)
    1. Organized crime—Mexico.   2. Organized crime—Political aspects—Mexico.
3. Organized crime—Mexican-American Border Region.   4. Mexico—Politics and
government—1988–   I. Bailey, John J.   II. Godson, Roy, 1942–   III. Series.
HV6812 .O74 2000
364.1'06'0972—dc21

                                           00-011649

Contents

v

List of Tables and Illustrations

Acknowledgments

The editors thank the William and Flora Hewlett Foundation for the generous financial support that made this book possible. Phil Williams of the University of Pittsburgh provided a useful overall critique of the book. Adriana Perez Mina, administrator of the Mexico Project at Georgetown, played a major role from start to finish. She tended to the planning and logistics for our authors' meeting and handled the communications among the editors and authors. She did a marvelous job in managing the flows of drafts, translations, corrections, and detail checking that went into the preparation of the final manuscript. Jeffrey Berman of the National Strategy Information Center also provided helpful support. Maria Granados, Lisa J. Kuhn, Nike Papadopoulos, Ann Pennell, Janette Stevens, and Jeffrey Villaveces contributed useful research assistance.

We also thank Agustin Gutierrez Canet, Susana Chacon, and Ricardo Macuzet of the Universidad Iberoamericana for hosting our authors' meeting in Mexico City. We note in passing that on the day of our meeting, July 7, 1997, an armed robbery occurred at the university's bank. Whatever doubts we might have harbored about the relevance and timeliness of our study were quickly dispelled.

Organized

Crime

& Democratic

Governability

Chapter 1

Introduction

John Bailey and Roy Godson

MEXICO'S GOVERNABILITY has been put to the test at several junctures since the mid-1980s.[1] But for the first time in many decades, there is growing concern about instability in the U.S.-Mexican borderlands. Not since the Mexican Revolution in the early 1900s and potential German threats to the underbelly of the United States in World War I has this sort of attention been focused on the region by observers on both sides of the border and in their respective capital cities. The reasons behind this interest in the region are largely economic and financial. They include the upsurge of bilateral trade spurred in part by the implementation of the North American Free Trade Agreement (NAFTA) in 1994; Mexico's financial crisis of 1994–1995; and rapid industrialization along the Mexican side of the border which in turn has fed increasing rates of mass migration and cross-border travel. But much of the interest stems as well from increased crime and corruption, which have spawned threats to governability in Mexico and in parts of the border region. Residents, tourists, businesspeople, and others with a direct personal interest in Mexico and the borderlands are concerned about this problem. But in addition, politicians, journalists, and academic specialists in Mexico City and Washington, D.C., as well as in other capitals, have become increasingly concerned about Mexico's complex transition and its implications for one of the busiest and more dangerous border zones in the world.[2]

Until recently, crime and corruption in Mexico and the borderlands were viewed as local law enforcement problems. That is to say, local criminals were blamed for corrupting certain local officials: police, customs, and immigration control officers on both sides of the border. Corruption among local officials was considered inimical to good governance, but it was not viewed by national political and economic leaders or by specialists in U.S.-Mexican relations as a major problem or as a threat to governability on either side of the border.

This limited perception changed gradually, however, beginning in the late 1980s and increasing in the 1990s. What started out as a law enforcement concern with drug trafficking in the mid-1980s has now come to be viewed as a growing threat to national security and governability on both sides of the border. This concern has become most pronounced in the high governmental circles of Washington and Mexico City. Over time successive presidents of both countries have come to recognize that, while drug trafficking is the major illegal activity, the range of criminal activities now extends well beyond drugs to include trafficking in arms, people, vehicles, financial instruments, environmentally dangerous substances, endangered species, and archeological objects, among others.

Moreover, criminal activities have become so large scale, widespread, and lucrative that the relevant officials from both capitals meet regularly to consider criminal threats to the economic, political, and social health of not only the residents of the border region, but to their countries as a whole.[3] In addition to regular bilateral heads-of-state and ministerial-level meetings, the United States and Mexico in 1996 created a high-level "Contact Group" to deal with the threat from organized crime to law enforcement and democratic governability. Key officials from the relevant agencies involved with intelligence, military, law enforcement, and financial matters meet in closed-door sessions to discuss strategic and tactical responses to criminality. Apart from these high-level discussions, we are seeing the proliferation of joint U.S.-Mexican programs to promote military, intelligence, and law enforcement cooperation.

Although few outside government are privy to the specifics of these programs, we can glean impressions from the public record as well as from extensive media reporting on aspects of this cooperation. On occasion, former government officials and academic specialists on both sides of the border have written or spoken about the growing threat of organized crime to governability and what they know of the responses of their respective governments. As a result, we can discern several perspectives or schools of thought about Mexico, the United States, and the borderlands. It is useful to summarize these views here to provide some preliminary interpretive guideposts. We elaborate them later in the introduction.

Crime and Governability: First Impressions

It is becoming increasingly difficult to find informed observers who view the past years through traditional lenses and perceive recent developments as merely an expanded challenge to local law enforcement. Such "traditionalists" would believe that by beefing up a police response internally in Mexico and by "hardening" the border, the problem can be mitigated if not eliminated. From this perspective crime is an aberration, which implies negligible systemic effect; thus the topic deserves little research or systematic multidisciplinary study.

The more mainstream interpretations now view the growth of crime and corruption in Mexico and the border region as part of a much larger and deeper set of problems that requires much more detailed study and attention. Proponents of this view see important systemic effects of criminal-political alliances on the broader political system and the bilateral relationship. By political-criminal alliances we refer to ongoing, complex networks of cooperation and exchange between criminal groups and political authorities—both elected and appointed—at different levels of government. Further, those who perceive ongoing criminal-political alliances see the problem set as rooted in deep-seated economic forces, institutional arrangements, and political culture that will require far more than improved law enforcement to effect any real change in the situation.[4]

Among those who believe the problems are deep rooted, we can identify two schools of thought. What we will call a "centralized-systemic" school sees a coherent, centrally guided system that links Mexico's political system with organized crime. In this view, political leaders control the webs of alliances from the top down. In contrast, a "fragmented-contested" school sees a much more fluid, complex set of relationships between the political system and organized crime. In this view, criminal-political alliances are dynamic and constantly changing, depending on a variety of circumstances. Control of the alliances by government officials is not a given; rather, criminals can take the initiative and assume control as well.

Among those who accept the centralized-systemic view, some perceive ultimate power to be in the hands of top formal authorities in the central government, while others see power shared between formal authorities and a parallel "shadow government." Proponents of the model of formal, top-down control emphasize that the complex party-government arrangements that became consolidated in Mexico in the 1930s and 1940s permit effective central control over virtually all significant legal and nonlegal activity. Stated simply, the perception is that the chain of control over crime and corruption runs from the president through the relevant security ministries downward through state governors' offices and justice ministries to connect with intermediaries of professional criminal leaders outside of government. Criminal organizations take their direction from political authorities. To win formal office is to assume the right to organize and benefit from business activity, both legal and illegal.[5]

A variation on the centralized-systemic perspective posits a shadow parallel system of government just below the surface, integrated into and run by most of the same people as the visible system. While the formally elected president retains ultimate control, the shadow actors exercise substantial power. This shadow parallel system, made up of a network of patron-client relationships, is symbiotically connected to the formal legal system. It controls many of the organized activities not formally tied to direct government control, including organized criminal activities throughout Mexico and in the borderlands.[6]

Proponents of the centralized-systemic perspective argue that high political leaders, even up to the level of the president, direct the legal, above-ground government as well as the shadow government that controls most organized criminal activities. The political leadership protects these organizations from both Mexican and foreign law enforcement organizations. These top Mexican leaders manage criminal activity in such a way as to reduce friction and instability among the criminals and between criminals and the Mexican and U.S. governments. They do this to ensure their personal wealth and the hegemony of the Institutional Revolutionary Party (PRI), as well as to ensure the relatively smooth functioning of the Mexican governmental system, even if from time to time officials are elected or appointed from non-PRI parties.

In contrast to the centralized-systemic view, others see multiple fragmented-contested political-criminal subsystems that threaten security and governability. Functional coalitions of actors from the political and criminal worlds are assembled at different levels and on a more or less ad hoc basis. Certain types of criminal activities can operate at a subnational level. This involves local and/or state judicial authorities in Mexico and on the U.S. side of the border region. Such activities include kidnapping, auto theft in the United States or Mexico with transportation across Mexico's northern or southern borders, and the smuggling of Mexicans (and also third-country migrants) across the U.S. border. Even in cases of local drug production (e.g., of locally or regionally produced synthetic drugs) a coalition could be assembled with the collaboration of police and customs officials at the state and local levels, operating independently from national political control. But as a general rule, the larger the scale and operation of illegal activity (e.g., smuggling cocaine), the more borders that will need to be crossed (as in Asian illegal migration through Mexico to the United States). And the more sensitive the commodity (e.g., arms smuggling to Mexico), the more complex, widespread, and higher the level of national involvement is likely to be.[7]

In this fragmented-contested image, there is no "Mister Big" or "Boss of Bosses" in either the political or the criminal world. Rather, political and governmental leaders at various levels—usually elected or appointed by the PRI—have benefited from and supported criminal organizations. Further, the power does not always flow from the top down or even from the political to the criminal networks. Power and influence have flowed in different directions, depending on particular circumstances and issues. At times, criminals threaten or coerce political authorities. At other times, political authorities extort and coerce criminals. Situational, fluid, ad hoc arrangements are more typical than top-down control.

This fragmented-contested image is consistent with imperfect control by central bureaucratic authorities over field operations. The image is also consistent with variable linkages between elected political authorities and organized crime. A national-level minister or a state governor personally may or may not be directly linked and benefit materially from police or judicial corruption. He may, however, benefit politically from local police involvement with and control of criminals, who may contribute financial support and stability in a given locale.

Whether the centralized-systemic or the fragmented-contested pattern of political-criminal collaboration offers the more accurate model of reality in the 1990s and continuing into the new millennium, it offers little reason for optimism that law enforcement alone is the principal route to reform. Increased Mexican-

U.S. military, intelligence, and law enforcement cooperation may produce some apparently positive results, but often these results are intended to deceive Mexicans and Americans who do not grasp the fundamental realities. Major reforms should be targeted at the police and judicial system, to be sure, but these will prove more effective and long lasting if introduced in the context of the broader modernization of the economic and political systems. Such changes in the broader context would include an extensive reform of the Mexican state, including the introduction of career civil service along with professional ethics into law enforcement and judicial procedures; and programs of civic education to promote a culture of legality.

It is unlikely that the transition to such reforms will be a peaceful one. This long, difficult, and costly reform agenda may initially produce greater violence as the stability of the old authoritarian order gives way to new institutions and values. In the long run, however, only systemic changes of these dimensions can ameliorate the effects of the criminal-political alliances. Also, a substantial reduction in the demand for illegal drugs in the United States would go a long way toward improving public security in both countries.

This book is an expansion of a previous study on the redefinition of national security in Mexico and the United States in the post–Cold War period. One of the conclusions from that book was that crime constituted a serious challenge to security and democratic governability.[8] Our present purpose is to bring together scholars and specialists, including current and former government officials, from both sides of the border to determine which if any of the models summarized here most approximates reality. This chapter defines terms, places the topic in a context of the dual political and economic transition in Mexico, and summarizes the contributors' main arguments with respect to the different images.

Organized Crime and Democratic Governability

The focus here is on the relationship between organized crime and democratic governability in Mexico and the U.S.-Mexican borderlands. Organized crime refers to primarily professional criminals with the following characteristics:[9]

1. They operate over a period of time. They are not individuals who come together for one or two "jobs" and then disband.

2. They have an identifiable structure and leadership which may vary, but there is a hierarchy and division of labor among the criminals. The hierarchies may be centralized with a pyramidal structure, resembling complex private- or public-sector organizations, or the groups may operate in loosely connected networks. At other times groups may operate more or less on their own and establish cooperative relationships or "nonaggression" pacts with other groups.

3. Their primary purposes are profit from illegal activities. These are activities that for the most part would be considered illegal in both the United States and Mexico.

4. They use violence and corruption to protect themselves from state authorities and potential rivals, and to discipline their own comrades as well as those whom they seek to exploit.

This broad definition might encompass a wide array of groups and activities, ranging for example from street gangs of varying size and degrees of aggressiveness to bands of cargo hijackers that operate in larger Mexican cities and principal highways to gangs that concentrate on car theft and smuggling. Implicit in our approach is a focus on the larger-scale types of organizations, especially the better organized groups engaged in drug production and trafficking, whose operations affect more than the immediate locales where they operate. Some of the more important of these organizations fit the notion of *transnational organized crime* in that they operate across national boundaries, affecting both state and private actors. Their activities also usually include money laundering and other financial crimes such as tax evasion and fraud.[10] We are concerned primarily with Mexican-based criminal organizations affecting governability in Mexico or in the United States, particularly the border region. We are also concerned with U.S.-based criminal organizations threatening governability in the U.S. border regions or in Mexico. At this stage, however, we are not primarily concerned with other criminal organizations operating in the United States or Mexico that have only tangential effects on governability in either country, for example, Chinese, Russian, Colombian, or Italian groups.[11]

Governability refers to the ability of a government to allocate values over its society, to exercise legitimate power in the context of generally accepted rules. It might be viewed in terms of a continuum. At one extreme are so-called failed states, which are marked by ungovernability, lawlessness, and even widespread violence. At another extreme are polities in which rules and norms are generally understood and supported by large majorities and where governments perform assigned roles effectively. In between there exists a range of cases in which societies operate at some acceptable level and governments exercise some effective degree of rule-making and implementation.

There are several fundamental criteria that help us think about the governability continuum:

Monopoly of legal coercion. Max Weber emphasizes the monopoly by public authorities of ultimate legitimate coercion in a society. State authorities exercise ultimate physical control over the national territory.[12] Again this is a relative matter. Not every square inch of territory will be effectively controlled by the government all of the time. But private, or extranational, groups cannot physically dispute control over territory in direct confrontation with the government. The state exercises ultimate monopoly over military force.

Administration of justice. Is law enforcement in the sense of public safety carried out by public authorities or by private individuals? Is punishment for criminal offenses meted out primarily by public courts or by private tribunals? Governability implies that rule adjudication in society is exercised by state authorities themselves following established rules. To the extent that criminals penetrate and corrupt the judicial process, a key requisite of governability is compromised.

Administrative capacity. To what extent are laws and regulations actually implemented with some degree of agreement with the intentions of policymakers? Or, are problems of administrative incompetence, lack of resources, or public and private corruption so serious as to effectively divorce the stated intentions of public officials—assuming these reflect real intentions—from bureaucratic behavior? A weak, poorly resourced public administration, especially one lacking a career civil service, is especially susceptible to corruption.[13]

Provision of minimum public goods. Governability can be assessed in part by the capacity of government to provide the basic services that make society function. Can government assure adequate roads, schools, health care, water supplies, public sanitation, minimum nutrition, and the like? This too is a relative matter, in the sense that expectations and demands vary from one society to another. Where the fiscal constraints of the dual transition (as discussed below) reduce government spending for social services, criminal groups can generate public support, even a degree of legitimacy, by supporting schools, housing, health care, and the like in local communities.[14]

Conflict management. Regardless of the particular form of government, a common requisite for governability is the capacity of institutions to channel and contain the sorts of conflicts and competing demands that are central to modern political life.[15]

Our particular interest is in *democratic* governability. The core dimension of democracy concerns procedures. Democracy is characterized by periodic elections—which are freely contested, with the maximum feasible participation of the citizenry—to select from among competing candidates the groups that will occupy significant policymaking offices. For citizen participation to be effective in choosing among competing candidates (a process usually structured by party competition), citizens must be able to exercise basic rights, including freedom of speech and assembly. In turn, these rights are exercised most effectively when buttressed by functioning institutions and appropriate values, operating in a supporting civic culture.[16]

We must look beyond the role of procedures to the importance of institutions in democracy. Guillermo O'Donnell argues that the minimalist procedural notions can include as democratic what he calls "delegative democracy." This refers to a form of democracy in which a strong executive, usually a president elected through procedures that meet a minimum definition of democracy, dominates the political system. This leadership exists to the detriment of creating effective, resilient institutions (such as legislatures, judiciaries, independent regulatory agencies, subnational governmental units, and the like) that can promote participation and accountability. The result is a fragile, brittle policymaking process marked by volatility and costly policy mistakes. O'Donnell sees forms of delegative democracy emerging in several of the recent Latin American examples, including Mexico, and in most of the former communist cases.[17] O'Donnell suggests that delegative democracy usually coexists with severe economic adjustment, as described below in the "dual transition." His argument interests us because he points to ways in which governability is limited by concentration of power in one actor alongside the relative weakness of other policymaking bodies. But the issue is not only weak institutional accountability. Without effective judiciaries, law enforcement agencies, and regulatory agencies, the very capacity of government to enforce the law is compromised.

Two other sets of concerns are germane, but their direct connections to the meaning of democracy and the relationships between crime and governability take us into terrain too complex to be covered here. These are (1) the degree of inequality among citizens and (2) national sovereignty, or the capacity of government to mediate between its society and the international system. It seems intuitively plausible that in highly unequal societies, such as Mexico's, the poorest strata lack sufficient resources (information, money, sense of civic competence) to operate effectively *as citizens* within the judicial or regulatory systems. Also, to the extent that laws or procedures are perceived to be imposed by extranational powers, the commitment of the citizenry may be reduced.[18]

Up to this point, we have defined transnational organized crime and conceptualized governability as a set of conditions along a continuum and have suggested corresponding criteria and "thresholds." Democratic governability refers to key procedures and the requisites that make them work. Among these requisites we have noted especially political accountability and administrative capacity. With these general considerations in mind, we can assess the criminal-political nexus in a context of rapid political and economic change in Mexico.

Dual Transition, Crime, and Governability: The Case of Mexico

The optic of the dual transition is useful in viewing the case of Mexico. The dual transition can be divided into two broad stages.[19] In Stage I, macroeconomic adjustment policies aim at reducing inflation and balance-of-payments deficits. In politics, attention focuses on the break from authoritarianism and the beginning stages of liberalization and democratization. In many cases, Stage I passes relatively quickly, often in a matter of months. With macroeconomic stability under way, Stage II emphasizes microeconomic measures designed to strengthen market forces, including policy measures, for example, to increase labor productivity and promote internal savings. Social welfare policies are also redesigned to target resources more effectively.

With the installation of democratically elected governments in Stage I, political reform begins its shift to longer-term issues in the consolidation of democracy. Often summed up in terms of "reform of the state," emphasis in Stage II turns to strengthening legislative, judicial, and administrative capacities, thus allowing these agencies to assume new roles, for example, in regulation. Administrative decentralization is often promoted and a variety of measures to cultivate a democratic political culture are undertaken. Advances in consolidation depend ultimately on strengthening the rule of law and on the transparency and predictability of administrative and judicial processes. It is important to note that Stage I reforms can show quick results, whereas the reforms in Stage II can take years, decades, even generations to accomplish, assuming there is no regression to economic populism and political authoritarianism.[20]

The Mexican government introduced Stage I-type macroeconomic changes beginning in the mid-1980s. On the external side, Mexico joined the General Agreement on Tariffs and Trade in 1986 and began a series of reforms to liberalize trade and investment, culminating in January 1994 in the North American Free Trade Agreement with the United States and Canada. On the internal side, reforms emphasized anti-inflationary monetary and fiscal policies, the privatization of the nationalized banks and numerous public corporations, and the deregulation of a variety of business transactions.[21]

Political reforms in Mexico came about more slowly, although in the realm of electoral politics important advances had been achieved by the early 1990s. The Stage I-type break from authoritarianism came incrementally, in a series of electoral negotiations at the state and local levels. The presidential elections of 1994 were viewed by many as a clear breakthrough; they were substantially cleaner— although not necessarily fairer—than any preceding national election. The 1997 congressional elections confirmed the trend toward electoral credibility and opened the way to a new agenda of Stage II-type reforms.[22]

Mexico's transition to Stage II-type reforms was seriously disrupted, however, by the peso crisis of 1994–1995, which brought on the country's deepest recession since the Great Depression of the 1930s. President Ernesto Zedillo's campaign agenda of proceeding from macro- to microeconomic reforms was quickly shelved in order to refocus on macroeconomic stabilization. His Stage II political agenda of decentralization, judicial reform, and administrative modernization was retained in principle but its implementation was substantially weakened. Some progress was recorded in decentralization (e.g., in education, health, and revenue sharing) but relatively little was accomplished with respect to judicial reform or administrative modernization.

Transitions of such profound breadth and depth, often originating in economic or political crises, create extraordinary societal turbulence and magnify the significance of criminality for the political system. The depth and suddenness of Mexico's economic and political reforms and the peso crisis produced profound shocks that exacerbated longstanding structural tensions such as unemployment and extreme maldistribution of wealth. Sergio Zermeño, a noted Mexican sociologist, has emphasized the pulverizing and pauperizing impacts of globalization, accelerated by neoliberal reforms, in creating the conditions for extensive social disorder. He notes that actors such as labor unions, producer associations, peasant organizations, and political parties have been profoundly disoriented and weakened by the effects of economic restructuring, which have reduced the actors' capacity to represent interests and manage relations with the government.[23] Criminality and public insecurity increased dramatically in the wake of the peso crisis of 1994–1995.

To illustrate the gravity of the problems of crime and public insecurity, Mexico's ministry of interior noted that between 1991 and 1997, crime rates increased at a faster annual pace than population growth, rising from 809,000 reported crimes to 1,490,000. Of the nearly 1.5 million crimes reported in 1997, the ministry suggested that probably an equal number went unreported. Further, "Crime has become increasingly violent and better organized. Criminal activities such as arms trafficking, hold-ups, kidnappings, vehicle thefts, and drug-trafficking have increased." State and local governments, which have jurisdiction over nearly 95 percent of all crimes, lack the resources to enforce the law.[24]

However, noted criminologist Rafael Ruiz Harrell raised important caveats about official assertions based on crime data provided by the government's statistics agency, the Instituto Nacional de Estadistica, Geografia e Informatica (INEGI). First, Ruiz noted that the official crime data from 1994 and 1995 were useless because they were incomplete and based on diverse categories. The 1997 figures were still incomplete by March 1999, the time of his analysis. The most recent complete year available to him was 1996, but these data contained gaps and inconsistencies with numbers reported by state justice ministries. He concluded that the margin of error in the official data reached nearly 17 percent.[25]

Recognizing serious problems with the data, Ruiz offered interesting observations nonetheless. Calculated on a per capita basis, Mexico's crime rate showed a 42 percent increase in 1995 over 1993, but the rate seemed to stabilize subsequently. More interestingly, the 1,671 crimes per 100,000 population reported in Mexico in 1996 equaled only about 29 and 33 percent of the European and U.S. rates respectively. If one shifts to public opinion surveys to correct for possible underreporting, quarterly surveys in the Federal District in 1996 showed that about 35 percent of the respondents reported having suffered from a criminal act. But this figure, Ruiz argued, is more or less in line with comparable surveys in Europe and the United States. Rather than claiming a national security threat, the more accurate generalization may be that crime in Mexico was especially prevalent in the Federal District and four other states, and that certain cities, such as the Federal District, Tijuana, and Ciudad Juarez, had serious problems of insecurity. In Ruiz's view, rather than the crime rate itself the more serious issue was the lack of law enforcement, which resulted in criminal impunity throughout the country.[26] That is, in terms of impacts of crime on governability, the key concern is a widespread view that government is incapable and/or unwilling to provide citizen security within legal, democratic procedures.

The Mexico City metropolitan area is by far the subregion most seriously afflicted by crime in the country. The Committee on Public Security of the Federal District's Legislative Assembly reported in 1997 that in Mexico City some 240 citizens were assaulted, murdered, or robbed every hour. Furthermore, in the Federal District robbery of vehicles or persons increased between 200 and 300 percent between 1989 and 1996. Automobile theft was surpassed only by drug trafficking in terms of its profitability for criminals. Problems of public security had reached the point that citizens were resorting to self-help by closing off streets to public traffic and carrying handguns. The Committee's data do not agree with the interior ministry's, however. The Committee reported that in 1996, at the national level some 2.1 million crimes were reported, and the estimate was that this number would increase some 7 to 10 percent in 1997. Mexico City was especially affected, with nearly 250,000 crimes reported in 1996 and the possibility of increasing to as many as 280,000 in 1997. As did the interior ministry, the Committee emphasized that these numbers refer to reported crimes, with the probability that the real number of crimes is substantially larger.[27]

Problems of crime and public insecurity threaten Mexico's governability, according to the criteria we have suggested.

Monopoly of legal coercion. Two types of developments are problematic. First, arms trafficking and the proliferation of well-financed and aggressive gangs have led to an increasing incidence of confrontations between criminal gangs and between these and state authorities.[28] Second, corruption among the police at all levels, and especially in the Federal Judicial Police, has severely reduced their effectiveness. Even more serious is the specter of the penetration and corruption of the Mexican army.[29]

Administration of justice. Mexico's complex judicial system is suffering from acute overload due to the upsurge of crime since the mid-1990s. Justice departments at the national and state levels are understaffed, with serious gaps in resources and training. Policy officials apparently lack effective control over police officers. Key problems include impunity from prosecution in real terms and inefficiency and corruption in the court system.[30]

Administrative capacity. Mexico's federal bureaucracy has long suffered from several key problems. The bureaucracy lacks a career service (with the exceptions of the military, foreign service, and Bank of Mexico) and served for years as a source of employment, especially for urban, educated youth. It was overburdened with programs to promote growth and provide social services, to the point that its complexity rendered it nearly incoherent. Some progress has been made in regulatory effectiveness at the national level. For example, tax administration has been substantially improved, although much remains to be done. In other areas, however, regulatory effectiveness is limited, as is the case with banking regulation, for example. Regulation at the state and local levels is weak or even nonexistent. The peso crisis of 1994–1995 effectively shelved efforts to modernize the administration. The key point is that political authorities lack reliable instruments through which to implement decisions.

Provision of minimum public goods. Federal government budgets have been cut back substantially since the mid-1980s and depressed world oil prices have reduced revenues in 1998–1999. Public investment has been reduced much more than current spending, in part to maintain essential services and to preserve employment. Even though education and health programs receive priority funding, they have barely kept pace with population growth. The fiscal situation of state and local governments is even more precarious. Even so, the federal government has substantially increased its investment in police and law enforcement.[31]

Conflict management. Much of the success in conflict management to date has been due to elite and mass commitment to an institutional, democratic route of transition, as seen especially in electoral reform and relatively clean elections. Although the commitment to a democratic route appears firm, the challenge here is to assure that criminal influence does not penetrate key actors (such as political parties or news media) and processes (such as candidate selection or elections themselves).

As noted, the dynamics of crime and public insecurity vary from one national setting to another. Mexico offers contrasting interpretations. On the one hand, the country has been governed by a highly centralized, hegemonic party system since the 1930s, which suggests the possibility that the political-criminal nexus operates in systemic fashion, managed more by government officials than by criminals. On the other hand, the country's size and complexity and the government's impressive bureaucratic inefficiency suggest the likelihood of lack of central control over, or even awareness of, the realities of law enforcement in the field. To simplify: (1) Are national-level political authorities inclined to combat criminality but effectively blocked because of bureaucratic incapacity? (2) Does the criminal-political nexus operate in a systemic fashion, bottom to top, or is it relatively confined to the security and judicial apparatus of state and local governments and to the field offices of national-level military and law enforcement agencies?

Contending Images of Criminal-Political Relationships

To sharpen the discussion and note the significance of the contributions by the chapter authors in this text, in this section we elaborate four contending images of the crime-governance relationships in Mexico and two other images relevant to the borderland regions of the United States. We summarize these images in Table 1.1. The key dimensions of the images are the degree of organizational coherence of both the criminal groups and the government; and the geographic and func-

Table 1.1 Mexico: Images of the Political-Criminal Nexus

	Bureaucratic Efficacy	Nature of Criminal Organizations	Scope of Criminal Activity
I. Contained Corruption	Limited central control; real control at subnational level of field offices, state, and local government Law enforcement variably effective (by police and military)	Dispersed, fragmented; subordinated to government	Subnational, local; focused on enforcement
II. Centralized-Systemic (Formal)	Effective central control by formal national government machinery Coherent, efficient law enforcement (by police and military)	Complex, hierarchical, disciplined; subordinated to government	Transnational; focused on enforcement, regulation, and other societal actors
III. Centralized-Systemic (Formal and Shadow)	Effective shared central control by formal national machinery and shadow groups Coherent, efficient law enforcement (by police and military)	Complex, hierarchical, disciplined; subordinated to government	Transnational; focused on enforcement, regulation, and other societal actors
IV. Fragmented-Contested	Weak, ineffective central control; bureaucratic infighting Law enforcement variably effective (by police and military)	Dispersed, fragmented, competitive; variably subordinate and superior	Transnational; focused on law enforcement with sporadic involvement with other societal actors

tional extensions of activity. (The latter considers whether the criminal activity is regionally focused or nationwide and reaching into the borderlands and whether it is limited to law enforcement or penetrates other spheres of political life.)

Mexico—Image I: Contained Corruption

Image I serves as a null hypothesis. It suggests that the linkage between organized crime and the political system in Mexico is primarily contained within the lower-level spheres of law enforcement and judicial administration, with only incidental spillovers into the broader political system. That is, criminal groups operate efficiently to apply corruption in order to neutralize police forces, including military units when these act as police forces. If that minimum level of effort is insufficient to avoid arrest or disruption of the illegal activity, corruption may be extended to include the judiciary. It is an unnecessary expense to attempt to influence other offices within the executive or legislative branches as it also is to influence the broader political system, including political parties, interest groups, media, or public opinion. Such "contained corruption" in this image would extend upward along effective lines of command within law enforcement bureaucracies to the points where real control is exercised over actual forces in the field, as opposed to reaching the highest levels of the organizations or to their formal politically elected or appointed overseers. That is, corruption would focus on neutralizing (or enlisting the support of) those operational forces that can physically impede or facilitate the acquisition and movement of illegal merchandise across some given geography.

The contained corruption image draws attention to the efficiency orientation of criminal groups (i.e., why spend more than necessary?) and the severely limited administrative capacity of government at all levels. Regardless of whether national top-level elected or appointed officials are aware of organized criminal activity, their ability to affect such activity is negated by bureaucratic incapacity (e.g., lack of trained career civil services) and—possibly—by lack of public pressures, as exercised through elections for example.[32] We are not aware of an in-depth study of opinion on this matter, but a leading Mexico City daily newspaper reports that although majorities of Mexicans consistently cite drug trafficking as a serious issue, only a small percentage list it as a priority concern. Surveys in September and December 1998, for example, showed that drug trafficking was mentioned by only 1 percent as the priority issue, while 31 percent mentioned the economic crisis, 15 percent cited unemployment, and 13 percent listed insecurity (street crime) as their main concern.[33]

Mexico—Image II: Centralized-Systemic Criminal-Political Linkages (Formal)

This image depicts the integration of relatively coherent criminal organizations with a relatively coherent governmental system. Top government officials detect criminal organizations and then subordinate them to their control. The simplest version of Image II is a chain of control and corruption that runs from the national presidency through key ministries (defense, interior, justice), through the field offices of the national bureaucracies located in the states, through state and local governments, and through judiciaries to connect with intermediaries of criminal organizations, who in turn exchange money and/or services for protection. The connecting linkages are formal government control supplemented by party discipline and by webs of patron-client ties. Consistent with this image is the "hierarchization of crime." That means that the most complex, extensive, and lucrative criminal activities (e.g., heroin trafficking) are organized by national-level authorities; intermediate sorts of criminal activities (e.g., auto theft, kidnapping) are managed by state authorities; and relatively minor activities (e.g., prostitution) are relegated to municipal authorities.[34]

In this image, the president as the key actor (either directly or by delegation to subordinates) appoints the relevant officers in the key law enforcement agencies, such as the justice ministry (PGR), the ministry of defense, and the interior ministry, who then make field assignments of the pertinent officials in the states. These officers in turn organize and/or manage the more important criminal activities in their jurisdictions. Rather than creating and managing one criminal organization, the political leadership works with multiple groups, giving it additional leverage over the gangs and taking advantage of the complexity and spontaneity of the appearance and alliance formation among groups. Control and coercion flow downward; money and services flow upward. Similar types of linkages are established in other key ministries, with the president (through subordinates) appointing key officials, who in turn manage processes that link government officials to criminal groups and activities. The image assumes that enforcement bureaucracies operate efficiently and are effectively coordinated from above to prevent accidental conflicts among them in field operations. Further, it assumes that the bureaucratic linkages actually work to connect national political leadership in the capital to field offices and that these in turn can actually regulate activities on the ground. Political authorities can employ resources from corrupt exchanges to further their political aims, whether personal, factional, or systemic.

Mexico—Image III: Centralized-Systemic Criminal-Political Linkages (Formal plus Shadow)

Like Image II, this image posits relatively coherent criminal organizations integrated with a relatively coherent government. In addition to the formal version, however, this image posits the existence of a shadow parallel structure made up of a network of patrons and clients that takes shape at some point within the government apparatus and subsequently operates alongside of, but functionally connected with, the formal bureaucracy. Powerful officials at some time and at some location high enough up in the law enforcement–security apparatus construct a network of agents that operates within and outside of formal bureaucracy to connect with criminal gangs in selected areas of the country to regulate the more significant political/criminal activities. The controllers of the shadow parallel government negotiate with the incumbent president and relevant formal political authorities at the various levels in order to regulate criminal organizations.

A recurring version of Image III explains the origins of these criminal-political networks. It emphasizes the role of an operational arm of the interior ministry's intelligence service, the Federal Security Directorate (Direccion Federal de Seguridad, DFS). Acting against leftist subversive groups (e.g., in Jalisco) in the 1970s, the DFS was granted virtual impunity. Some DFS officers allegedly formed alliances with criminals, including drug traffickers, to carry out their anti-leftist mission. The criminal-political networks thus created operated more or less coherently until the mid-1980s, when the DFS was disbanded in the wake of scandals surrounding the torture-murder of a DEA agent and his Mexican pilot.[35]

The shared characteristic of Images II and III is the coherence and discipline of both the criminal organizations and the government agents. Image III is a more complicated notion, in the sense that formal and informal networks interact. Further, both images build on the hierarchical, patron-client nature of the Mexican political system. That is, loyalties in the system are based on strong personal ties between leaders and followers that reach from the local to national levels. Both images locate the center of power in a single figure, the president, or a limited number of actors, the president and the shadow manager(s). Resources acquired from corruption are available for both personal and political purposes.

Mexico—Image IV: Fragmented-Contested Political-Criminal Linkages

This image depicts segmented, fragmented, and opportunistic criminal-political cooperation at various levels. These coalitions are assembled at the initiative of government officials or of criminal leaders at different levels of government and on an ad hoc basis. The coalitions vary by types of criminal activity. Some activities can operate in a fairly decentralized and ad hoc form, involving local and/or state police and judicial authorities. Activities of such groups might include bank robbery, kidnapping, hijacking, auto theft, prostitution, or the smuggling of un-documented migrants. As the scale of activity increases in terms of actors, geo-graphic extension, and money involved, the higher up within government resides the level of official protection. Drug trafficking implies more complex coalitions with higher-level involvement, but even this is variable. In cases that involve mari-juana or synthetic drugs (locally or regionally produced), coalitions could be as-sembled with combinations of police at state and local levels in coordination with federal police, but possibly operating independently from national-level political control. Trafficking in heroin and cocaine (the latter foreign produced) implies complex transnational communications and transport, which suggests protection (or tolerance) from national- and international-level police, military, and trans-portation authorities.

Image IV is consistent with incomplete control exercised by central bureaucra-cies over field operations. The image is also consistent with variable linkages be-tween elected political authorities and organized crime; that is, political authori-ties on their own volition may or may not be linked to police-judicial-criminal corruption. It is also a dynamic image, suggesting ongoing coalition making among officials at various levels. It is consistent as well with coalitions that in-clude extra-governmental actors (e.g., former government officials). It can ac-count for patterns of relative stability (coalitions put in place by actors early in a presidential or gubernatorial cycle and buttressed by extra-governmental webs of patron-client linkages), as well as instability (coalitions put under pressure by presidential or gubernatorial successions). The image also fits with our under-standing of the disruptions and dislocations brought on by the dual transition, discussed above. Image IV allows the possibility that specific governmental actors at any level may be disconnected from criminal operations. That is, criminal-polit-ical networks can be "built around" specific officials. Also, the image suggests the fluidity and incoherence that permits accidental or intentional clashes among criminal groups and among government agencies. Criminal activity also takes on a more fluid geographic mobility, taking advantage of particular actors in differ-ent parts of the country. Finally, in contrast to Images II and III, Image IV is volatile and evolving and it allows the possibility that criminal leaders may gain the upper hand over government officials under certain circumstances.[36]

U.S. Borderlands—Image V: Marginal, Ad Hoc Corruption

Differences in political institutions and law enforcement capacity create a different context to develop images for the U.S. borderlands. Two such images are summarized in Table 1.2. Image V suggests that the penetration of U.S. law enforcement or judicial agencies by organized criminal groups is limited to occasional, isolated instances involving officials who are acting alone or in small groups. Criminals seek to insulate themselves as much as possible from law enforcement and submerge themselves in particular ethnic or racial subcommunities. Border control officers or law enforcement officers in the counties and municipalities along the border who are acting as individuals may commit corrupt acts on an ad hoc basis. Maverick law enforcement officers in the interior communities may commit corrupt acts in isolated incidences. But corruption is not ongoing or widespread in law enforcement agencies and does not reach into the judiciary.

The main assumptions underlying Image V are that U.S. law enforcement is relatively professionalized, the kinds of bureaucratic checks and controls employed by modern bureaucracies are relatively widespread, competitive and pro-

Table 1.2 Borderlands: Images of the Political-Criminal Nexus

	Bureaucratic Efficacy	Nature of Criminal Organizations	Scope of Criminal Activity
V. Marginal Corruption	Effective federal and state supervision of field offices Effective border control forces and state-local police	Dispersed, fragmented; sporadic contact with law enforcement; subordinate to government	Transnational, subnational, local; limited to police and border control forces
VI. Decentralized, Targeted Corruption	Ineffective federal and state supervision of field offices Ineffective internal checks on border control forces and police	Patterned and continuous activity; subordinate to government	Transnational, subnational, local; affects police, border control, judiciary and local government of field offices

fessionalized media maintain a degree of surveillance, and the electorate punishes corruption (which builds in automatic electoral checks). Also implied in Image V is that the borderlands regions offer the privacy and freedom of movement with which criminal groups can operate relatively unobserved by law enforcement.[37]

U.S. Borderlands—Image VI: Decentralized, Targeted Corruption

Transiting the U.S.-Mexican border is the main hurdle for criminals. Organized smuggling bands target officials in U.S. border control agencies. U.S. Customs Service officers at points of entry are a priority target, as are U.S. Border Patrol officers, who police the territories between points of entry.[38] Also, state and local police in the counties along the border can be targets. The corruption may involve individual officers or teams of officers and may be complex and sustained over a period of time. Contributions by criminals to the election campaigns of county police chiefs may project corruption into the broader political arena, but at a local level. In the interior communities of the borderlands, criminal gangs may target law enforcement officers on a sustained basis. Corruption may penetrate the judicial system as well, on either an ad hoc or sustained basis. Penetration of the prison system may also be extensive and sustained.

Previewing the Findings: An Overview of the Chapters

How do our findings relate to the images? The chapters that follow proceed from broad overviews of the political-criminal nexus in Mexico to discussions of partial aspects of the phenomenon, specifically campaign finance and key law enforcement agencies such as the attorney general's office and the Mexican army. These discussions are followed by chapters on the borderlands, with two contributions providing Mexican and U.S. perspectives on the border itself, followed by a discussion of the political-criminal nexus in the State of California.

Working from his twenty-nine years of service with the Federal Bureau of Investigation (five of these assigned to the U.S. Embassy in Mexico City), Stanley Pimentel attempts a broad synthesis of the criminal-political nexus in Mexico, drawing on the theoretical work by Peter Lupsha. According to Lupsha, Mexico's mature authoritarian system of the 1950s–1980s resembles what he calls the "elite-exploitative" model, one in which political authorities systematically use criminal groups for their personal gain as well as to acquire resources for the functioning of the political system. In such a system, political authorities identify successful criminals and subordinate them to political control through police or military instruments. Then the criminals, according to Pimentel, are "milked" like "cash cows" as long as they are useful. Once they are no longer useful, the criminals are prosecuted or liquidated.

Through confidential interviews with senior Mexican law enforcement officials who have firsthand experience, Pimentel provides detailed descriptions of the mechanisms by which control is exercised by political authorities and corrupt exchanges are carried out between criminals and law enforcement officials. Pimentel's descriptions of the mature system most closely resemble our Image II, a coherent, competent government bureaucracy that operates through key ministries from the very top downward to systematically organize and exploit criminal organizations. He also reports the possible significance of an Image III-type "shadow manager," a former senior government official, but does not develop the point. Pimentel emphasizes the important changes brought about by the democratic transition of the 1990s, which—in its early stages—has resulted in the breakdown of traditional controls and practices but without the construction of modern police and legal institutions. In this setting, which resembles Image IV, police are ineffectual and largely corrupt and criminal groups have become more violent and aggressive, leaving "no one in control." Pimentel offers an agenda of political and administrative reforms that are needed to confront the growing problems of criminality.

Luis Astorga, a researcher at the Institute for Social Research of the National Autonomous University of Mexico, uses a sociological-historical perspective to develop the following arguments: (1) Political-criminal cooperation in drug trafficking dates from the early twentieth century; it was concentrated in Mexico's Northwest (especially Sinaloa), and the dominant pattern of trafficking typically involved high government officials' taking the lead to organize criminal activities. (2) The changes brought by the Miguel Aleman administration (1946–1952) strengthened national-level involvement by police and military intermediaries in drug trafficking, creating a system that remained more or less intact until the acceleration of democratic reforms in the late 1980s.

Whereas Pimentel emphasizes culture to account for behavior, Astorga points more toward structural and institutional variables. He suggests that criminality is a socially constructed category and thus subject to change over time and to manipulation that reflects the relative power of different actors. The Harrison Narcotics Act of 1914 criminalized trafficking in opiates in the United States for the first time, and perceptions of criminality by U.S. officials have typically been forced onto Mexico over the years. Similarly, perceptions about drugs and gangsters have changed over time, as has the view of criminal-governmental alliances.

Astorga's historical perspective brings out the importance of key coincidences. The Mexican Revolution brought disorder and ungovernability to northern Mexico at about the same time that drug trafficking was outlawed in the United States. The consolidation of power by victorious groups in Mexico's north coincided with Prohibition in the United States (roughly 1920–1935), which laid the foundations for criminal-political cooperation in Mexico and the border region. The institutionalization of Mexico's civilian authoritarian regime in the 1940s and 1950s, abetted by the U.S. Cold War outlook, in effect nationalized what had been regional patterns of politically controlled criminal enterprises. The Cold War outlooks also contributed to a permissive environment for the interior ministry's DFS. The breakdown of the authoritarian system since the mid-1980s in turn coincided with the upsurge of cocaine smuggling and the dramatic accumulation of power by drug traffickers, creating possibilities for the first time that criminal gangs could gain the initiative over government.

Astorga describes a kind of "double diaspora" of criminal families from the northwestern state of Sinaloa. The major antidrug operations by the army and police in the late 1970s may have been successful, but they also had the effect of scattering gang leaders from Sinaloa to other states, notably Jalisco (Guadalajara). Subsequently, the scandals surrounding the murder of a U.S. DEA agent in Guadalajara in 1985 traumatized U.S.-Mexican relations and resulted in another scattering of criminals into other northern states, thus contributing to the formation of still more criminal organizations, most notoriously the Arellano Felix gang in Baja California. Like Pimentel, Astorga sees a watershed in the democratic transition of the late 1980s and posits a troubling scenario of possible alliances between criminal groups and hard-line, authoritarian politicians. In all, Astorga's account points to a centralized-coherent interpretation (Image III), giving way to a contested-fragmented perspective (Image IV) with the democratic reform.

Moving from general to partial views, Leonardo Curzio, of the Center for Inter-disciplinary Research in Sciences and Humanities of Mexico's National University, investigates links between criminals and the broader political system by looking at sources of party and campaign finance. Like Astorga, he notes the importance of coincidences. Increased flows of money from drug trafficking in the mid-1980s coincide with the dual transition. The expanded costs of political campaigns re-sult, in part, from heightened electoral competitiveness. This in turn is a conse-quence of cleaner elections as well as President Zedillo's decision to reduce gov-ernment support for the official party, both of which grow out of the democratic transition.

Curzio weaves an argument from a series of hypotheses based on little solid empirical evidence, which he readily acknowledges as an inherent limitation in this sort of inquiry. His argument is based for the most part on examples, anec-dotes, and public statements. He draws extensively on the case of the 1994 guber-natorial campaign in the southeastern state of Tabasco. That case, which—like several others—was never satisfactorily resolved, was exposed and documented by opposition party leaders. The Tabasco case, and Curzio's analysis more gener-ally, might be interpreted as support for our contested-fragmented image (IV), in the sense that a particular alliance of state-level PRI officials allegedly was formed with business and criminal groups, joined—possibly—to a broader, national-level coalition of party officials to fund a national campaign. He also argues plausibly that the 1996 national campaign reform law, which emphasized generous public funding for parties and campaigns, was propelled in no small measure by Presi-dent Zedillo's stated concern about the potential for criminal infiltration of par-ties and elections.

Curzio's discussion suggests the hypothesis that democratic reform that leads to a more effective, responsive, and participatory form of government may have the paradoxical effect of inducing criminal organizations to expand their targets of corruption and penetration to include electoral campaigns and legislative offices. That is, democratic governance that fits our minimalist procedural defini-tion is no sure antidote to criminal influence; such influence may even expand in the early stages of the transition.

Important to the effort to assess political will and governmental capacity is the administrative efficiency of key national agencies, especially the Office of the Attorney General (PGR) and—given the militarization of law enforcement in the 1990s—the Ministry of Defense. Based on personal observation from her service on the attorney general's staff, Sigrid Arzt, a Ph.D. candidate at the University of Miami, sketches the political context surrounding the appointment of Antonio Lozano, a leader in the center-right opposition National Action Party, as attorney general at the outset of the Zedillo administration in December 1994. She analyzes the ambitious reform project that Lozano attempted, unsuccessfully, to implement during his tour in office (1994–1996). Arzt documents the organizational and operational deficiencies of the attorney general's office, highlighting two important themes.

First, training and professionalization have been badly neglected in what she calls the agency's "operational forces," that is, the Federal Judicial Police, the public prosecutors, and the technical experts. The lack of training necessarily undermined the administrative reforms undertaken. Second, the growing reliance in the 1990s on the military to assume law enforcement duties, although understandable given the dire situation of criminality and lack of adequate civilian police, produced important negative consequences. The military were unprepared for police roles, and their involvement in law enforcement created problems of human rights abuses and circumvention of legal procedures, which together vitiated efforts to promote a culture of legality. Also, some military officers proved susceptible to corruption in much the same way as civilian police. Like Pimentel, Arzt describes patterns of corrupt exchanges that affected the assignment of PGR officials to key regional posts. Arzt's picture is not completely negative, however. She suggests that the creation of the Organized Crime Unit within the attorney general's office in 1996 was an important advance.

For our purposes, though, Arzt's analysis clearly demonstrates the problem of administrative incapacity. That is, the quality of personnel, organizational capacity, and resources are lacking to connect effectively the political guidance at the top with effective police operations in the field. In this sense, her findings cast doubt on an image of governmental coherence and, although we get glimpses of systematic patterns of corruption, they seem to point more toward Image IV (fragmented-contested) than either III or II.

Raul Benitez, a prominent scholar of civic-military relations based at the Center for Interdisciplinary Research in Sciences and Humanities of the National University, analyzes the Mexican army in a context in which it has been assigned extensive roles in law enforcement while simultaneously confronting significant guerrilla operations in various regions of the country. At the same time, the army is buffeted by broad forces of democratic change, including electoral transparency, alternation in power, and defense of human rights. Like Arzt, Benitez notes that the army's police role triggered constitutional and legal debates and complicated the army's doctrinal guidelines to preserve public order. Ultimately, the recognition that criminal activity does threaten public order and that the civilian police are completely inadequate, along with the army's strong institutional discipline to presidential and, increasingly, constitutional control, provides sufficient justification for involvement. Even so, Benitez maintains that the law enforcement roles have damaged the army's image in public opinion, as a result of human rights abuses and allegations of extensive corruption, and such criticisms have created tensions in the officer corps.

Benitez brings to light some of the contradictions of political reform for the improvement of law enforcement. For example, he argues that decentralization, however important for democratization, actually undermines governmental capacity to enforce the law. He notes as well the practical problem of how reforms introduced into an established authoritarian system often have the perverse effect of corrupting the new elements rather than reforming the old system, a point that Francisco Molina also makes with respect to the customs police. Victories by opposition parties have not led to important advances in law enforcement, as demonstrated by the cases of Baja California, where PAN has governed since 1989, or Chihuahua, where Partido Acción Nacional (PAN) governed in 1991–1997, or in the Federal District under a Partido de la Revolución Democrática (PRD) administration.

In all, Benitez's analysis suggests that an army is not an answer to confronting criminality, especially organized crime, and that continued reliance on the army runs the risk of drawing the military into alliances with political and criminal groups. Though not unambiguous, Benitez seems to draw a picture that is consistent with a fragmented-contested image (IV).

Luis Ray Sadler and Francisco Molina offer complementary views of the border from U.S. and Mexican perspectives. The views complement one another in recognizing that smuggling and the corruption in which it thrives are deeply rooted in a series of structural, cultural, and institutional conditions. Sadler is a historian by training, with lengthy practical experience on border-related boards and commissions and head of the Department of History at New Mexico State University; he notes that smuggling has thrived since colonial times and gained impetus virtually from the time a border was established between the United States and Mexico in the 1820s. Market dynamics is the main variable to account for the volume and direction of goods and services smuggled, whether these be munitions, people, export crops, drugs, or consumer durables. Changes in laws primarily affect the profitability of smuggling, as was the case with the outlawing of opiates in the United States in 1909, Prohibition in the 1920s, and the stricter criminalization of drug trafficking and illegal migration in subsequent years. This was the case as well with the adoption of high tariffs for consumer durables by Mexico in the 1930s, which strongly spurred southbound smuggling.

Sadler describes customs of informal cooperation by Mexican and U.S. law en-forcement agencies from the 1920s to the 1970s, cooperation that gave way to bu-reaucratic rigidity, especially on the U.S. side, as the border gained greater na-tional attention from the 1970s to the present. He is skeptical about U.S. efforts to control the border through bureaucratic means. He asserts but does not docu-ment the point that corruption in U.S. border control agencies is a growing prob-lem, thus suggesting support for our borderlands Image VI (decentralized sus-tained corruption). But Sadler's main point is that markets rule. One implication is that as long as the Mexican economy shows slow growth or even recession and the U.S. economy and laws generate robust demand, smuggling and associated il-legality will continue to thrive along the border.

Francisco Molina, a native of Chihuahua, served as director of Mexico's na-tional antidrug institute during 1994 to 1996. He describes the border region as distinct from both Mexican and U.S. societies, with its own peculiar vocabulary and outlooks and with extensive webs of family ties that reach across national boundaries. Molina points out that U.S. markets for prohibited goods and serv-ices have long fueled illicit activities along the Mexican border, as has been the case with liquor, drugs, and prostitution. The long history of smuggling created experienced organized crime groups that readily turned their talents to drug trafficking. Molina emphasizes aspects of border culture that create a facilitating climate of tolerance for criminal activities and he describes the structure and behavior of varieties of criminal gangs, ranging from street corner delinquents to complexly organized polycrime organizations. The picture he draws includes gangs that resemble the Sicilian Mafia in their hierarchy and discipline.

Molina also provides clues about the mechanisms through which international connections are forged between Mexican and Colombian gangs. He notes the corruption of the Mexican border police and within the Mexican army, and he also questions whether corruption of U.S. border control agencies is a factor in the facility with which both drugs and weapons so easily transit the border. The complexity and dynamism of the gang structure that Molina describes seem most consistent with our Image IV.

Elias Castillo, winner of journalism awards, including Pulitzer Prize nominations, and president of the Mexico Group in Palo Alto, and Peter Unsinger, professor of criminology at San Jose State University, describe dynamics of Mexico-related drug smuggling and distribution gangs in California. They depict an extensive network of Mexican-origin and recent-immigrant gangs that they suggest operate largely in isolation from mainstream California society, disconnected from the political system. This is a point of some controversy to those Mexican critics who are skeptical that U.S.-based, American-dominated criminal groups would allow such immensely profitable operations to be run by Mexicans.[39] Castillo and Unsinger describe how shifts in market supply and demand account for changes in patterns of drug smuggling from Mexico. U.S. criminals were the critical middlemen in supplying the U.S. drug market until the 1970s, when technological changes in heroin processing increased both the purity and ease of smuggling of Mexican "brown" heroin. At that time, Mexican smugglers increasingly dominated drug distribution, at least within the western and midwestern United States. The authors describe differences among Hispanic groups and emphasize that drug smuggling and distribution is handled not by Mexican Americans (those who have resided in the United States for generations) but rather by Mexican nationals and recent Mexican immigrants. They suggest that family and regional ties help to provide the trust necessary for complex, decentralized transactions. Their description of gang structure in the drug trade suggests segmented, small-scale operations largely acting independently in a cell structure that resists easy dismantling by police. By emphasizing gang isolation from society, the authors support our borderlands Image V—marginal, ad hoc corruption.

Part I

Crime and Governability
in Mexico

Chapter 2

The Nexus of Organized Crime and Politics in Mexico

Stanley A. Pimentel[1]

THIS CHAPTER EXAMINES the associations between organized crime and politics in Mexico from the 1960s to the mid-1990s. In order to understand how this nexus evolved, I must first consider the relevant historical and cultural contexts. Following this, I examine how the organized political and criminal elements came together in the contemporary period to work in a collaborative pattern and how organized crime was, for a period of time, controlled and managed by the political authorities. A theoretical framework developed by Peter A. Lupsha is particularly helpful in interpreting the Mexican case.

My argument is that three centuries of occupation, exploitation, and civic neglect by Spain, and a century of local dictatorships by revolutionary leaders, could not then allow a democratic civic society to evolve overnight. An agreement by several fighting factions to put aside their weapons and to come under the rule of one political umbrella, beneficial to all, began with the formation of an official party in 1929 that has now become the Partido Revolucionario Institucional (PRI). The PRI, a political monopoly, has been a "patron-client," authoritarian type of system for seven decades and has used its social control forces (military, police, and internal security agencies) to control, tax, and extort the organized criminal elements. The political authorities provided immunity from prosecution for the criminal groups while obtaining money for development, investment, and campaign funding for the party, as well as for personal enrichment.

The criminals were expected to pay and obey the authorities, and if they became a liability or could no longer produce, they were either "liquidated" or incarcerated.

Over time, however, the relationship between political officials and criminal groups was dramatically altered. By the late 1980s, changes such as the advent of concern for human rights, the North American Free Trade Agreement (NAFTA), global communications, a more educated middle class demanding democracy, and the opposition parties winning important positions made it virtually impossible for the political authorities in power to control the organized criminal elements. As a result, the criminals began fighting back by killing anyone they believed opposed them, including law enforcement officials and prosecutors. With no professional law enforcement and no effective system of laws capable of combating these criminals, the results are disastrous for the Mexican society. Drastic measures must be taken by the Mexican government to combat these organized criminal elements and to successfully destroy the political-criminal nexus that has remained. Creating an elite professional law enforcement task force to work with a national criminal intelligence clearinghouse is a beginning. Empowering members of such a task force with the proper tools, equipment, and laws so that this elite group can actively pursue the criminal organizations is also needed. Their task will be to identify and attack the weaknesses of these organized criminals and their partners, such as seizure of their assets and imposition of lengthy prison sentences, in order to break the cycle of the political-criminal nexus.

Historical Legacies of Authoritarianism and Instability

Speaking at a Bankers' Convention at Cancun, Quintana Roo, Mexico, on February 7, 1997, President Ernesto Zedillo promised to make Mexico a "country of laws" and to build public confidence in the justice system. He stressed that one of his top goals was to shore up Mexico's democratic institutions. He went on to state that "we do not have conditions now guaranteeing our security nor have we achieved the full state of law that is required for Mexico's development." In an interview with the *Chicago Tribune* published on July 20, 1997, President Zedillo spoke of the urgent need to introduce a "government of the rule of law" and expressed his desire to free the country of official corruption. He went on to state that "corruption is not a phenomenon that came about a few years ago but, unfortunately, has been around since the colonial times within our cultural traditions and certain practices."

The Mexican political system, "New Spain," evolved out of three centuries of occupation, exploitation, and civic neglect by the European colonial powers and a century of local dictatorships. The basic fact is that Mexico was under the "paternalistic and repressive control of Spain, which discouraged political self-government, stifled individual economic initiative and suppressed intellectual ambition."[2] Spain was interested in souls, gold, and silver, but not necessarily in that order. For generations, Mexico was ruled by a viceroy who governed the colony as the personal representative of the Spanish Crown: "He lived in a palace, maintained a court and all forms of royal pomp and prestige, and appointed all officials with the king's authority, and supervised the economic, religious, intellectual, and social affairs of the colony. The Viceroy headed the Colonial Government, was supreme judge and made and enforced the laws. To see that he functioned honestly and efficiently, the Viceroy was often spied upon by a 'Visitor General' sent by the Crown to report on colonial matters."[3]

The Spanish colonials became the propertied class, along with the Catholic Church, whose mission system provided the means of administration and social control in the outlying areas. While the viceroy and governorships were initially in the hands of Iberian-born, then local, creole elites (those born in Spanish America of European parents), administrative units, town and city councils, and magistrates were run by *mestizo* (mixed indigenous-European) elites. Limited and weak administrative control by Spain, the harsh topography, and slow communications allowed for local autonomy and upward mobility among the mestizo leadership, as well as the evasion of royal edicts and taxes. In spite of all the Spanish laws imposed on New Spain, "political corruption flourished, especially when the Spanish Crown, after the sixteenth century, decreed that public offices could be sold at auction to the highest bidder. In this way, many incompetent and corrupt individuals got into colonial offices."[4]

At the same time, local corruption and the sale of offices allowed the landed oligarchy to gain control over the rural administrative offices as access to higher positions. Once entrenched there, nepotism and graft extended into the patron-client system, which became the embedded norm, and the motto "Obedezco pero no cumplo" (I obey but do not comply) became the operating code of the leaders of New Spain. As a result of these systems of control, the "inevitable outcome of three centuries of exploitation and repression by the Spanish, was revolution, which stirred Mexico to its foundation and resulted in the severing of ties" to the motherland.[5] Four centuries of authoritarian rule could not be transformed into a democratic civic culture overnight. It is a struggle that still confronts and configures Mexico today.

Its "beginnings as an independent nation in 1821, when she cut her last ties to Spain, were inauspicious. Because of the lack of self-rule under Spain, the general poverty and illiteracy of the inert masses, and the preponderant economic and political powers of the army, the Church, Mexicans were not prepared to rule their own house. The shift from a colony to a republic meant only a change of rulers for the common man . . . the tensions merely shifted" from the Spanish born to the creole and from the creole to the mestizo.[6] Roughly a century of instability, foreign invasion, dictatorship, and revolution followed Mexico's independence in 1821. First came a "war of reform" that led to nationalist rule by Benito Juarez, followed by a brief period under the European-imposed ruler, Maximilian (1864–1867). After this came Juarez's efforts to implement liberal laws in a period called the Restoration (1867–1876), which was followed by the dictatorship of Porfirio Diaz (1876–1910), who fortified Mexican unity. Unity collapsed into revolutionary convulsions (1910–1920), during which time a succession of *caudillos* (strongmen) fought for control of the national government and the promulgation of the 1917 Constitution. Out of this instability came the creation in 1929 of the ruling party, initially known as the Partido Nacional Revolucionario (National Revolutionary Party, PNR), the forerunner of today's PRI.

The current political system in Mexico was begun in 1928–1929 after the assassination of Alvaro Obregón, the revolution's victor, its strongman, and president. The incumbent president, Plutarco Elías Calles, and his successor, Emilio Portes Gil (1928–1930), worked together to convene "all political factions into one imposing party, the PNR, which was financed by a 'kickback' from the pay envelope of every government employee."[7]

Calles recognized the historic opportunity and his unique responsibility to achieve a comprehensive political agreement, create the new political institutions for a modern Mexico, and leave behind the raw violence that had characterized personal politics . . . to establish and maintain control over the main forces and actors in Mexican politics. To achieve it, all the accesses to decision-making centers and all the roads to economic, social and political mobility passed through the party, the formal and operating structure of the 1929 political agreement. The party became the only gatekeeper of access to power, closed and out of reach to those on the outside who would never enter. A monopoly of access to power was created.[8]

And so for the next seven decades, the PRI, operating under a patron-client hierarchy, has distributed patronage, contracts, jobs, educational opportunities, social services, and other benefits to its loyal adherents via its governors, trade unions, and occupational associations. Various power centers, cliques, and alliance systems within the oligarchy would vary positions and offices in alternate administrations, all with a strong "trickle down" to the people. Upward mobility, education, and opportunities for economic success were available to the loyal, when they attached themselves to the right patron and were able to stay in the stream of rising party stars.

Presidential control over his successor and influence over gubernatorial selections and state financing, along with what was basically a "rubber-stamp" legislature and judiciary, centralized power in the PRI and Los Pinos (the presidential residence). The presidential clique and the party leadership, together with the security apparatus (formal security agencies, the police, the attorney general's office, and the military), possessed both the power and capacity to make their collective will felt throughout the country. Presidentialism, a term frequently used to describe Mexico's political system,

has caused so much harm to the country, particularly in the last few *sexenios* (six-year presidential terms) and is a product of the control the President of the Republic has exercised over PRI congressmen and senators. The authoritarianism, the discriminatory application of the law, the centralism, the corruption and the impunity are all products of placing all the state power in one solitary person: the President of the Republic.[9]

During the PRI's monopoly of power, actors such as the media and the Catholic Church have been co-opted and become a part of the political system. Early on, the PRI removed the Mexican military from the center of power by promising great rewards, exercising civilian oversight over their food and supplies, and rotating the zone commanders every two to three years. "Senior officers were encouraged to enrich themselves with assorted business opportunities, sinecures and favors, and even illicit activities, such as contraband, drug trafficking and prostitution, were tolerated. . . . At the same time, the government protected the armed forces from media criticism," making the military a "sacred cow."[10]

Also at the disposal of the president was the Secretaría de Gobernación (Ministry of Government, or Interior), the second most powerful position next to the presidency, "with its broad responsibility for preserving the country's political stability . . . in charge of managing the political arena where both the opposition and the PRI perform."[11] Within this ministry was the Federal Security Directorate (DFS), which was responsible for investigating matters affecting national security and other duties as directed by the president. The DFS, which was staffed by the elite Presidential Military Staff Guards (Estado Mayor Presidencial, EMP) and by paramilitary experts, was at the ready to do as the president commanded or to use the president's name when it suited their purpose.

With these tools at their disposal, and with their many coalitions of interest groups and alliances with other powerful institutions, the president and the PRI leadership enjoyed virtually absolute power. "Myriad pyramids of power are thus superimposed on the larger hierarchical pyramid: everyone except the President is both boss and servant . . . (where) the process spawns political cliques—known as mafias—that are loyal to the President but compete fiercely with each other. Without them, the system of loyalties could not work."[12] As a result of these loyalties to bosses and ultimately to the president, institutions have not become professionalized, nor can there be any checks and balances to offset the corruption and complicity ingrained in this system. The PRI has successfully permeated the entire system of living in Mexico so that everyone—the police officer on the street, the mayor of the city, the governor of the state, the Minister of Finance, or the attorney general of the nation—are all indebted to the party bosses, and ultimately to the president. No controversial action could be taken by one patron without checking with his or her patron, and on up the line. Many decisions that normally would be made by a deputy secretary would be referred to the president, who appointed that individual, for the final say. And since there is "No Reelection" of the president, governors, mayors, congressmen, and senators, everyone must "make hay while the sun shines" to ensure a larger nest egg when they are no longer in a position to obtain the benefits of office. Carlos Hank Gonzalez, former Secretary of Agriculture in the Carlos Salinas administration, former mayor of Mexico City, and a well-respected PRI stalwart, probably said it best when asked about his accumulation of wealth and his status as one of Mexico's richest: "A politician who is poor, is a poor politician."

The Political-Criminal Nexus: Theory and Practice

Peter A. Lupsha has developed a theory that helps interpret political-criminal relationships in the Mexican case. He posits two basic patterns of criminal-political relationships: the "stage-evolutionary model" and the "elite-exploitation model." According to Lupsha's stage-evolutionary model, the most common progression in the relationships between organized crime and the political system is that most organized crime groups tend to evolve through three stages: the predatory, the parasitical, and the symbiotic. In the predatory stage, the criminal group is usually a street gang or group rooted in a particular territory or neighborhood, such as the gangs in Los Angeles, Chicago, or New York. Criminal gangs evolving from the predatory stage into the parasitical stage have developed a corruptive interaction with the legitimate power centers, such as occurred with La Cosa Nostra in the United States during the alcohol prohibition days of the 1920s. Political corruption, which accompanies the provision of illicit goods and services, provides the essential glue that binds the legitimate sectors with the underworld criminal organization. The third, or symbiotic, stage evolves when the relationship between the criminal organization and the political system becomes one of mutuality, where the political and economic systems become dependent upon and subject to many of the services the criminal organizations have to offer. The mob's control of the Fulton fish market, the construction industry, and the sanitation department in New York City are prime examples of this stage.[13]

This dynamic evolution of organized crime in the stage-evolutionary model is one in which the criminals follow an illicit parallel ladder of upward mobility and over time seek to legitimize their wealth and status for themselves and their children. These criminals actively seek niches in the interstices of the law where they can enrich themselves and at the same time buy into the political and economic systems to minimize risks of arrest and loss of wealth. From governmental and citizen perspectives these organized criminal enterprises provide desired economic services, such as gambling, prostitution, illicit alcohol and drugs, yet are part of an underworld that is accepted but not catered to.[14]

Lupsha's second model of organized crime, the elite-exploitative model, is one in which the organized crime enterprises are not treated as useful or necessary evils but rather as "cash cows," to be manipulated and exploited by political authorities. This model most accurately describes what we observe in Mexico, where organized crime becomes a source of funding and illicit enrichment for the political elite and their social control agents. Drug traffickers in these settings, after achieving some entrepreneurial successes, are sought out by the system and taxed and disciplined into their role within the system. Although corruption is a key factor in both of these models, in the stage-evolutionary model it is initiated by traffickers in pursuit of insurance and protection. The legitimate social control actors in this model may accept payoffs and even seek them, but they rarely become the initiators of trafficking or its reinforcers.[15]

In the elite-exploitative model, the traffickers are under pressure from the legitimate social control agents—indeed they are forced—to accept and sell loads of seized drugs, and they are constantly threatened and taxed by those agents, who are passing percentages of this tax to higher-level officials. These criminals are rarely permitted to retire from the game; they are either killed or imprisoned and other family members are allowed to take over. In this model, the organized criminal system is called upon to support the oligarchy. Control and initiation come from the top, from the so-called legitimate power holders and their social control agents, and the drug lords, like good "cash cows," are protected, milked (taxed), and when no longer useful, imprisoned or sent to the slaughter, to continue the analogy.[16] "Nevertheless, these groups continue to work with renewed efforts, which demonstrate that, contrary to common belief, the drug trafficker's power is limited; they are disposable pieces, and as part of the unwritten rules, are utilized for convenience, either by the State or their real bosses."[17]

We see in the case of Mexico a more or less clear representation of the elite-exploitative model. Political authorities used social control agents to organize and regulate drug trafficking. Traffickers were manipulated and disposed of to suit the needs of political officials. Over time, however, traffickers grew more powerful and the political system became more pluralistic, but not institutionalized. In these circumstances, drug traffickers gained greater autonomy of action—

and grew more violent and aggressive in their dealings with both state and society.

A case can probably be made that the first association between an organized criminal group and a politician in Mexico occurred when Hernan Cortes and his marauding band of soldiers from Spain marched into Tenochtitlan (current Mexico City) and captured the Aztec capital and its emperor, Moctezuma. Despite the fact that Moctezuma had previously offered Cortes and his organization gifts of gold, silver, and jade in hopes that they would leave, Cortes is said to have remarked, "The Spaniards are troubled with a disease of the heart for which gold is a specific remedy."[18] For our purposes, however, the first time that one can truly observe in Mexico the evolution of the criminal-political nexus is during the early 1900s, when the United States attempted to put a stop to the contraband of drugs, whiskey, and arms with its Mexican neighbor.

The business was so lucrative that it raised the attention of several powerful politicians such as Colonel Esteban Cantú, Governor of the Territory of Baja California Norte from 1914 to 1920. In customs reports from Los Angeles in 1916 sent to the Department of the Treasury, he was mentioned as one who gave out concessions to exploit the opium trade in exchange for important sums of money. The cost of a concession was $45,000 (U.S. dollars) and the monthly rent was between 10,000 to 11,000 dollars.[19]

As long as there has been a United States–Mexican border, there has been smuggling between both countries. Goods smuggled out of Mexico into the United States have included marijuana, heroin, and more recently, cocaine, while refrigerators, televisions, automobiles, and weapons have come into Mexico. Many of these goods were purchased by the average citizen; however, the great bulk were smuggled by organized crime elements who have had family-run businesses for generations. These families have produced all the major organized crime figures, such as Miguel Angel Félix Gallardo, Rafael Caro Quintero, Juan Garcia Abrego, Amado Carrillo Fuentes, the Herrera family, and the Arellano Felix brothers of the present day. Most of these had their humble beginnings in the 1960s in the drug trade.

In the 1960s and 1970s, opium poppy and marijuana were grown in abundance in the western parts of Mexico, where "politicians, business people, police and peasants all knew who was planting poppy seed. . . . The police knew who were the producers. . . . The Chief of Police was the one who controlled the 'percentage' in exchange for tolerating (the trade) or for support. . . . Knowing the Chief of Police meant closeness to the Governor."[20] What began with a local, home-grown organization paying off the officials of the local "plaza" (informal police jurisdiction) grew into a national organized crime organization paying off high-level political authorities. Originally, under the concept of the plaza, the drug trafficker or smuggler bought his or her "license" to operate from the local police chief, military commander, mayor, or the individual who had been given authority in that area by the PRI: "Payments went to locals who passed part of it up to the patrons they owed their positions to. Should a trafficker have a major business success with resulting notoriety, he would then likely be visited by the *judiciales'* (state level agents of law enforcement) and later by *federales'* (agents of national police agencies) and operating 'franchises' would have to be also purchased directly from these agencies."[21]

One of the sources I interviewed for this chapter reported that the Mexican government, particularly the Ministry of the Treasury (Hacienda), has not provided a budget to other government institutions, such as the Mexican Attorney General's Office (PGR) or the Federal Judicial Police (PJF), and these agencies have had to find their own way to obtain operating funds. For many years, these agencies have assigned their personnel to their offices (plazas) throughout Mexico, expecting them to perform their duties with honor, while providing little or no funding to do so. These officials arrive at their new posts and must find ways to "earn" money so that they can pay their personnel, pay for their office expenditures, and survive on their meager salaries. According to Source "A" it was generally through the arrests of organized crime figures and the seizures of their contraband goods (such as stolen cars, drugs, weapons, or television sets) that these individuals were sent to jail and their goods confiscated and turned over to Hacienda. The drugs would be turned over to the prosecutor for destruction, while Hacienda would sell the contraband items and give 40 percent of the profits of these sales to the federal law enforcement officials. It was in this manner that the police survived. Source "A" indicated that very often the police official in charge of the area would simply confiscate contraband from the crime figure and submit the goods to Hacienda for a payment; the official would then require the crime figure to sign over the deed or title of his house or car to the law enforcement official or a relative. "A" blamed the Mexican government for not providing the law enforcement officials with much-needed funds, training, and equipment to perform their duties in an honorable fashion. According to "A" the hierarchy has looked the other way, knowing its personnel were extorting monies, properties, and gifts to administer justice while illegally enriching themselves.

"A" further observed that, since the PGR/PJF hierarchy in Mexico City was not in a position to earn a decent wage, the commanders in the field would donate to La Copa (essentially passing the hat around), by which a percentage of the field profits was sent to superiors in Mexico City, usually on a monthly basis. "A" explained that since Mexico City was declared a free zone (not controlled by anyone), the hierarchy in the Federal District relied upon donations from the field commanders to supplement their incomes. This tradition had been carried on for decades and it was not until approximately the mid-1980s, with the establishment of the National Commission on Human Rights and with the complaints of the criminals lodged against the PGR/PJF officials, that the custom changed. "A" indicated that until this time, the police or military had dictated the terms of the plazas to the organized crime figures and had exerted control over them. However, with the new concern about human rights, the police and military commanders could no longer exert control over the criminals, and many of the experienced commanders resigned for fear of going to prison. Thus, many plaza holders became servants to the crime figures and literally became part of the organized crime scheme, rather than attempting to control or prosecute the criminals.

"A" noted that in the late 1940s, President Miguel Aleman "devalued the Mexican Generals" by creating 300 when there had been only 20, thereby having 300-plus generals looking to share "the spoils" of the country. As has previously been stated, military zone commanders obtained monies and gifts from drug traffickers and other organized criminals within their zones in exchange for protection and/or immunity from prosecution. The zone commanders have generally coordinated through intermediaries with the PGR/PJF officials on the "levies of funds" to be obtained from organized crime.

A second informed source, "B," told me that the PGR Ministerio Público Federal (Federal Prosecutor, MPF), who is typically assigned to one location from four to six years, is generally the intermediary between the drug trafficker, the PGR/PJF hierarchy, and the military. This arrangement is usually made through the attorneys working for the drug traffickers or organized criminals. Rarely are the senior government executives involved in the negotiations with criminals.

Suitcases filled with money are passed from the criminals through their lawyers to the MPF. He then passes it to his superiors, who in turn pass it on to their superiors as far away as Mexico City. Both "A" and "B" advised that while the PJF was directed by Rodolfo León Aragón and Adrián Carrera Fuentes (1990–1994), they regularly sent their immediate subordinates in official PGR aircraft to pick up the suitcases filled with money and gifts obtained from the organized crime elements by the PGR/PJF plaza holders throughout Mexico. These suitcases were later disbursed among Aragón and Fuentes, to their superiors in the PGR/PJF, and ultimately to Los Pinos (the presidential residence) to a "slush fund" account.

Details of this slush fund were brought out during the extradition hearings of former PGR Deputy Attorney General Mario Ruiz Massieu in U.S. District Court, Newark, New Jersey, in 1996. When questioned about the source of money in a seized Houston bank account, Ruiz Massieu claimed that he had received a number of bonuses from President Salinas, the largest being 800,000 pesos (approximately $240,000 at the 1993 exchange rate). Documents presented at the extradition hearing by the PGR attested to the presidential accounts and the awarding of bonuses to PRI members.

"A" asserted that many believe the Mexican military has been exempt from acting in complicity with organized crime. However, evidence to the contrary is the February 1997 arrest of the former division commander, and former commissioner of the PGR's National Institute to Combat Drugs (INCD), General Jesús Gutiérrez Rebollo, who was charged with protecting a major drug cartel leader, Amado Carrillo Fuentes, and his organization. Allegedly, in exchange for gifts such as luxury apartments, vehicles, jewelry, and money, Gutiérrez provided protection to the Carrillo Fuentes organization while attempting to dismantle the rival Arellano Felix drug trafficking organization of Tijuana. Witnesses have testified at the Gutiérrez Rebollo hearings that drug trafficker Amado Carrillo Fuentes was in possession of PGR credentials allegedly provided by Gutiérrez Rebollo. (Carrillo Fuentes died at a clinic in Mexico City on July 4, 1997, after undergoing surgery to alter his appearance.) The role played by the PJF and former DFS agents with organized crime has been abundantly portrayed in the media. However, "the information about the military collusion with drug traffickers is less known . . . and surely, their participation is more than what has been 'filtered' by the media. . . . The 'generals' are not necessarily those who are the visible heads."[22]

Source "A" advised that La Copa had been a traditional means of corruption within the law-enforcement institutions of Mexico. However, in the mid-1970s to the early 1980s, the DFS, in the name of national security and with total license granted by the presidential office to attack the enemies of the system, took corruption to a new level with its greed and dictatorial powers. "DFS's primary mission in the 1960s was as an anti-guerrilla force to combat the National Revolutionary Civic Association (ACNR), and later the Party of the Poor and the Mexican People's Party. As the guerrilla organizations mobilized in the cities, DFS formed the White Brigade (La Brigada Blanca) . . . to neutralize them . . . The White Brigade is said to have tortured, killed and 'disappeared' hundreds of Mexicans considered threats to the regime."[23] While getting rid of the guerrilla threat to the country, the DFS personnel with their "death squads" combined their counterinsurgency activities with active participation in the drug trade, particularly in the Guadalajara region.

From its inception, DFS had interactions with drug traffickers. . . . Atonio Zorrilla (Director of the DFS in the 1980s) signed the DFS and Gobernación Agent Identification cards that Rafael Caro Quintero and other members of the Guadalajara cartel were carrying when they were arrested. According to the revelations of the Camarena (DEA Agent kidnapped, tortured and killed by drug traffickers in 1985) trials, DFS Comandantes and ex-Comandantes even became participants and investors in the Guadalajara cartel's plantations and trafficking ventures.[24]

Once the guerrilla movement was stopped by the DFS, the complicity between the drug traffickers and the DFS reached unprecedented levels in the mid-1980s. Mexican newspaper reporter Manuel Buendía was killed in May 1984, and DEA agent Enrique Camarena Salazar and his pilot were kidnapped, tortured, and killed by traffickers the following year. Buendía allegedly came into possession of a videotape showing high-ranking government officials meeting with drug traffickers. Buendía was ordered killed by his friend and confidant, Jose Antonio Zorrilla Pérez, who at the time was head of the DFS. Zorrilla Pérez was said to have political ties to the interior minister when Buendía began publishing details in a Mexican newspaper of the drug traffickers' connections to high-level police, politicians, and businessmen.[25]

Source "A" noted that Zorrilla's predecessors had been from military backgrounds, and therefore disciplined, and had held in check the many organized crime figures. According to this source, Zorrilla, as head of the DFS and a career politician, believed he was all-powerful and an untouchable executive of the PRI. He ordered the assassination of Buendía and was even rewarded by the Interior Ministry and designated a candidate for a PRI federal deputy position. However, "A" advised that public opinion subsequently led to a decision in 1990 by then-President Carlos Salinas de Gortari that Zorrilla be tried for the Buendía murder. Zorrilla was sentenced to forty years in prison.

As a result of these two well-publicized events and at a time when the media were linking governors, military officers, and even President Miguel de la Madrid to drug traffickers, de la Madrid ordered the dissolution of the DFS in late 1985. As a result, several ex-DFS commanders continued their involvement in drugs. In particular, Rafael Aguilar Guajardo would become a major drug cartel leader in the Juarez, Mexico, area until his murder in 1993 in Cancun.

Source "B" stated that until approximately the mid-1980s, the local plaza dealt with the organized criminal elements in the region, and these in turn dealt only with the authorities of that area. The plaza holder generally received instructions from Mexico City, either through the mayor or the governor or from the director of the PJF or DFS. The financial terms would be dictated to the organized crime figures. However, Rafael Caro Quintero, head of the Guadalajara drug cartel, broke all the rules of the "game" by personally approaching the secretaries of defense and interior. According to "B," until this time, no organized crime figure had ever dared approach a high-level government official, as all negotiations between Mexico City and the plaza had always been through intermediaries of the region. "A 1988 District Court affidavit in the State of Arizona states that in 1984 an informant told the DEA that a consortium of traffickers including Rafael Caro Quintero, Juan Esparagoza Moreno, Jaime Figueroa Soto, Manuel Salcido and Juan Quintero Paez paid ten million dollars to the Mexican Secretary of Defense, General Juan Arevalo Gardoqui, for protection."[26] A note from the Second Section (Intelligence Section—Mexican Army) to the secretary of defense, dated March 4, 1997, lists persons linked to drug traffickers in the 15th Military Zone, Guadalajara, Jalisco. During an investigation carried out by the military in 1991, Ruben Zuno Arce, the former brother-in-law of former President Luis Echeverría, was found to have been involved with drug traffickers.

General Juan Felix Tapia, formerly in charge of the 15th Military Zone, now retired, was an associate and protector of Ernesto Fonseca Carrillo, alias Don Neto, and has received monies and gifts directly from him or through the intermediary, Lt. Colonel Jorge Garma Diaz (fired), or through another drug trafficker, Roberto Orozco. It is said that Rafael Caro Quintero gave him (General Felix Tapia) a dark red Grand Marquis and another to Colonel Beltran Guerra. It has also been noted that General Arévalo ordered that Garma Diaz be given access to a car and driver, and that Felix Tapia was closely associated with Ruben Zuno Arce.[27]

Zuno Arce is presently incarcerated in the United States, following a 1990 conviction by a federal court in Los Angeles for complicity in Camarena's murder.

A third informed source, "C," advised that for approximately the past thirty years, the seeding, cultivation, and sales of marijuana and heroin and the smuggling of cocaine have been carried out by reputed Mexican drug traffickers. However, all of these traffickers were acting in concert with the governing powers of the state, namely the governors, the military, and the police forces, and these in turn collaborated with their patrons in the hierarchy of the PRI. "C" emphasized that *no one can act without protectors* (nadie sin protectores) in the patron-client relationships, which have existed within the PRI for the past seventy years. "C" noted that for the past thirty years, politicians and organized crime have worked hand in hand—the politicians providing criminal organizations with protection from prosecution or competition from rivals in exchange for money and gifts. Oscar Lopez Olivares, alias El Profe, a lieutenant of former drug kingpin García Abrego, stated:

Drug trafficking . . . is a matter completely handled by the government, from the protection that is given to the marijuana cultivations, everything is duly controlled, first by the Army, next by the Federal Judicial Police, and even the fumigators of the PGR . . . there is no doubt that police agencies have been the protective arm of the principal drug barons. . . . At the same time, these (barons) have received protection from high level politicians.[28]

"C" noted that those who step out of line or are not in agreement with the governing forces are jailed or killed, while new clients are found to provide the protectors with the necessary cash and gifts. "C" went on to say that nothing happens in Mexico that is not known by the protectors; therefore, when a government official denies knowing the location of a badly wanted fugitive, he is lying.

As an example, all three informed sources agreed that certain officials within the Mexican government were aware of the whereabouts of the Gulf Cartel leader and former FBI top ten fugitive, Juan García Abrego, in the 1990s, and could have detained him when he was being sought by U.S. authorities. However, these officials chose not to cause his arrest inasmuch as they were being paid directly or indirectly by García Abrego and he had not as yet become expendable. It was only after García Abrego had in fact become a liability to the Mexican government that he was allowed to be captured and turned over to the U.S. government in January 1996. PGR officials familiar with the capture of Juan García Abrego allege that the PJF commander in charge of the García Abrego investigation received $500,000 and a new bullet-proof Grand Marquis vehicle from another major cartel leader for arresting García Abrego. Source "B" reported that this PJF commander was assigned to Tijuana after the arrest and expulsion of García Abrego, with orders to prosecute the Arellano Felix drug trafficking organization. Instead, he received several million dollars from them to allow them to continue their operations in Tijuana.[29] Based on her study of the García Abrego organization, Yolanda Figueroa asserts that "no one doubts that the Gulf Cartel (García Abrego) is a part of the power group. It is impossible to move tons of cocaine, launder thousands of millions of dollars, maintain a clandestine organization of several hundred armed persons, without a system of political and police protection . . . [It is] a clear example of how a criminal organization interrelates with a power group."[30]

The three informed sources separately corroborated that the sale of offices within the PGR/PJF has been done generally through a deputy attorney general, who was purposely selected by the PRI hierarchy and named by the president. (One Mexican attorney general stated that President Salinas did not allow him to select his own deputy attorney general.) In addition, one former PGR delegate (much like a U.S. attorney for a district) informed me that a deputy attorney general told him that the plaza he was taking over cost $3 million, plus a payment of $1 million per month rent, and that he should pay up front. The delegate said he told the deputy attorney general that since he had been selected by the president, he was not going to pay.

Two of the informed sources pointed out that during his tenure former President Carlos Salinas selected three individuals to coordinate Mexico's counterdrug efforts. The three have been reportedly linked to drug traffickers by the media.

Important positions such as the PGR delegate or deputy delegate in Tijuana or Juarez could cost up to $3 million for the concession. The delegate in turn would pay $1 million per month, payments to be made to the PGR hierarchy, and ultimately to Los Pinos. These monies were provided, of course, by the organized crime elements. Source "C" confirmed that portions of the payments collected during the Salinas administration by the PJF directors would ultimately reach President Salinas' private secretary, where the monies would be placed in secret accounts to be used as the president or the PRI hierarchy saw fit. Positions in other non–drug producing/less populated states cost only $30,000 for the concession and a few thousand dollars per month payments to the higher authorities. Sources "A" and "B" report that the sale of offices continues to this day (August 1998) in the PGR/PJF.

Two of the informed sources corroborated that selective law enforcement of organized crime activities took place during the past thirty years. Organized crime figures went to prison only after much hue and cry from the United States; when that individual became a liability to the Mexican government, such as in the case of García Abrego; or if the political situation warranted a "sacrificial lamb" to appease the U.S. government, such as during the weeks prior to the "certification process" by the U.S. Congress in March of each year. The sources reported that as long as the criminals maintained a low profile, paid their dues each month, and did not create any problems for the police, the law enforcement authorities would not prosecute them. "In Mexico, control was in the hands of the State . . . which in determined circumstances . . . especially when there are political pressures from the United States . . . (Mexico has been) obligated to sacrifice laborers (who are) easily replaced, but without weakening the drug organization to the point of placing its existence in danger."[31]

Two sources stated that 1992 marked the beginning of the "limousine service" in which the military, the PGR/PJF, and state judicial police officials began providing protection for drug shipments to the border area. Most often, the road blocks implemented in an area by the military, the PGR, PJF, or the local authorities are to safeguard the passage of the drug shipments and not necessarily for the detection of contraband. Through intermediaries, the plaza holder will be notified when a drug shipment is expected and is instructed to set up the checkpoints. The sources indicated that one plaza holder will not necessarily know that another plaza holder in another state or region has coordinated the shipment of drugs to the next area. To facilitate smooth operations, orders will come from Mexico City to the appropriate "jefe" (boss) in the plaza to supervise and ensure the safe transhipment of the merchandise through his or her area.

The sources went on to explain that not only was organized crime expected to consistently pay, but they had to continually keep the plaza informed of their activities, their associates, and their rivals—particularly those who were not paying or had not received the authority from the plaza to operate. The three sources stated that once a productive relationship had been developed between the organized crime figure and the plaza, the crime figure would try to keep that official in place for a long period by making the plaza holder look good to his superiors. "The trafficker was expected to assist the police and the political system by providing grist for the judicial mill (i.e., pinpoint or inform on rival traffickers) as well as public relations materials to give the U.S. drug enforcers. Thus, while the trafficker could gain protection and warning information, the police could gain credit, praise, and promotions; the political system gained campaign monies and control; and the U.S. obtained statistics, to justify a job well done."[32]

"B" advised that many organized crime figures are marrying police officers or prosecutors to further protect themselves from persecution and prosecution. The three sources noted that organized crime leaders have insulated themselves further by recruiting family members, trusted friends, and others through intimidation exerted by their attorneys and enforcers to carry out their trade. "B" and "C" advised that most of the organized crime figures' money does not leave Mexico, but rather is invested in real estate, apartments, houses, financial markets, construction and road building firms, drugstores, tourism projects, and, of course, paying for protection.

The question is then asked, if the Mexican government has been a patron-client type of system, who is the ultimate patron? One informed source has stated that the person manipulating or orchestrating the PRI hierarchy behind the scenes, much like a puppeteer, is a former secretary of interior who has maintained extremely powerful control over the principal members of the PRI through favors, promotions, and blackmail. This individual has been able to manipulate and control the PRI hierarchy for so many years because of his astute ability to play one political interest against the other and yet maintain the loyalties of the players. Other sources agree that this individual is powerful; however, they suggest that a select few long-time, central figures of the PRI have also exerted control over its members for the past forty years.

We have examined how organized crime evolved in Mexico and how the organized crime elements were utilized by the political system. "In other words, traffickers have been perceived as creatures used by the dominant political class to do its dirty work, (and) not as independent social agents or barbarians trying to take by force the strength of the State through corrupt strategies directed at unpolluted officials at different levels."[33] Organized crime figures are in business for the money. The more money they can make, the more they can legitimize their status in the community, the region, and the nation. The Mexican drug traffickers are known to have built roads, churches, schools, and medical centers in their communities. Others, like García Abrego, sent their children to the United States to be educated. In this manner they can legitimize their status in the region at the same time they obtain protection and immunity from the authorities. According to the informed sources, these organized crime figures have not sought political positions nor do they seek publicity in the media. Cartel leaders such as García Abrego and Carrillo Fuentes bought newspaper and magazine businesses to try to keep their names out of the press. PGR officials advised that they have established that many newspaper persons receive salaries from organized criminals in order to keep their names out of the paper, just as the PRI has "purchased" newspaper reporters to publish stories favorable to that party.

Disorder in the Political-Criminal Nexus

July 6, 1997, began a new era for the country of Mexico. For the first time in almost seventy years, the PRI was no longer a majority in the chamber of delegates and it had lost two additional governorships to the opposition PAN (the National Action Party) and the mayoralty of Mexico City to the Revolutionary Democratic Party (PRD). For the first time, the PRI would have to learn how to share legislative powers with the opposing parties and not be a "rubber-stamp" to the president as it had been for so long. At the same time, Mexico has undergone

significant erosion of institutional authority. There is less power at the center, even in the presidency, than there used to be. . . . In effect, Mexico has been witnessing political disintegration at two distinct levels—among its uppermost institutions, and within the political class. These developments intersect with each other and multiply their mutual effects. In this fashion, they set the scene for the ascendancy of the country's new-age drug barons. . . . The deterioration of Mexico's long-standing system tends to magnify the political significance of drug traffickers, since they face relatively few constraints on their action.[34]

Bluntly put, at the present time no one is in charge. The traditional methods of control from the president down through the PRI hierarchy, and through the social control agents over organized crime, have deteriorated to the point where criminality is rampant, a number of political murders have not been resolved, and kidnappings for extremely large ransoms have gone unresolved for years. The transition taking place from authoritarianism to democracy in the last five years has been extremely difficult to navigate. The organized crime figures, realizing this lack of control, know that they will not be touched by lawful authorities and therefore are going after their competitors and assassinating the police officers and prosecutors who are serious enough to go after them. And so, "no one is confronting the mafias or serious crime for one simple reason; everyone, in whatever police agency, knows who is killing whom and why. But they will not investigate for one simple reason: It is better to delay it (investigating) or face assassination by one's own police comrades."[35]

The mass firings of federal, state, and local police in the 1990s aggravated the situation by placing more individuals on the street who were hungry to make ends meet at any cost and have joined the criminals or banded together to form their own enterprises. "By 1995, according to an internal Interior Ministry report, there were an estimated 900 armed criminal bands in Mexico of which over 50 percent were made up of current and retired members of law enforcement agencies."[36]

Because of the well-established patron-client systems that ruled Mexico for so many years and kept major crime in check, there was no perceived need for a career civil service system. Therefore, with the exceptions of the army, foreign service, and Bank of Mexico, no professional government institution exists today. That lack of a professional career and a civil service system for the police and judicial services has placed an unfair burden on these groups to administer justice. The lack of training, the lack of a decent wage or possibility of promotion, and the institution's inability to provide the necessary tools for an investigation (i.e., cars, phones, gas, per diem, as well as adequate laws) leads to corruption on the part of the institution. When the institution does not provide the tools for the official to carry out his or her duties, then that official must seek out ways, generally through corrupt practices, to pay for services to the public institution.

In addition, through intimidation, coercion, and bribery of judges, major criminals are having serious charges dismissed, allowing them back on the street to continue their criminal activities. The authorities at the state and national levels are "outgunned, outmanned" and undercut by the corruption and intimidation by the criminals. President Zedillo has repeatedly stated that criminals present the number one threat to the national security of Mexico. In addition, urbanization, multinational corporations, global communications, internationalization of finance and financial controls, the North America Free Trade Agreement (NAFTA), and the creation of an educated and viable middle class with democratic expectations have all contributed toward weakening the authoritarian system of governance in Mexico.

For almost seven decades, "corruption enables the system to function, providing the 'oil' that makes the wheels of the bureaucratic machine turn and the 'glue' that seals political alliances"[37] and brought Mexico relative calm. From the foregoing, it would appear that:

Corruption and complicity appear to have been carefully organized. If this is so, they have to be considered as institutions serving precise and specific goals of the existing Mexican political system. . . . They integrate the political elite, reward loyalty to the Presidency, serve as a real and permanent threat for those not conforming to the rules and provide a vehicle for economic and social mobility. However, the set of institutions created in 1929 no longer respond to the needs of a society in the process of modernization. Many of the institutions that had functioned in the past, have become dysfunctional and now threaten to thwart Mexico's further development.[38]

Indeed, the change from authoritarianism to democracy will be a difficult challenge for Mexico and there could be a period of ungovernability as we are witnessing today. A recent newspaper article aptly stated, "There currently exists in Mexico an alarming political vacuum. We are trapped in the midst of a transition from a presidentialist and centralist system that no longer functions, toward a plural democratic system that has not been consolidated. The violence, the insecurity, the lack of dialog, and the permanent political tension that we live are all products of that power vacuum and from the lack of a profound democratic reform."[39]

For Mexico to regain its streets and the confidence of the public, drastic judicial and law enforcement changes must be implemented, first by professionalizing the social control agencies and the judiciary, and second by modifying the laws to be able to attack the organized crime problems effectively and efficiently. At the helm of the PGR, PJF, and other national law enforcement agencies must be strong, honest, and experienced individuals and an equally strong and honest staff with experience in law enforcement who will remain in place for many years. The professionalization of law enforcement is critical, and to achieve this the recruitment, selection, and training processes must be upgraded and maintained, with better salaries, incentive programs, and career opportunities. These institutions must operate with checks and balances to ensure that the performance and integrity of the public officials will be above board and open to public scrutiny. An impartial device for monitoring the performances of public officials, with the power to discipline and punish offenders of the public trust, must be established. Legislative oversight must be implemented to ensure compliance, public scrutiny, and continuity in the professionalization of police and law enforcement. The operations of law enforcement must be transparent and coordinated to address the major crime problems of the community. Task forces must be established to attack organized crime elements, gather intelligence on corrupt organizations, and dismantle these by seizing their assets and incarcerating their members. Profits realized from the seizure of assets should be returned to the police to augment its budget for training and equipment. Judicial reform is a must in order to attack organized crime. Passage of legislation to utilize undercover agents, informants, electronic monitoring devices, and effective witness protection programs and funding for such initiatives is required. Banking laws must be strengthened to make money laundering and frauds serious criminal offenses.[40]

There is no respect for law enforcement authorities in Mexico. There is a need to instill in the community a sense of trust by which each citizen can expect respect, honesty, and integrity from public servants. The institutions must work with the community to improve relations and to instill a sense of trust toward the police. On the other hand, the police and the prosecutors must gain the public's trust by not accepting or demanding bribes, by being professional and courteous, respecting the civil rights of each citizen, and working with the community to make it a safer environment. Extensive crime prevention programs sponsored by the government and the private sector should be implemented and should address all age groups.

President Ernesto Zedillo, in an address to the nation on November 30, 1997, stated that he shared the nation's indignation over rising crime and pledged to crack down on organized criminals and police corruption. He promised to send draft legislation to the Congress that would reform the Constitution and Mexico's antiquated laws to stiffen penalties against criminals and to make it more difficult for criminals to avoid judicial actions. He intended to launch a nationwide crusade against crime and violence by: (1) legislating rigorous laws to punish the criminals; (2) profoundly transforming the law enforcement institutions and their personnel; (3) greatly increasing the economic resources for law enforcement efforts; (4) mobilizing society toward a culture of lawfulness; and (5) instilling in society an awareness that all crimes must be punished, whether at the local, state, or national levels.[41]

The future of Mexico is full of perils, with many competing interests. On the one hand, there are those who want democratic change with equal participation of all political parties; then there are the so-called dinosaurs of the PRI who do not want change under any circumstances and who will fight change with their known methods of corruption and complicity. Also resisting change are the organized criminals, competing among themselves for fiefdoms through kidnappings and murders. Finally we have those caught in the middle of all the above, the majority of hard-working and honest Mexican citizens striving for tranquility and justice. As Mexico's Nobel Laureate, Octavio Paz, said:

We are witnessing the end of the PRI system, which could pave the way to a multiparty system; but if we don't achieve that, if the different forces don't succeed in agreeing on a peaceful transition toward a new political situation, we will have demonstrations, possible violence in the countryside and the cities, internal fighting, or something like that . . . in the long run, the forces of openness, modernization, and democracy will prevail, but it will be a very painful, very difficult road.[42]

Appendix: *Comparative Models of Organized Crime**

Model One: The Stage-Evolutionary Model of Organized Crime

I. The Predatory Stage

Examples: Street gangs; outlaw motorcycle gangs (early period); Vietnamese gangs.

II. The Parasitical Stage

Examples: Italian American organized crime in general; many Colombian organizations; many Bosnian groups.

III. The Symbiotic Stage

Examples: Italian American organized crime in private sanitation, Fulton fish market, and construction industry in New York City; certain labor unions; Japanese Yakuza; Chinese triad organizations in Southeast Asia; Cali cartel in Valle de Cauca.

Model Two: The Elite-Exploitation Model of Organized Crime

I. Entrenched Dominant Elites

Dominant political party, military, political-economic, security apparatus. Russian Nomenklatura; key regime actors; serious criminal communities.

II. Tax and Extort

Major national, transnational, and regional organized crime groups and drug traffickers.

III. For Hard Currency, Internal Development and Investment, Campaign Funding, and Personal Enrichment

This system is controlled by operators and collusion at the top. Examples include Burma, Mexico, Pakistan, and Russia.

Some Indicators of the Elite-Exploitation (E-E) Model Compared with the Stage-Evolutionary Model of Organized Crime

• Organized crime entrepreneurs are viewed as "cash cows" to be "taxed, exploited, and manipulated by the political system's agents and institutions of social control."

• Organized criminals are rarely permitted to retire from the game. If they are, other family members take their place in the system.

• The children of organized criminals rarely establish legitimate careers totally separated from the business of crime. Money laundering fronts are about as far as they get.

• The agents of state institutions of social control plan and initiate criminal acts ranging from sale of seized drugs to murder.

• Extrajudicial acts and actors are a basic part of the system.

*The above models and indicators were developed by Professor Peter A. Lupsha.

• Seized drugs and other contraband tend to be used and sold, not destroyed, despite "Potemkin-like" displays of destruction.

• When elites change, organized crime group leaders tend to be replaced, and the former leader is arrested, extradited, or killed.

• When contraband seizures are made, generally no arrests are made.

• When arrests are made, these are generally the lowest level of personnel of the criminal organization.

• Offices (positions) are sold, especially those in lucrative ports of entry in drug/contraband/import areas.

• The elites' willingness to commit crimes and use threats and torture creates a conspiracy of silence among organized criminals even after arrest or extradition.

• There are embedded expectations of kickbacks and payments up the chain of command. Thus, extortionist behaviors permeate every level of organization and spread across the system.

Little of the above is commonplace in the stage-evolutionary model.

Chapter 3

Organized Crime and the Organization of Crime

Luis Astorga

Introduction

AS A METHODOLOGICAL PRINCIPLE, the study of a subject should begin with critical examination of the sociohistorical origin of inherited categories and patterns of perception. Doing otherwise limits one's understanding of the subject. In the case of illicit drugs and drug traffickers, the current prevailing discourse can make uncritical thinkers believe that what is said is true and has always been true and that the future is already laid out. People talk about the war on drugs, drug trafficking, drug traffickers, cartels, federation, Colombianization, organized crime, national security, and the like as if these categories had meaning in themselves. All of these categories of perception are sociohistorical constructions or intellectual creations that have been successfully imposed by those who invented them. This is so not because they provide better explanations, but to a great extent because of those persons' social status and their ability to make their perceptions take precedence over those of their competitors. The universe of thought in which these categories gain their meaning began to become more clearly defined at the beginning of the twentieth century with the birth of the new modern prohibitionist era, which was actively promoted by different U.S. administrations. The Shanghai Conference on Opium Control in 1909 was the starting point for this.

Over time, drugs, the social agents who deal them, and their activities have been conceptualized in various ways. The current prevailing discourse includes categories of perception that have been established at different times and in different places. Curiously, heterogeneous realities have led to a trend toward the homogenization of concepts, making them universal, and toward a type of conceptual imperialism. Historical analysis of each individual situation makes it possible to determine the social uses of different drugs over time and the perceptions people have of those drugs and their users. Such analysis also helps identify the words that have been invented to designate the substances, social agents, and conceptual patterns that have served as reference points in understanding the relationship among users. It also allows for the observation of changes and external influences on the determination of categories and patterns of perception in concrete cases.

As for organized crime, one must research both the sociohistorical process that made it possible at a given time to criminalize activities that were previously legal as well as the social agents who—depending on the location and time, from outside or inside legitimate power structures—organized those activities using a business rationale without regard for conventional ethical concerns. Regarding illicit drug trafficking, in each instance one must study the skill and ethical willingness of certain social groups, inside and outside the state or the hegemonic political power, to directly or indirectly organize and control this activity that has been outlawed since the beginning of the twentieth century. Organized crime is a category that encompasses several factors: (1) the number of participants and perceived scale of illicit operations; (2) the level of business development and organization attributed to the social agents who live off of the illegal business or who at some point participate in that business; and (3) the danger these participants may pose in specific situations for the existence or effective exercise of the rule of law.[1]

The clandestine production of and demand for prohibited goods are two aspects of a complementary relationship. Contraband is a strategy of selling illegal or legal goods through fraudulent means. When this trade takes place between countries with different laws—one that prohibits certain goods and another that does not—there are legal repercussions. So in a sense, prohibition creates the crime and the criminal. As for the sale of drugs, it can either be a legitimate commercial activity with goods made profitable by demand, or it can be illegal when the goods and those who trade them cross the border between countries with different legal codes to conduct their business. What is criminal on one side is legal on the other.

In the face of this contradiction, the more powerful country will try to impose its vision of the phenomenon and change the laws of the weaker country accordingly. That was the situation that began to emerge between Mexico and the United States after the U.S. Congress passed the Harrison Narcotic Act in 1914, which imposed certain controls and restrictions on the production of opium for smoking; there were no similar measures in Mexico. Another example, but of the opposite circumstance—that is, of free trade, was the situation that forced China to surrender to the interests of English opium traders in the nineteenth century.

There may be preexisting ignorance when conducting this business, that is, social agents are neither perfectly rational nor perfectly informed. When the act is voluntary and agents have prior knowledge of the legal implications, there can be multiple reasons for engaging in it. These may range from deeming illegal drug trade to be an economic activity like any other to viewing it as a means for survival or a full-time profession, thus making it worthwhile to risk one's freedom or even one's life. The person is aware of the risk; however, the nonconformity of the established measures, the expected profits, and the hope for success outweigh the negatives.

There are various reasons why prohibitionist laws are passed in a given society, including the perceived need by decision makers—which is not necessarily shared by the rest of society—to establish strict controls on certain behaviors and practices of some inhabitants, which they oppose. Other reasons include the existence of a widespread conviction that such laws are necessary, internal social pressure stimulated by influential groups, and external political pressure, among others.

The prohibitionist measures that began in 1909 continued on their course in other forums, such as the International Opium Convention that was held in The Hague in 1912. The U.S. government passed the Harrison Narcotic Act in 1914 with the same intentions. The Mexican government began to participate in these international forums in 1912, adopting the proposed measures. Opium poppy was cultivated in Mexico and large amounts of opium were imported for medicinal use. Nonetheless, the prohibitionist mentality was not as developed in Mexico as it was in the United States; the consumption of opiates was not as extensive in Mexico and thus was not a cause for great concern. In addition, the country was in the middle of a revolution. It simply did not have laws similar to those of its neighbor to the north, and preparing such laws was not an urgent matter among the political forces battling for power. National prohibition of the cultivation and marketing of marijuana did not occur until 1920, and for opium poppy it was not until 1926. Smugglers immediately saw the chance to do business and did not deny themselves that opportunity. Those most involved in this trade at that time were Mexican residents of Chinese origin, although they were not the only ones. The northern part of the country became a strategic zone for the production of and traffic in drugs.

The goal of this chapter is to present some significant cases that illustrate the particular features of this historic process in Mexico. I develop two main points. First, contrary to the conventional wisdom that now considers drug trafficking in Mexico as relatively recent and illegitimate from the start, research in archives and newspapers shows how long it has existed and some of the sociohistoric conditions that made it possible to transform a legitimate business into a prohibited one. It also shows that in Mexico there are well-founded reasons for thinking that this business originally flourished because of the boost it was given from within the regional power structures in production and trafficking areas, starting precisely at the time when the United States outlawed opium. The monopoly of political power beginning in the 1920s by the victorious revolutionary forces, and the lax ethics of some of its representatives and heirs in public administration in subsequent decades, facilitated the success of the business.

Second, the mechanisms used by those in political office to control the business changed in the 1940s with the arrival of civilians in power. From that time on, the National Security Police (DFS) and the Office of the Attorney General (PGR) were the main institutions responsible for combating drug traffic, for regulating it, and for serving as a structural intermediary between traffickers and those in political power. The traffickers, who were historically subordinated to the hegemonic political power, showed greater relative autonomy only when the old power structure began to show signs of deterioration in the 1980s and 1990s as the political opposition gained ground.

Baja California

In the 1910s, the dealing of contraband illicit drugs was already sufficiently profitable to attract the attention of powerful politicians, such as Colonel Esteban Cantú, Governor of Baja California (1914–1920). In reports from customs authorities in Los Angeles (1916) to the Department of the Treasury and the Department of State, he is named as having granted leases for opium trafficking in the region he governed in exchange for large sums of money. The price of a lease was $45,000 and the monthly rent for trafficking ranged between $10,000 and $11,000 (U.S. dollars). He is also said to have been addicted to morphine. Gambling and prostitution were other sources of revenue for his government and for Cantú himself. In 1917, an amendment to section XVI of article 73 of the Constitution was approved, giving Congress the authority to dictate laws in fields like public health. One of the main concerns was the sale of substances that "degenerated the Mexican race," such as opium, morphine, cocaine, ether, and marijuana. According to customs sources in Los Angeles, what Cantú seized he subsequently sold in the United States with the help of his father-in-law's family.[2]

Governor Cantú (judge and jury) was a pioneer of the tradition between revolutionary politicians and those who succeeded them of conducting private business from public office, regardless of moral considerations and the illegal nature of the activities. Opium trafficking was simply one more business that his political power and ethical disposition allowed him to conduct with greater chances of success and impunity than other persons. Those who wanted to deal in the big league had to do so with him. In other words, the traffickers' power was subordinate to the political power of the governor. Technically, Cantú was a trafficker only from the U.S. point of view because poppy culture and its illegal commerce were not prohibited in Mexico until 1926.

Displaced by the victorious revolutionaries from Sonora, Cantú was replaced by General Abelardo L. Rodríguez, who was put in charge of military operations. Rodríguez was subsequently made governor and some years later served as acting president of Mexico (1932–1934) and then as governor of Sonora in the 1940s. General Rodríguez owned the Casino Agua Caliente in Tijuana, which at that time was frequented by figures such as Babe Ruth, Charles Chaplin, Rita Hayworth, and even Al Capone, and he took advantage of his position during the years of prohibition in the United States to make his fortune.[3]

The possible conflict between organized crime and governability—a recent concern in Mexico—was nullified by those in political power who controlled the largest illegal business. From that time on, the "usual suspects" in wholesale drug dealing were prominent politicians, particularly the governors of northern states and persons close to them and members of their government or of police agencies. The majority of influential traffickers who were not members of the political class were political protégés, not the politician's godfathers or controllers. In other words, the traffickers were perceived as being used by the dominant political class to do their dirty work, not as independent social agents above that class, nor were they viewed as barbarians trying to seize the power of the state by force or through corruption strategies aimed at officials at different levels who were clean.

It is useful to take a closer look at some other early examples from the fringe area of a history of suspicion that goes on today, the history of the ongoing tension between the spirit of the law and the spirit of deceit.

On May 18, 1931, Dr. Bernardo Bátiz B., a health officer in Baja California Norte, sent a report to the head of the Department of Health in Mexico City, in which he mentioned the talks he had held with U.S. authorities in Los Angeles on the "lamentable traffic in opiates" in the border region. He stated that he had reached the conclusion that the direction of the trafficking was more from the United States to Mexico than vice versa and that both he and narcotics supervisor Harvey Smith thought that the large-scale traffickers resided north of the border. They were also suspicious of the behavior of veteran health workers in both countries. He noted that Governor Carlos Trejo y Lerdo de Tejada had told him confidentially that "the Mexican police were accomplices of the drug traffickers." He suggested "credible, energetic, and on-going action" to remove the "inclination to judge with disdain the actions of Mexican authorities on drug issues."[4] Dr. Bátiz's curious concern was surprising, since he himself chose to reveal the governor's confidential information.

Almost two months later, on July 13, 1931, Dr. Rafael Silva, head of the Department of Health, wrote a letter to Governor Trejo defining his position on statements allegedly made by personnel from his office, saying that the governor was named as someone who promoted "narcotics trafficking" or who did not help to pursue traffickers. Dr. Silva was surprised by the news and stated that he and the governor had known each other and been friends for some time. He assured the governor that no one from his office had made public or confidential statements to that end. He also overrode "any lower-ranking employee who may have stated an opinion not only without having full knowledge of the facts, but also without having the jurisdiction and competence to do so on this subject." He informed the governor that investigation had begun into "lower-level narcotics employees," in search of proof to take legal action against whomever was found responsible for the accusations against the governor.[5]

A confidential memorandum (dated September 4, 1931) to Dr. Silva from Francisco Vázquez Pérez, head of Legal Services of the Health Department, informed him that the recent attacks on Governor Trejo in the Chamber of Deputies had been made by Deputy Bátiz, the brother of the health officer in Baja California, "thus making it easy to deduce that he received the data on narcotics trafficking in Baja California that he transmitted to the Chamber from him." The memorandum stated that this information was being forwarded so that he "would kindly bring it to the attention of the president of the republic, so that the attorney general may make:

I. The appropriate decision on the events attributed to the government authorities in Baja California.

II. The appropriate decision on the possible revelation of details on drug trafficking made by the health officer in Mexicali to Deputy Bátiz."[6]

Weeks earlier, on August 19, 1931, Deputy Bátiz had sent a report to Dr. Demetrio López, head of the Service of Chemistry and Pharmaceuticals. One of the paragraphs of his text refers to Trejo in pointed terms:

Undoubtedly, the Governor, following Mr. Santoyo's (Secretary General of the Interior in Baja California) indication, and more surely by the arrival of the Inspector of Chemistry and Pharmaceuticals, S. García Remus, and the notice from the military authorities, whom Inspector García Remus asked for assistance, felt obliged to pursue drug traffickers. This was nothing more than a distraction. A few isolated arrests were made, which were wildly exaggerated in the press, in order to make the government's work in that area seem very worthwhile.

Bátiz mentioned a note published in the Mexico City daily *El Nacional* on the ninth of that month, in which Antonio Gabucio, personal secretary to Governor Trejo, had discovered a "mafia" headed by Domingo Pérez Vázquez, the health inspector. According to Bátiz's investigations, the latter was a drug trafficker, "which the people who appointed him knew. With the help of the elements put at his disposal, he pursued individuals who were competing with him in his business." In opposition to the account given that Pérez was not a government employee, Bátiz stated that he was a trusted employee who had attended numerous official ceremonies and, on one occasion, had even accompanied Antonio Gabucio. Bátiz said the statements "were being made merely to mislead, while the narcotics trafficking continued ever more intensely and was shielded by officials. Only when people fall into disfavor because of their greed does something happen like what happened to Pérez Vázquez." His own summary of events was as follows: "One of the drug traffickers supported by the administration decided to work for himself, and it ended poorly."[7]

In the 1940s in California (United States), the world of organized crime included figures such as Mickey Cohen, who began his career with Al Capone in Chicago. Cohen's name is linked to others such as Harold "Happy" Meltzer—who had special contacts with Salvatore Duhart, the Mexican consul in Washington, who made arrangements with Mexican customs to traffic opium—and his associate Max Cossman, also known as Max Weber, or "Step and a Half." In his study of the CIA's involvement in drug trafficking, Alfred McCoy asserts that Meltzer joined forces with Mickey Cohen. He does not mention "Bugsy" Siegel, from the Luciano-Lansky group; however, he does say that Meltzer failed in his Mexican endeavor because he did not have adequate political contacts. Luciano, on the other hand, had solid political power in Sicily and the support of criminal groups in Marseilles and Corsica. In Marseilles, his associates enjoyed the support of the city government and the CIA.[8] According to Harry Anslinger, Siegel and Virginia Hill negotiated with Mexican politicians in order to be able to finance the cultivation of opium poppy in the northwestern part of the country.[9] In Baja California Norte, Enrique Diarte emerged as an important opium trafficker operating in Mexicali and Tijuana. In 1944, Diarte was killed near Tijuana, a murder that Cossman was accused of masterminding. In the 1950s, Cossman—under the name Francisco Mora—made frequent trips to Culiacán, Los Mochis, and Mazatlán to purchase raw opium, which he paid for with fake jewels and counterfeit dollars. Cossman is attributed with having funded the activities of a band of traffickers in Sinaloa headed by Rodolfo Valdez, also known as "El Gitano," who was a gunman for the landholders from the south of the state and who killed the governor of Sinaloa, Colonel Rodolfo T. Loaiza, in 1944. Cossman, also known as "the king of opium," was apprehended, jailed, and sentenced in Mexico City in 1949 and escaped from prison twice. His wife brought morphine and heroin into the Lecumberri prison in rubber bags underneath her clothing.[10]

Chihuahua and Coahuila

The smuggling of prohibited drugs in the northern border area began to be a cause for political concern at the highest levels of the federal government, as is evident in the following historical reconstruction.

At the beginning of the 1930s, in a letter to General Eulogio Ortiz, military commander of the state of Chihuahua, that was neither dated nor signed, the sender referred to the general as a "friend and nephew."[11] The tone and content of that letter lead one to believe that it was sent by President Pascual Ortiz Rubio himself. It expressed concern over "the increase in national and international narcotics trafficking along the rail line joining Mexico City and Ciudad Juárez." For that reason, he said he ordered the Department of Health to conduct a meticulous investigation and to punish those found responsible. He reported that the department had hired Juan Requena, a "secret agent," and two others to handle the matter, all of whom, he adds, "are currently in Torreón." Predicting the consequences, he stated, "in charging those found responsible, the agents will undoubtedly run into the difficulty of damaging important interests and will certainly need the assistance of federal forces; I implore you to give orders providing them with all the necessary support through the forces under your command."

Inspector Requena sent a report, dated July 20, 1931, on his investigation to the head of the Department of Public Health.[12] In that report he noted the results of his work in Ciudad Juárez, then the capital of Chihuahua, and in Torreón over a period of three months and ten days—since April 10, 1931. The above-mentioned letter to General Ortiz must have been sent at some time between those two dates.

The task assigned to Requena and his agents does not appear to have been easy or simple. In May 1931, during their stay in Ciudad Juárez, General Enrique Zertuche González firmly reminded federal health officer Dr. Alberto Jacqueminot that he had not delivered the weapons that Requena had deposited in his office—which apparently were confiscated—despite the verbal orders he had been given. The doctor defended the actions of the federal health officers, who were "authorized to proceed as they did when carrying out a difficult task in which they may easily be putting their lives on the line," and the doctor answered Zertuche González vigorously in writing that he received orders only from the head of the Department of Health, which he had never been given verbally.[13]

On June 4, 1931, Requena received orders from the head of the Department of Health to transfer to Torreón and was told to announce his departure from Ciudad Juárez in the following terms: "The agent appointed by the federal government to monitor the illicit trafficking in narcotics in the city has received orders from higher up to work on a mission in the City of Los Angeles, California." He was asked not to divulge his destination to anyone and "that he be totally discreet and ensure that the newspapers do not publish anything on the work you are to carry out in that city, in order to make your actions more successful."[14]

The results of the investigation by Requena and agents Piña and Baca were summarized in a confidential memorandum from the Department of Public Health (June 16, 1931).[15] Torreón was listed as being the "main center for narcotics trafficking in the populations linked together by the rail line from Mexico City to Ciudad Juárez and for the international trafficking carried out in this city." It stated that the agents had located the main traffickers and were merely waiting for hard evidence to take legal action against them. However, the most relevant statements are outlined in three points:

I. "One of the main culprits, Antonio Wong Yin, who is Chinese, is in constant contact with the Municipal President of Torreón, Mr. Francisco Ortiz Garza.

II. He is also the 'compadre' of the Governor of the State of Coahuila, Mr. Nazario Ortiz Garza.

III. General Jesús Garzía [sic] Gutiérrez, the Head of State Operations, who resides in Torreón, has dealings with another one of the narcotics traffickers."

Given the above, the agents had to suspend their investigation pending new instructions, since they feared they did "not have sufficient support from civilian and military authorities in the state." There were grounds for that concern.

In his report, Requena mentioned that many of the narcotics traffickers in Ciudad Juárez "have or had the support of civilian and federal authorities."[16] He spoke of several Chinese men in the city of Chihuahua who supplied their fellow countrymen in Juárez and of an American couple doing large-scale trafficking and making trips by plane. He mentioned a person named Luis, or "El Texano," who was deported from the United States and was the supplier for many of the traffickers in the border city. He further stated that he knew of connivance between civilian authorities and railway employees in the cities of Chihuahua, Parral, Jiménez, and Piedras Negras. As for the traffickers, he stated that they all "have a complete espionage service with elements prepared to do anything."

Regarding Enrique Fernández, "the ace trafficker in Juárez," Requena wrote that on one occasion he was sent to Las Islas Marias for a "vice crime" and was "saved" by the acting governor of Chihuahua (1929–1930), Luis León (Secretary of Agriculture and Development in Calles' cabinet and Secretary of Industry, Commerce, and Labor for Ortiz Rubio). He added that Fernández, who had six police officers in his service to protect him night and day and a "well-organized mafia," was in Mexico City and walked with a limp. He wrote that his brother Antonio had been accused in Torreón of being a drug trafficker and addict, along with Samuel Chew, a Chinese man. Finally, he writes: "Antonio Wong Yin (the owner of the Chinese Casino in Torreón, who was accused of vice crimes on several occasions) is a close friend of the current governor of the state of Coahuila and is his 'compadre.' The Governor used to be the Municipal President, a position held today by one of his brothers in Torreón, and I myself witnessed Antonio Wong Yin being close to the Municipal President and other authorities for two days." He attached a list of over eighty names of the main drug traffickers and dealers from the capital and other parts of the country. Among those topping the list were Simón and Antonio Fernández, Daniel Gutiérrez (El Chiquito), José Hernández, and Francisco (Paco) Pérez. He further mentioned that in Topia, Durango, "there is a large amount of land on which opium poppy is cultivated." In addition, an American told him that he suspected that the Chinese in the region engaged in manufacturing opium.[17]

More precise data on the criminal history of Enrique Fernández Puerta, known as the Al Capone of Juárez, were published by police reporter Salvador Martínez Mancera between November 1937 and January 1938. Fernández began his career by smuggling alcohol and counterfeiting dollars. He then took up drug trafficking. According to the journalist, Fernández "eventually controlled city hall and was a stepping stone for making many individuals who worked for the government in Chihuahua wealthy, including three governors."[18] He strengthened his power as strongman of Ciudad Juárez during the term of Deputy Governor Roberto Fierro (1931–1932). At the end of Fierro's term, the brothers of the official candidate for governor, General Rodrigo Quevedo, seized city hall in Juárez and declared war on Fernández. General Quevedo served as governor from 1932 to 1936 and was mentioned in a letter to the Senate "left wing" and to the Permanent Committee of the National Congress from Fernando Orozco, a candidate for governor of Chihuahua, as the protector of Quevedo's brother José, the municipal president of Ciudad Juárez, "in the illicit trafficking in opiates."[19] At the end of 1933, Fernández was shot and wounded. After receiving that message, he and his men fled to Mexico City, where he was later killed in Guardiola Park by gunmen hired by the Quevedo brothers, or so it was said.[20] In 1937, General and Doctor José Siurob, head of the Department of Public Health, referred to Ciudad Juárez as "possibly the most dangerous center where traffickers operate who are corrupted by Allende el Bravo's gangsterism and defend their trafficking with gunfire."[21]

The point of these vignettes is to suggest that there is evidence that a pattern of control by politicians over criminals is more accurate than the contrary thesis that posits the traffickers' "penetration" of the clean, transparent, and virginal field of politics. A few years after the prohibition of marijuana (1920) and opium poppy (1926), the reports of two officials, Requena and Dr. Bátiz, both of whom were in a position to know what they were talking about, clearly showed that in the business of drug trafficking there was solid ground for believing in the connivance, protection, and support of authorities, even high-level ones. The observations by these officials illustrate what could be deemed to be the origin of an endogenous development within the power structure, not an exogenous, parallel, or unrelated one, as is the more widespread perception today.

Sinaloa

The most significant case of the crime-politics nexus of the 1940s took place not in the border states in northern Mexico but rather in the northwest, in the state of Sinaloa, where opium poppy had existed since at least the last quarter of the nineteenth century. When the prohibitions began in the 1920s, the cultivation of opium poppy was primarily concentrated in four states: Sonora, Sinaloa, Chihuahua, and Durango. Traffickers from Sinaloa showed greater dynamism in developing their business and were able to consolidate their positions at a time when few people anticipated that it would boom in future decades.

In 1947, journalists for the Mexico City daily papers *Excélsior, El Universal,* and *Ultimas Noticias* named General Pablo Macías Valenzuela—Secretary of War and the Navy from 1940 to 1942 and governor of Sinaloa from 1945 to 1950—as controlling or protecting opium trafficking in the state he led.[22] His defenders claimed that this was a campaign orchestrated by his political enemies, who years earlier had accused him having masterminded the assassination of then-governor of Sinaloa, Colonel Rodolfo T. Loiza, in 1944. Months before these articles attacking Valenzuela appeared, Harry Anslinger, the head of the U.S. Federal Bureau of Narcotics and a delegate to the United Nations Commission on Narcotic Drugs, had declared that Mexico was the main supplier of the opium consumed in the United States. He also said that high-level state authorities in drug-producing areas had dealings in the drug business. The accusations against Valenzuela emerged during the preparation of the antidrug "campaign" by the administration of Miguel Alemán, which was started by the Office of the Attorney General in 1947.

Sinaloa was portrayed in the press as "the most brazen center for trade in opiates." Culiacán, the state capital, was described as the "opium smugglers' base of operations." The municipality of Badiraguato, the main producer of opium poppy, was dubbed "opium central" and the "hideout for hundreds of hoodlums." It was also published that for at least twenty years (since 1927) the governors of Sinaloa had been "accomplices in opium production." It was said that many people referred to Governor Valenzuela as "one of the ringleaders of the gang of traffickers." Federal officials asked the press to "avoid insolence, exaggeration, and lies that may hinder the success of the investigations or unduly compromise the country's prestige." The tension decreased after President Miguel Alemán's trip to Chihuahua and Sinaloa in the second half of November 1947. Two days after the president's visit to Mazatlán, Valenzuela issued an official communiqué rejecting the accusations made by the press, which he called "extremely offensive," "slanderous," and "extravagant fantasies." Nothing was proved, but suspicions remained. The governor completed his term, and in 1951 was appointed to head Military Region I, the headquarters of which is in the Valley of Mexico, and to run the Military Camp Number One in 1952. The main opium trafficker of the time, Miguel Urías Uriarte from Badiraguato, was captured and released shortly thereafter, and it was said that he was protected by the authorities.[23]

Sonora

The banks of the Yaqui, Mayo, Concepción, and Moctezuma Rivers and the Altar region were mentioned in press accounts as places where opium poppy was grown. General Abelardo L. Rodríguez was the governor of Sonora at the time of the accusations against Macías in Sinaloa. He considered Sonora to be exclusively a trafficking state, although he could not deny the existence of production fields in some of the above-mentioned locations. Days before the Macías case broke, the rumors heard in the PGR and published in the national press said that two northern governors were "involved in narcotics trafficking"; however, a second name was never given. In a note sent from Hermosillo, a journalist from the *Excélsior* stated that Sinaloa was the center of drug trafficking.[24]

In Sonora, the head of the Social Prevention Police and other agents under his command were accused of permitting the planting of opium poppy. In the municipality of Soyopa, the Mexican Federal Judicial Police (MFJP) discovered and destroyed a 4,000-square-meter irrigated plot near the ranch of Francisco Landavazo, a Mexican congressman. Among those detained was a cousin of the congressman, who was an officer in the Social Prevention Police. The land was occupied by the municipal president of Soyopa, J. Dolores Moreno, who fled upon the arrival of federal agents. According to neighbors, Landavazo was "one of the largest drug traffickers who (controlled) opium production in the region."[25]

Northern and Central Mexico

In the northern states, governors and other politicians were suspected of being involved in drug trafficking, and the situation was not very different in the capital of the country. Carlos I. Serrano was named in a confidential document sent on September 4, 1947, by the U.S. Embassy in Mexico to the secretary of state, based on a report by Maurice C. Holden, assistant military attaché. Holden reported on the recent establishment of the National Security Police (DFS), a political police force under the command of the president, with authority over all other police forces and the authority to investigate drug-related matters. Serrano was a senator and leader in the House and a close advisor to President Miguel Alemán and the true head of the DFS. Also mentioned in the report were Marcelino Inurreta, the official head of that organization, and Lieutenant Colonel Manuel Magoral, the third in command. All were listed as being involved in drug trafficking. The report stated that Magoral controlled marijuana trafficking in Mexico City. It recorded the suspicion that these individuals requested information from the U.S. government and used it to get rid of their competition and control the business. Treasury Department calculations on drug trafficking in Mexico at that time ranged between $20 million and $60 million (U.S. dollars) annually. The American military attaché compared the DFS to the Gestapo because of the powers it had been given and the extremely dubious background of those persons recruited to form it. The legal attaché of the U.S. Embassy indicated that it was too early to determine who would dominate in the DFS—the FBI-trained officers he deemed to be good or those well known for being bad.[26]

Until 1947, the Department of Health was the institution responsible for the antidrug policy, and so the agents who destroyed prohibited crops were from the Health Police. Given the vastness of the territory on which there were plots and the small number of agents, it was physically impossible for them to fulfill their task. However, that was not the only problem. In 1937, the head of the Department of Health himself commented that "in the past" the agents were paid with the drugs they seized, which, of course, they then sold. Some of the elements that helped strengthen the inclination of individuals and groups—both in and out of positions of power—to traffic illicit drugs included the increased demand for drugs during World War II; the aforementioned shortages and practices of health department agents; the testimony of specialized agents and health officials; and the constant suspicion of powerful politicians who perpetuated their inherited ways and enjoyed the impunity stemming from belonging to the governing elite.

Starting in the 1930s there were proposals for the PGR to manage antidrug activities. At that time, President Cárdenas supported the health authorities. In the postwar period, the U.S. government stepped in more aggressively as a leader on the international scene for determining the specifications of the antidrug policy. They did so because of concerns over the possibility of increased drug trafficking and consumption resulting from the habits acquired by the soldiers and the resistance by producers and traffickers to giving up such a profitable business. In this context, the first civilian president since the Revolution, Miguel Alemán, appointed the PGR as the institution responsible for drug issues, beginning in 1947. Meanwhile, the Mexican Army was in a full "campaign" or "fight against drugs" to support the PGR, primarily by destroying growing plots. Because it had more resources, and as the only institution capable of covering the entire country—but formally and legally subordinated to the PGR—the army was in a key position for mediation, containment, or control of the producers and traffickers and the Mexican Federal Judicial Police (FJP), the DFS, and those in political power. From that time on and for several decades, the secrecy of the military institution, the mutual protection of political families belonging to the official party, and the law of silence drew attention exclusively to accusations against the traffickers, police agents, commanders, and other low-level officials who were accused of corruption or of protecting or being traffickers.

It should be noted that of all the northern border states, only Chihuahua was a large drug producer after the 1940s. Another drug-producing state not along the border, but closely linked to the American market through agricultural exports since the beginning of the twentieth century, was Sinaloa, which became the home base for the most powerful, visible traffickers in the country. From then on, the most spectacular raids to destroy illicit crops, such as Operation Condor in the 1970s, contributed to crop replacement and the exodus of experienced growers and traffickers to other states, ready to meet the growing demand of the American market.

An informant recruited by the DEA in 1986, who claimed to have worked in the DFS from 1973 to 1981, stated that some of the commanders in the DFS itself had advised and organized the traffickers in Sinaloa so they could play in the big league, using Jalisco as a base, after Operation Condor.[27] This version of the story was abandoned by U.S. authorities in order to broadly disseminate the thesis of drug traffickers' "penetrating" power structures. Miguel Angel Félix Gallardo, the main trafficker from the mid-1970s to 1989—the year he was captured in Guadalajara—was a pioneer of cocaine trafficking in Mexico and had special contacts with the Colombians. He began his career as a judicial police officer in Sinaloa and (in the 1960s) as a bodyguard to the governor of that state, Leopoldo Sánchez Celis, who was also the best man at his wedding. Félix Gallardo, who stood as best man for the former governor's son, was killed when arranging to visit his godfather in prison in Mexico City. This event is more revealing when one notes that most of the groups of traffickers currently in operation were from this organization and were headed by Sinaloans. What has been lost over time, or rather has been hidden, is the name or names of the political patrons of each of the groups. The "penetration" thesis assumes that the traffickers had autonomous backgrounds, or at least assumes a reversal of the traffickers' relationship of dependence on political power and their subordination to that power beginning at a given time.

Prohibition and Violence

At different times, the violence in drug trafficking has been compared to that which broke out in the United States during Prohibition. Al Capone and Chicago are frequently mentioned as a shorthand reference to a basic historic event, which became a paradigm for illicit business. For example, Enrique Fernández Puerta was known as the "Al Capone of Juárez" in the 1930s, and Culiacán, the capital of Sinaloa, was described in the 1950s as "Chicago with gangsters in huaraches." Sicily and the Cosa Nostra, or Medellín, Cali, and the Colombian traffickers also have certain preferences among the professional labelers. One characteristic of the discourse on drugs was the mechanical use of categories of perception borrowed from other fields and situations, regardless of the country and the particular characteristics of the society in question. Another was the variety of names used to describe this phenomenon and the social agents before the stage of conceptual universalization and homogenization.

Some names from the 1920s that were associated with the illegal drug trade are: plundering criminals, despicable drug dealers, public poisoners. From the 1930s: international narcotics mafia, gang, underworld, international bands or rings. From the 1940s: internationally and nationally organized bands, bands of drug traffickers, international band of traffickers, and international trust. From the 1950s: racketeers and international narcotics bands. From the 1960s: international organization of drug traffickers. From the 1970s: mafia of the *gomeros* ("gum makers"). From the 1980s and 1990s: cartels, drug trafficking mafias, organized crime, federation. Criminalized in the 1920s in Mexico, drug trafficking very quickly became associated with the international market. Of course, there are smaller groups that traffic within the country; however, the largest ones operate on the international scene. The discourse that perceives this phenomenon as being part of organized crime or that uses this category of perception as part of its universe is to a great extent a product of the 1980s and 1990s, the beginning of the post–Cold War era.[28] From the beginning, the names used implicitly considered two aspects: crime and organization.

The firefights between traffickers and police officers and the military grew in direct proportion to the increase in the demand for drugs, the expansion of the market, and the arrival of a new generation of traffickers. Deaths of those on the side of the law were of the lowest ranking officers in the respective agencies. At the end of the 1960s, there appears to have been a shift in the implicit rules of the game, since those killed were higher up in the hierarchy. Instead of mere agents or common soldiers, it was no longer rare—although not very common either—for heads of the judicial police or commanders to be killed, particularly in drug-producing states or those where there was intense trafficking. For example, Major Ramón Virrueta Cruz, the head of the judicial police of Sinaloa, was killed in Culiacán on June 6, 1969. Alfredo Reyes Curiel, deputy chief of the judicial police of Sinaloa, and Major Gustavo Sámano, military advisor for Operation Condor, were killed in 1977 in that same city.[29] However, there is still widespread doubt about whether they died fulfilling their duties or because they were playing a double game. The gross statistics do not make these qualitative distinctions. The bands were breaking their old codes and were openly fighting among themselves in broad daylight in urban areas where innocent civilians were killed in the crossfire.

The comparison with Prohibition-era Chicago went back to the front pages of the press in Sinaloa, since it was in that state where the problem first manifested itself with the greatest force. The federal and state governments felt the situation merited military intervention. Former governor Sánchez Celis, who was no stranger to this subject, stated that in his day there was no need to call in the troops, implying that the situation could have been resolved politically by state authorities. Some thought the unbridled violence of the 1970s had exceeded tolerable limits and the local government's ability to control it and that therefore a spectacular raid, a larger military operation, was necessary. Others felt that it was nothing that could not be resolved through political negotiation, in other words, the situation in itself was not ungovernable and the traffickers were not more powerful than the authorities. Rather it was due to the political ineptitude of Governor Alfonso G. Calderón in imposing minimum rules for peaceful coexistence. In his administration, Sánchez Celis is credited with having told traffickers, whom he knew very well: "Get out from Sinaloa; kill each other somewhere else. Do not work here anymore."[30]

Who's in Charge?

Beginning in 1985, the year in which Enrique Camarena, a DEA agent, and Alfredo Zavala, a Mexican pilot, were kidnapped and killed, the U.S. government put more political pressure on the Mexican government. More than ever before, stories of complicity between the traffickers and police and high-level officials came to light. Some of those persons were apprehended, tried, and sentenced; others were merely named, but hard evidence was never presented against them, and they continued their political life. Yet to this day some of them still do not dare travel to the United States. The traffickers accused of these murders, Rafael Caro Quintero and Ernesto Fonseca, were captured almost immediately, but it took four more years to capture the "Chief of Chiefs," Félix Gallardo. The oligopoly of Sinaloan traffickers, which already had representatives in Ojinaga—such as Amado Carrillo[31] in Pablo Acosta's group—was apparently weakened, but not for long since other groups broke loose from it and extended their bases of operations to other states. In a few years, these "splinter groups" proved to be at least as powerful as their predecessors.

In addition to Pablo Acosta's group in Ojinaga, in Tamaulipas Juan García

Abrego's group was consolidated. It grew rapidly during the Salinas administration (1988–1994) but was weakened when his term ended. Since the 1920s, the drug-producing and -trafficking areas of the country have been primarily dominated by northwestern traffickers, particularly those from Sinaloa. The strongest competition ever for the oligopoly of Sinaloan traffickers came from a border area with a long tradition of smuggling, but which until then had not been much of a factor in drug trafficking. One of the key figures in reestablishing the power dynamic among the groups of traffickers in the country was the then commander of the PJF from Tamaulipas, Guillermo González Calderoni. He led the police raid that killed Pablo Acosta (1987),[32] arrested Jaime Herrera Nevares and Jaime Herrera Herrera (1987),[33] captured Félix Gallardo (1989), and, according to an undercover FBI agent (SA 2620-OC) operating within the organization of traffickers in the Gulf, Calderoni was García Abrego's protector and partner, or at least had been since 1986. Accused of "inexplicable" enrichment in 1993, Calderoni fled to the United States, where he is currently a member of the witness protection program. When faced with possible extradition to Mexico, the former commander revealed that he worked as a political spy for Raúl Salinas, the brother of the former president, who, in turn, is suspected of having protected García Abrego and is currently (2000) in prison for various offenses. These include illicit enrichment and the murder of his former brother-in-law and general secretary of the Institutional Revolutionary Party (PRI), José Francisco Ruiz Massieu. Calderoni threatened to "remember" a great many things if the Mexican government insisted that he be extradited.[34]

García Abrego was captured in 1996 and was immediately deported to the United States, because Mexican and American authorities had agreed that he was born in the United States and thus was a U.S. citizen, despite other proof indicating that he was born on a ranch in Tamaulipas.[35] President Zedillo justified that decision to legislators in a private meeting (as some attendees leaked to the press) by arguing that Abrego was a very dangerous figure and that he could carry out a destabilizing raid in a short period of time. The spokesperson for the president denied this account.[36] Interestingly, when the search for García Abrego was on, there were no desperate acts of violence from someone who felt persecuted and cornered or who had the destabilizing power he purportedly had. Furthermore, the most sensitive economic indicators did not move in a way that caused concern during the search for him or after he was captured. Either García Abrego was an example of nationalism and civility, since there was neither capital flight nor blind violence, or the authorities or those leaking the information exaggerated the story.

The Arellano Félix brothers in Tijuana and Amado Carrillo in Ciudad Juárez were all originally from Sinaloa. According to authorities, the former were kin-related to Félix Gallardo, and the latter was kin-related to Ernesto Fonseca Carrillo and became the undisputed masters of their respective territories. The Arellano brothers were involved in the murder of Cardinal Posadas in May 1993 because of a "mix-up," according to the official version. They were also named as the master-minds of a failed murder attempt on Amado Carrillo in November of that same year, as well as successful attempts against a long list of other important police chiefs. After García Abrego was captured, American authorities named Carrillo the most powerful drug trafficker in Mexico and the world. To develop and con-solidate his position, he seems to have favored distributing money rather than bullets, of course without rejecting the law of the "goat's horn" (AK-47).

Several unsuccessful military raids on the Arellano brothers were launched. Then, in February 1997, the head of the National Institute to Combat Drugs (INCD), General Jesús Gutiérrez Rebollo, was jailed, accused of protecting Car-rillo even before he reached this position.[37] Carrillo, the traveling, cosmopolitan trafficker, was pursued and fled and hid; he would be sighted either in Russia or the Middle East, or in South America and the Caribbean. He had become invisible in Mexico several years earlier and was able to go undetected by U.S. authorities on his frequent trips to Las Vegas,[38] by Israeli authorities on his trip to Jerusalem, and by Cuban authorities. He officially died from side effects of a medicine ap-plied after plastic surgery to change his appearance in a clinic in Mexico City.[39] It is strange that Carrillo chose to have the surgery performed in the capital where he was sought most, when he could have had the surgery anywhere in the world where he traveled without any problem. Was it a suicidal act, supreme unaware-ness, the greater challenge, or was it simply the place where he would be best pro-tected?

With Amado Carrillo's departure from the scene, reports about murders along the northern border, particularly in Ciudad Juárez but also in Tamaulipas, where García Abrego's successor appears to be operating silently and unspectacularly, have begun to appear in the press. The new outbreak of violence is likely the result of fights between rival trafficking groups for control of the market and hegemony in drug trafficking in Mexico.

Conclusion

The foregoing discussions present at least five stages in the development of drug trafficking in Mexico. The first is the formation and consolidation of the postrevolutionary state. In that stage, prominent members of the governing political elite or people very close to them—especially in the northern states that produce prohibited commodities or that are trafficking sites—are mentioned as directly controlling drug trafficking, among other activities. In some instances there is direct testimony from Mexican and American authorities; in others, there is only suspicion. The problem in moving beyond mere suspicion, in the past and today, is that those suspected were (are) both judge and jury.

The second stage began in 1947, when the PGR took over from health authorities in the antidrug area. That same year the DFS was established and granted authority to act in this field. In addition, the army was more openly involved in the task of destroying plots where marijuana and opium poppy were grown. In this way, police forces, which were primarily but not exclusively civilian, became the structural mediator between the hegemonic political power and the drug traffickers. They were given authority but not absolute autonomy to operate in the business to their benefit. They established mechanisms that made institutional control possible and simultaneously extended the social groups that could benefit economically. This was the definition of the maxim: "I don't want you to give it to me, just show me where to get some."

The third stage runs from the end of the 1960s, in particular from the second half of the 1970s, to the first half of the 1980s. A greater number of documented cases of violence occurred among traffickers and between them and the police and military. During those years there was increased demand for marijuana and cocaine in the American market. President Nixon implemented Operation Intercept in 1969, and in northeastern Mexico the army began to participate more visibly and spectacularly in Operation Condor, which officially began in 1977. It became difficult to effectively control the new generation of traffickers and their larger number, within the socially tolerable limits of violence.

The fourth stage began in 1985, with the assassination of DEA agent Enrique Camarena and Mexican pilot Alfredo Zavala. For the first time, American authorities publicly named politicians and high-level police and military officers as protectors of drug traffickers. The president of the United States, Ronald Reagan, promoted the "war on drugs," and in 1986, the year in which the annual certification process for producing and trafficking countries began, he declared drug trafficking a threat to national security. Mexico joined the neoliberal economic current and subscribed to the Reaganite view on drug issues. At the end of the 1980s, the PRI began to lose important political positions when Ernesto Ruffo of the National Action Party (PAN) became governor of Baja California. There were additional examples of the break with the old methods of controlling criminal groups, especially in the states where the political opposition was gaining ground, such as Chihuahua, Jalisco, and Baja California. It seemed as if the displacement of the PRI in some regions had accelerated the dismantling of the mechanisms for mediation between those in political power and the traffickers. The assassination of Cardinal Posadas, Luis Donaldo Colosio, the PRI candidate for President, and José Francisco Ruiz Massieu, the General Secretary of the PRI, were without a doubt signs that the governing class had broken its own rules and that "hunting season" had begun.

In short, and this is the fifth stage, what we are witnessing in Mexico at the end of the 1990s and into the new millennium is the accelerated breakup of the postrevolutionary political system, of a structure based on the concentration of power in the institutional presidency, of the existence of an official party that has governed for almost seven decades, and the subordination of the legislative and judicial branches to the executive. This caving-in of the old system and the emergence of a new correlation of national political forces following the legislative elections of July 6, 1997, make it possible to end traditional control mechanisms. For example, the control agents such as the police and the army served as structural mediators between the hegemonic political power and the traffickers, but they acted under political control, as operational bodies regulating the market and the number of traffickers necessary for the business's scale of operations.

This accelerated breakdown of the old system has created conditions in which the traffickers can express their rebellious spirit, their desire and capacity for autonomy, and their will to throw off the customary patterns of submission. They do not necessarily seek to take over the political power that shielded and nurtured them; but they do want to be considered among the major players in the new game with its new power relationships. They seek to improve their bargaining position in the reorganization of a business that will continue, given the realities of illegal drugs: strong criminalization and high demand. This is the case even with the introduction of the military into the antidrug effort, as for example in the case of Chihuahua in November 1995 and the subsequent expanded militarization of antidrug law enforcement.[40] Even so, the traffickers' economic power does not translate automatically into political power, as "spontaneous sociology" would have it. Put another way, the one that pays does not necessarily rule alone: the obligation may remain to pay for the "franchise" and to continue operating, more or less as in the early years of the 1900s. And even if that actor does rule, it is not absolutely or at all levels, all the time.

Recent changes in the correlation of forces in Mexico have created a context in which democratic forces have not been able to consolidate or to impose the rule of law over the working agreements among power groups, including both established and new bands of traffickers, that do not respect democratic civility. This might lead to an extreme scenario, in which an understanding might be reached among some ex-members of the DFS, the Judicial Police, and the army, along with hard-line PRIistas (both in and out of power) and traffickers to join forces and employ the drug trade to generate resources. These resources would enable such a coalition to exercise influence in a variety of ways, possibly to complicate or even reverse the democratic transition, since a democratic system would presumably expel criminal-political alliances from government and subject them to stricter controls. The power that organized crime has attained in present-day Russia shows that alliances among those displaced from the old order are hardly fictitious.

Influential PRIistas of the hard line, including governors, ex-governors, high-level former and current bureaucrats (some of whom have been identified in the national and foreign media as connected with drug traffickers) with the ambition to assemble a coalition that might support a presidential candidacy could form alliances among themselves and with like-minded currents in the military. Some of the military actors might hold commands in the antidrug campaigns. These elements would be in a strong position to finance such a project, but conceivably as groups within the military seeking their own political space. Such a scenario, carried to a negative extreme, would suggest an effort to resuscitate an authoritarian system that defies death. In sum, the problem of organized crime and governability, in this case drug trafficking, is closely related to the particular forms in which crime has been structurally and historically organized. Understanding that dialectic is the first step in imagining possible solutions.

Chapter 4

Organized Crime and Political Campaign Finance in Mexico

Leonardo Curzio

ONE OF THE MOST DEBATED topics in modern democracies relates to financing the activities of political parties. In North America, Europe, and Latin America, this issue is high on the political agenda. Furthermore, in some countries, irregular contributions have resulted in widely publicized scandals, and, in others, in intense legal-political controversies in order to establish legal frameworks to promote more equal electoral competition. Restrictive regulations or controls on funding received by political institutions have been modified recently. Countries have undertaken these reforms in order to diminish the bias of illegal or illegitimate funding of political parties.

Recent practices of political competition have spurred the progressive commercialization of electoral campaigns, which in turn has required an extensive flow of resources to enable the parties to function.[1] The need for money, generated by rising campaign costs, lies at the root of the increasing relevance of this theme. In fact, illegal financing of parties is only sparsely covered in the specialized literature.[2] Traditionally, the possibility that more powerful economic groups could control party structures was emphasized because it was thought that parties would be used as an instrument of oligarchic control or as a lever to transmit sectorial or foreign interests.[3] Similar concerns about party financing are also reflected in laws that regulate campaign contributions, establishing explicit prohibitions against money from private companies or foreign interests above specific limits.

However, little has been said about the possibility that money coming from organized crime might make its way into the political system through financing of political parties. But this is a topic that requires careful attention. As stated by Peter Lupsha: "In several nations organized crime has turned into a key political actor, an interest group, a sectorial player that must be taken into consideration by the legitimate political system."[4]

It is not easy to conclusively establish links between organized crime and political systems, but there are indicators occurring in certain circumstances that can be used to establish areas where they complement each other.[5]

What do criminal organizations need to operate in a country? First, they need police protection. They also need financial mobility and protection to launder their earnings and bring them into the legal economic system. Political protection is harder to see, but it is also important in creating a powerful buffer against law enforcement and judicial authorities if they decide to move against a criminal organization. These minimal necessities are what prompt criminal organizations to infiltrate government and corrupt public officials to win the complicity or tolerance needed to continue or expand criminal activities.

It seems reasonable to suppose that if $300–500 billion, according to varying estimates, is laundered worldwide each year, some part of that is going to disappear into the political systems of the countries suffering the plague of organized crime.[6] This is made more likely by the fact that financing political activities demands enormous quantities of money. The illegal funds being shuffled from country to country in search of a place to be invested or otherwise protected are not all attributable to organized crime. In general terms, the money may have three origins: tax evasion, governmental and transnational corruption,[7] and organized crime earnings.[8]

The purpose of this chapter is to analyze the possible links between organized crime—especially drug trafficking—and political activity in Mexico. We will first analyze the evolution of organized crime into a national security problem. Once we have established this, we will study the ever-controversial question of what has come to be called "narco-politics." In Mexico the issue of narco-politics is at the center of four recent episodes of national importance. The first is the investigation into Raul Salinas Gortari, brother of the former president, for money laundering and other crimes. The second are rumors that drug money found its way into

President Ernesto Zedillo's campaign coffers. The third is the breakdown of consensus between the government and the president in negotiations on electoral reform. The fear of organized crime infiltrating the political system was so great in the early 1990s that the reform authorized a more than 1,000 percent increase, in nominal terms, in political party financing. The fourth episode focused on campaign spending in November 1994 by Tabasco Governor Roberto Madrazo, who according to the Mexican attorney general's office spent more than $36 million, some of which came from Carlos Cabal Peniche, a fugitive ex-banker with links to drug trafficking. In the conclusion, I will try to establish a relationship between organized crime and governability in contemporary Mexico.

Politics and Drug Trafficking in Mexico

In the last several years, there has been a debate over whether Mexico is a "narco-democracy." The term was popularized by Eduardo Valle, better known by his nickname "The Owl." The Owl was a leader of the Mexican left who represented the National Democratic Front, known by its Spanish acronym FDN, on the federal electoral board in 1988. When Jorge Carpizo was appointed attorney general in January 1993, Valle was named his special advisor for drug trafficking issues. He later fled to the United States under the protection of the FBI. In 1995, he wrote a controversial book entitled *The Second Shot: Mexican Narco-Democracy.*[9] Valle enjoyed some influence in the press, but this later declined. Nevertheless, his allegations of Mexican narco-democracy have had an impact in major publications, as reflected in the widely cited article by Silvana Paternostro.[10]

Beyond what Valle has written and stated, Mexico has become the base for some of the world's biggest criminal organizations. The existence of powerful criminal groups can be found in a variety of academic and official documents.[11] These groups are involved in a range of illicit activities but their main focus is on drug trafficking.

Drug trafficking and related activities like money laundering have risen in priority on the Mexican and U.S. security agendas, and on the bilateral agendas of both countries. In Mexico, the illegal drug trade has gone from being a problem restricted to certain regions (like Sinaloa or Jalisco) to having a direct impact on the country's national security.[12] It quickly became a problem that reached beyond Mexico's borders, affecting three spheres simultaneously: subnational, national, supranational.[13]

The complexity of the problem is reflected in the ways that the fight against organized crime has been undertaken. First it fell within the purview of state forces. As a result, narco-trafficking corrupted the judicial system, police, and even politicians in some states. For example, the former governor of Jalisco, Flavio Romero, is under investigation for money laundering.[14]

Narco-trafficking eventually became too big for the local sphere, and because of the size and the risks that it represented, federal security forces joined the fight. Soon after, allegations began surfacing that the federal police, judges, and politicians were also implicated in drug trafficking. This was when the Mexican and U.S. presses began reporting that General Arevalo Gardoqui, the former Defense Secretary, along with former Mexico City police chief Arturo Durazo and former Interior Secretary Manuel Bartlett and members of the now-disbanded Federal Security Directorate had some ties to organized crime.[15]

In this same period, suspicions were raised that sectors of the Mexican government protected drug traffickers, and the security problem became more serious. An effect, or perhaps a cause, of the situation was the growing tension over the issue in U.S.-Mexican relations. Godson and Olson sum it up well:

For many years, U.S.-Mexican cooperation, or lack of it, was the subject of ongoing controversy and recrimination. This was exacerbated by the Enrique Camarena case, where Mexican drug traffickers, with the possible complicity of some Mexican state and federal officials, kidnapped and tortured to death a U.S. DEA agent stationed in Mexico. The controversy surrounding the murder, the alleged cover-up, and the U.S. seizure in Mexico of one of the alleged perpetrators of the torture/murder, seriously damaged bilateral relations for years. Hence not only does Mexican organized crime undermine the Mexican government's ability to rule, it also undermined U.S.-Mexican relations. Although relations have improved, the potential for Mexican criminals to sidetrack cooperation and aggravate an already sensitive political environment is likely to remain a major problem for years to come.[16]

The nearly simultaneous inaugurations of Carlos Salinas and George Bush as presidents of their countries in 1988–1989 began the process of easing tensions between the two nations. Salinas de Gortari gave high priority to fighting drug trafficking. In 1990, he unveiled his National Drug Control Program, in which he gave "a top priority in the national agenda to fighting drug trafficking."[17] Still, the problems linked to drug trafficking persisted. The case of Admiral Mauricio She-leske, the former secretary of the navy, who was relieved of his duties after suspicions were raised that he was linked to the drug trade, once again fueled the debate over the extent of the illicit trafficking. The firing of Ignacio Morales Lechuga from the attorney general's office in January 1993 and the naming of Jorge Carpizo to replace him appeared to open a new chapter in the fight against drugs.

Carpizo's appointment as attorney general in effect marks a break in relations between drug trafficking and the government. He later told the Mexico City daily *Excélsior* that his departure from Mexico to be ambassador to France resulted from, among other things, threats that he had received from the drug cartels.[18] Whether or not circumstances reached that extreme, it is fair to assume that during his administration the interests of the drug traffickers and the attorney general's office appeared to diverge. Carpizo thoroughly purged the federal judicial police commanders, exposed procedural irregularities by the police that favored drug traffickers, and began an anti–drug trafficking propaganda campaign.

There is a particularly telling event that to this date remains shrouded in mystery: the assassination of Cardinal Jesús Posadas Ocampo at the Guadalajara airport on May 24, 1993. The official story is that the cardinal was gunned down because he was mistaken for a drug kingpin. In some government circles, however, the murder was understood as a threat or a warning from the mafia not to break the "traditional understanding" that existed between the security forces and drug traffickers. There are still others who believe that the real reason for the assassination was that the cardinal had been given copies of documents taken from the office of Justo Ceja, a secretary to Carlos Salinas de Gortari, that allegedly linked the Salinas family to the drug cartels.[19]

Posadas's murder not only was the first in a series of assassinations of high-level Mexicans but also sparked a debate about links between security forces and organized crime. Relations between the two would go beyond the question of why it was necessary for organized crime to move into the highest circles of power to a much more basic point: The interests of certain drug cartels coincided with the interests of some in the country's highest political spheres.

The apparent divergence of interests between the drug cartels and the Mexican government during the Salinas administration seemed to be a valid view until his brother, Raul Salinas de Gortari, was accused of various crimes (including money laundering) that appeared to link him to organized crime. We will leave aside the details of Raul Salinas de Gortari's case for reasons of space, but it suggests a clear nexus between criminal interests and the highest spheres of power in Mexico. Surprisingly, Salinas was successfully prosecuted and sentenced to a fifty-year prison term.[20]

The failure to prosecute—or impunity—for certain drug-related crimes in Mexico may arise from deliberate cover-ups or negligence. In either case, it is clear that virtually all significant drug investigations began outside the country. In fact, the DEA began the probe into Raul Salinas de Gortari's alleged money laundering, and police investigators in Switzerland and Great Britain broadened it. The case of Mario Ruiz Massieu is even more clear. The former deputy attorney general left Mexico legally with no arrest warrants issued against him. The U.S. authorities arrested him and went to work trying to ascertain the origin of the millions of dollars in his bank accounts.

The case of Carlos Hank González remains one of the most controversial. The former secretary of agriculture has a fortune of nearly mythic proportions (no one knows how much) and has been accused by the press of having direct ties to the drug trade. As of this date, Mexico has never investigated him.[21] The U.S. embassy in Costa Rica confirmed that Carlos Hank González and his son Jorge Hank Rhon are under investigation by U.S. law enforcement for allegedly participating in drug trafficking and money laundering.[22] This became public knowledge when President Miguel Angel Rodriguez, at the time Costa Rica's presidential candidate from the Social Christian Unity Party, allegedly accepted a contribution from Hank.[23] The scandal received international press coverage, and most of the articles at least hinted that Hank had some sort of ties with dirty money from organized crime.[24]

Other cases have been widely discussed without any real conclusions. A *New York Times* article accused the former governors of Morelos and Sonora, Jorge Carrillo Olea and Manlio Fabio Beltrones, respectively, of having links to traffickers. They reacted angrily and sought damages from the New York paper. To support the allegations, lawyers for the reporters produced two sworn statements from former members of the DEA's El Paso Intelligence Center as proof of Beltrones's and Carrillo Olea's involvement. New scandals piled on to old ones. In the 1997 elections, Vicente Teran Uribe, a candidate for the post of mayor in Agua Prieta in Sonora, was described by the *Dallas Morning News* as one of Mexico's most important traffickers. The source was a report from the El Paso center, and, according to the DEA report, Teran Uribe was not being sought by Mexican police.[25]

The Zedillo administration has been dogged persistently by the allegations of narco-politics. Although no cabinet minister has been directly implicated, there have been cases like those of General Jesús Gutiérrez Rebollo, Mexico's former drug czar, which demonstrate the ability of organized crime to penetrate the country's highest decision-making circles.

It is clear that organized crime has infiltrated sectors of the Mexican political system, but there is little hard evidence. In this regard, the question that Jorge Chabat asked in 1994 remains unanswered several years later: "Can we not say that the institutional pillars of the Mexican government are taken advantage of [by drug-trafficking]?" At that time, Chabat wrote: "The relative tolerance of drug trafficking probably derives from the fact that it in itself doesn't threaten stability, given that its ends are not political and given that the unfinished modernization of the Mexican state leaves open space for corruption generated by drug trafficking."[26]

Perhaps institutional development to strengthen the rule of law and more energetically fight the mafia, along with international supervision of that fight, has made it harder to buy protection from the Mexican police and judicial system. These new conditions could explain why criminals are seeking protection from some sectors of the political system that oppose both a new legal framework (the 1996 law against organized crime, for example) and the Mexican government's greater willingness to grant extraditions to the United States and to promote closer cooperation between the two nations in the fight against drugs. But currently there is no evidence that such a strategy is being pursued by criminals. Nevertheless, several recent incidents suggest areas of analysis into the channels that organized crime may be using to penetrate deeper into the political system. To do this, we should look into the financing of Mexico's political parties, and that of the Institutional Revolutionary Party (PRI) in particular.

The Financing of Mexico's Political Parties

The issue of financing political parties is one of the biggest debates in the Mexican political transition. There are three primary areas of focus:

1. Lack of fairness in political competition.[27]

2. Oligarchical tendencies and shared loyalties between economic and political powers.

3. Financial infiltration by organized crime.

There is little solid information on how the PRI finances its campaigns. As Oscar Hinojosa wrote in one of the few articles available on this subject: "Financing is without a doubt one of the most delicate areas in the history of the PNR-PRM-PRI because this is where the essence of any official party is found: its financial dependence on the government."[28] The mystery that has historically surrounded the PRI's finances hides a well-known secret. The symbiosis between the party and the three levels of government was a constant for several decades. The government's material and human resources were placed at the disposal of PRI candidates. This was considered normal for decades. The PRI became one of the "public" dependencies that consumed the most resources.[29]

But as the opposition gained more political clout in national life and, parallel to this, the electoral system was cleaned up, the question of unfairness in the electoral process came to the fore. Criticism of the traditional political system focused on the government's illegal financial support for the official party. Faced with this new situation, the PRI began to explore new forms of financing.

The 1994 election reopened the controversy over campaign expenditures. The fact that the PRI spent 80 percent of the combined expenditure by all campaigns caused a scandal that remains divisive. (See Table 4.1 for a breakdown of campaign expenditures.) Still, the PRI's astronomical campaign budgets had been exposed before in local elections, like the 1992 election in Michoacán.[30] The report on the 1994 election was written by the Federal Electoral Institute (IFE). IFE's elec-

Table 4.1 Expenditures of Parties in the 1994 Mexican Presidential Campaign

Party	Expenses (pesos)	Expenses ($ millions)	Percentage of total
PAN	43,003,758	12.6	10.37
PRI	324,681,340	95.4	78.28
PRD	6,286,604	1.8	1.52
PT	4,637,703	1.3	1.12
Others	36,167,400	10.6	8.71

Source: *The 1994 Federal Electoral Process* (Mexico: IFE, 1994), 246.

toral advisors included doubts about the amount and origin of the resources used by the PRI and the lack of serious accountability of the other parties' finances.[31]

Miguel Alemán—the treasurer of PRI—acknowledged that the party's campaign expenses "required between [US Dollars] $300 and $500 million." The cap on the public subsidy was about $70 million, and individual contributions were restricted to about $700,000.[32] If we take Alemán at his word, the difference between the maximum and minimum is enormous. But even if we take the minimum figure, there is a $230 million difference between public subsidies for the PRI and the money its treasurer stated was needed. Where did this money come from? In legislation to regulate campaign financing, in addition to public financing, three other sources may be considered: quotas or other financial support from party members, donations from supporters, and building a system of trusts and financial investments. The debate centers not on financing from party members but on donations, some of which were made surreptitiously and others that were clearly illegal.

One of the most publicized charges was that of the former director general of Aeroméxico, Gerardo de Prevoisin, who was accused of embezzling $72 million from his company. The New York Times reported that de Prevoisin donated $8 million to the PRI.[33]

Another highly publicized incident, reported in detail by journalist Andrés Oppenheimer,[34] was a dinner given on February 23, 1993. The event was hosted by then-President Carlos Salinas de Gortari for the country's richest business leaders at the home of Antonio Ortiz Mena, a former Treasury Secretary and a long-standing bridge between the political and business communities. Some of the invitees were people who had benefited from the privatizations of government businesses. They were asked for a "voluntary donation" of $25 million each. At first, the dinner and discussion of party finance were closely guarded secrets. Then the Mexico City daily El Economista published the names of the attendees, the agenda, the discussions, and even the reactions of the participants to the proposed donations.

The scandal was huge, and even major personalities like writer Octavio Paz jumped into the debate. The Nobel Prize Laureate wrote:

The question of democracy is vital for the vast majority of Mexicans. Now, the transition that Mexico is making toward becoming more democratic and pluralistic demands a reform of all political parties, the PRI most of all. It has been and is the party of the government; it must separate itself and win its autonomy. But independence will be impossible as long as it receives a government subsidy. A week ago we learned that—to achieve this separation—a group of business leaders offered the PRI a donation of several hundred million dollars. The cure was worse than the disease. It is critical that limits be set on donations that individuals make to political parties. Democracy is a system founded on credibility, and thus it is urgent that we re-establish credibility in Mexico, breaking with years and years of bad habits and irregularities.[35]

The press report on the dinner caused the termination of the financing scheme. Even so, Porfirio Muñoz Ledo, who was the PRD president in 1994 and his party's leading negotiator in the 1996 electoral reform, commented that the famous dinner "to pass the collection plate" to the best-known business leaders was in itself a money laundering operation. Or, put another way, the PRI had collected a large amount of money that it could not explain and exposed the meeting to establish a legitimate source for the funds. Muñoz Ledo seemed to believe that the PRI decided that a business/political scandal was preferable to a scandal over embezzled government monies given to the party or, still worse, a narco-scandal.[36]

As Mexico's political transition has progressed, it has become harder for the government to channel its customary support to the PRI. The opposition parties showed as early as 1993 that they could effectively compete with the regime and so the cost of financing the official party machinery has risen substantially. The increasing autonomy of the media has also made it difficult for the government to manipulate public finances without getting caught. As Andrés Oppenheimer wrote:

The PRI needed the money badly, and not just because it wanted to avoid an embarrassment during the electoral race over the massive financial help it had long received from the government. After decades of functioning like a de facto government agency that got its money directly from the Finance ministry, the PRI was discovering that the flow of government funds was running dry. A few months earlier, Finance Secretary Pedro Aspe had sent a memo to party president Borrego informing him that the central government would no longer finance the party's needs. . . . Aspe, a conservative economist . . . had explained his memo to Borrego as part of the government's overall policy of reducing public expenses. . . . The party needed to generate its own resources.[37]

If this hypothesis is true, it is probable that the PRI has seen a dramatic drop in resources, including government support for campaigns. It is very likely that the party is looking into other revenue sources that include more or less voluntary donations from business sectors. And finally, there are those like Pedro Pérez who argue that the loss of the PRI's governmental support could lead to solicitation of drug trafficking resources to finance campaigns: "Having reduced the official donations that keep the system alive . . . [the PRI] appears to have started to lean toward drug trafficking money to preserve its privileges."[38]

In any case, the events in question and the PRI's position with respect to how to finance the amounts needed for campaign expenditures show that for the PRI, and the government that it created, demonstrating a source for the funds was a major problem for national and international credibility. Since it was an enormous amount of money, much of it in cash, drug trafficking cannot be ruled out, as we will see later in the attorney general's probe of the Tabasco case. But, what evidence exists that criminal elements were getting involved in campaign financing? The case of Tabasco is particularly interesting because it provides clear evidence of how the PRI finances its campaigns.

The Case of Tabasco

On November 20, 1994, Tabasco held the most controversial elections in the history of the state. Andrés Manuel López Obrador, gubernatorial candidate of the Party of the Democratic Revolution (PRD), challenged the result, alleging irregularities before and during the election. The PRD leadership in Tabasco then decided to organize a march on Mexico City to demand that the electoral results be reviewed.[39] The PRD marchers arrived in the capital several days later. In Mexico City, López Obrador, who met them there, "mysteriously" received several boxes of documents on PRI campaign expenditures in Tabasco.[40] In June 1995, López Obrador, now a PRD leader, and other party members filed a formal complaint with the federal attorney general's office against Tabasco Governor Roberto Madrazo Pintado alleging embezzlement and abuse of power.[41] These charges were based on the alleged expenditure of almost $238 million pesos (about $68 million) on his campaign. The plaintiffs also alleged a possible violation of federal laws, including those barring use of public funds for campaigns.

To support his allegations, López Obrador turned in the twenty-one sealed cardboard boxes containing eighty-nine files. The contents of the files varied: there were check vouchers, payment records, check stubs, receipts, bills, notes, and memos. The job of going through all of this material was turned over to Auldarico Hernández Jerónimo, the PRD senator from Tabasco. Once that review was complete, a real investigation began. The attorney general's office requested that federal investigators be named to decide whether any crime had been committed.

In response, the Tabasco governor, together with Pedro Jiménez León, the speaker of the state legislature, and state district attorney Andrés Madrigal Sánchez, went before the Supreme Court and sparked a constitutional controversy by asking it to declare invalid all the previous findings and the attorney general's investigations related to the case. They argued that the probe was federal interference in local affairs. Governor Madrazo said he was defending states' rights, but public opinion was of the mind that someone had something to hide. On March 26, 1996, the Supreme Court resolved the constitutional controversy by ruling that the federal entity, in this case the attorney general's office, had jurisdiction to continue its investigation of López Obrador's complaint.

The attorney general's office went to work and, after interviewing PRI leaders in Tabasco,[42] came up with the following results:

1. The PRI state committee directorate in Tabasco spent $128 million pesos ($36.5 million) between June 7 and November 20, 1994, alone.

2. It was impossible to determine the origin of most of the funds managed or apportioned by the PRI in Tabasco since payments were made in cash. Thus, in those cases it was impossible to determine whether federal laws against embezzling federal funds were violated. Nevertheless, it was possible to determine that money came from:

a. Lomas Mil S.A. de CV ($12.44 million pesos). This company's board of directors includes people linked to criminal activity by Carlos Cabal Peniche, individuals such as Paul Karam Kassab, who has previously been under investigation for money laundering.[43]

b. A company called San Carlos World Trade ($1 million pesos), also linked to the same person.

Between them, Cabal and Karam contributed $13.44 million pesos to a PRI financial board (Fideicomiso PRI F-2939-1) operating in Tabasco from August 5,

1993, to November 11, 1994. The board's technical committee was made up of Roberto Madrazo, president, and Oscar Saenz Jurado (the state's finance secretary for the PRI in Tabasco) as vice president. The fiduciary institution was the Banco Unión, whose president of the board of directors at that time was Carlos Cabal Peniche.[44]

The case of fugitive banker Carlos Cabal Peniche is one of the most controversial. The origin of his fortune has come into question since the government sold him the Banco de Cédulas Hipotecarias in an auction as part of the privatization of the banking system in 1991. After a series of mergers with other banks, Cabal created the Banco Unión. Suspicion grew when Cabal bought Del Monte Fresh Produce using virtually fraudulent financial practices. By the time Cabal put a $1.06 billion bid on Del Monte Foods, questions over how he got rich were everywhere.[45] But the deal fell through, and Cabal disappeared. He was located in Australia in 1998, and is currently being extradited to Mexico. As with Cardinal Posadas, there has been no investigation to determine whether Cabal used his banks to launder money, as the press has speculated.

Returning to the financing of the PRI campaign in Tabasco, given the attorney general's findings on Cabal's contributions, what defense does Roberto Madrazo have? The governor said that he spent 3.8 million pesos on his campaign, less than the 4 million allowed by law. He also released a report on his expenditures that is shown in Table 4.2. Madrazo said that these were his campaign expenditures and that the rest of the money was used elsewhere. In sum, it is difficult to determine the origin of more than 114.6 million pesos (U.S. $32.7 million) used to finance PRI activities in 1993–1994.

The governor of Tabasco said that Cabal never contributed to his campaign and concluded that the money given to the PRI campaign funds was part of the

Table 4.2 PRI Campaign Expenditures in Tabasco's 1994 Governor's Race (pesos)

Government financing	1,152,412
Contributions from party activists	238,580
Contributions from supporters	1,150,000
Contributions from self	1,229,849

Source: Roberto Madrazo, "Precisiones," in *El Financiero*, June 18, 1996, 46.

party's national strategy, begun in 1993 and not limited to Tabasco, to raise money for its ongoing political programs. Roberto Madrazo concluded: "Since 1993, when there was neither a campaign nor a candidate, the Tabasco PRI, like its counterparts in other states in the republic, received countless contributions from individuals through a campaign finance board created *ex profeso* to make them transparent."[46]

As if they had been expecting them, the governor's explanations failed to convince many sectors of public opinion. When told of the files, José Agustín Ortiz Pincheti, a magistrate from the Federal Electoral Institute in 1994, said: "For the first time, we see clear evidence of how the financial political entrails of Mexican politics are managed."[47] In any case, Madrazo's arguments sought to relieve him of any direct responsibility by making it very clear that the money was used by all the PRI campaigns that year. However, nothing he said shed any light on the origin of the funds. Faced with this lack of clarity, each sector felt free to create its own hypotheses on the origin of the money. CODEHUTAB (Consejo de Derechos Humanos de Tabasco, or the Tabasco Human Rights Council), a Tabasco nongovernmental human rights group close to the PRD, asked for an investigation into the possibility that the money had been embezzled from a fund earmarked to aid Mexicans hurt by PEMEX's activities as required by a recommendation from the federal National Human Rights Commission (recommendation 100–92).[48]

A national newspaper suggested that the money could have come from business. Although the business group COPARMEX always appeared willing to support Madrazo and dismiss the PRD accusations, there are two elements to consider. The first is that some business leaders told reporters from the daily *La Jornada* the following: "Madrazo's campaign didn't ask for our cooperation, it was real extortion. If we didn't we wouldn't be able to work."[49] The second was that the COPARMEX president in Tabasco was Carlos Madrazo Cadena, the governor's cousin, who was removed from his post for accepting two checks for 82,500 pesos[50] from the PRI for the "quick count" that the business group carried out in the November 20, 1994, elections.[51]

The debate over the recipients of the funds was huge. In the boxes of documents discussed by the weekly magazine *Proceso* there was evidence that journalists and academics were in Tabasco at the PRI's expense. The uproar was such that columnist German Dehesa denied his involvement.[52]

The boxes of campaign finance records were turned over to the treasury secretary who, through federal district attorneys, failed to find evidence of criminal behavior in the operations investigated by the attorney general's office and banking authorities.[53] The rest of the documentation was sent to Tabasco authorities, and the first federal circuit court with residence in Villahermosa ruled that there was no evidence to press charges against Roberto Madrazo for excessive campaign expenditures.[54] That was the end of the court proceedings. Still, questions remained on the political side. The Tabasco case dominated negotiations on the 1996 electoral reform and decisively influenced the drafting of new legislation regulating financing for political parties and the budgets approved by the 1997 campaigns, which will be discussed in the next section.

Debate over the 1996 Electoral Reform

The electoral reform approved in late 1996 was supposed to be a "definitive" reform, according to the president. Despite this and the hopeful signs that pointed toward a consensus on the constitutional aspects of the reform, the president could not convince the main opposition parties to implement laws even though the government and the parties spent months making a series of wide-ranging concessions in hopes of getting a consensus.[55] In the end, the PRI deputies approved the reforms without opposition support. The biggest sticking point was financing for the parties. There had been agreement that public financing would predominate over private financing, but there was no agreement on amounts.[56] The opposition believed that the limits were excessive both in absolute and relative terms (see Table 4.3).

Table 4.3 Public Financing of Political Parties

Party	Amount (pesos)	Amount ($ millions)	Pesos spent per vote in 1994
PAN	520,799,290	66.0	59.8
PRI	873,343,620	110.0	51.6
PRD	388,450,456	49.0	69.2
PT	186,254,292	23.0	207.0
Others	164,071,800	20.7	83.7

Source: Estimates from *Voz y Voto*; quoted in *Reforma*, November 15, 1996, 11A.

In 1986, the Mexican constitution was amended to state that it was in the public interest to finance political parties and that the parties had the right to public financing for their activities.[57] In fact, under the constitution, the parties' public financing must predominate over other sources of funding.[58] The distribution of public funding is as follows: 30 percent is distributed equally to support ongoing activities while the rest is divided proportionally according to party representation in each of the political formations.[59] For campaign expenditures, the parties are given an amount similar to that received for permanent expenditures, but only in election years.

This means that public financing takes precedence over private financing under the new legislation. The parties can accept private donations, but they are limited. In the case of the 1997 election, the ceiling was $84,500 for each of the 300 deputies and a maximum of about $22 million for the senators.[60] Public financing is allocated as follows: 30 percent is divided equally among the parties and division of the remaining 70 percent depends on each party's showing in the most recent vote for the Chamber of Deputies.

The increase in public financing for political parties was not politically acceptable for three reasons. In the first place, a conflict arose between a public treasury dedicated to cutting costs in all areas and the prodigious amount of money going to the parties. Second, the amount appropriated to finance the parties was about the same as that spent on public security. Vast sectors of Mexican society disagree with the concept of spending the same amount of money to finance political parties and to fight crime. It is widely known that crime has become one of the most important issues on the public agenda in Mexico, while political parties have considerably less impact on society. And third, the amount of money involved and the pace of its growth is spectacular, as is shown in Table 4.4.

What prompted the government to accept the huge political cost of authorizing so much public financing for political parties? There are two possibilities. The first is that the PRI realized that increased monitoring by opposition parties and society at large meant that it would have less access to illegal funds for its activities and hence decided to crack open its books. If this is true, it means that the party backed such a huge expenditure so that it would not be forced to cut spending that had previously come from a variety of government agencies' budgets or from other means. While the PRI claimed that it had spent a total of $95.4 million in

**Table 4.4 Increases in Public Financing of Political
Parties, 1992–1997**

Year	Amount (pesos)	Amount ($ millions, rounded)
1992	86,174,205	28
1993	135,175,644	41
1994	201,308,002	58
1997	2,132,917,000	267

Source: For 1992, 1993, and 1994: *Memoria del proceso electoral federal*,
IFE; and for 1997: Budget of IFE, 1997.

1994, including both public and private financing, the public financing alone for
1997 was $110 million. In other words, the party received enough to mount a real
campaign without upsetting businessmen, or having scandals in the newspapers
or bills coming in after the election.

The second is the perception of the risk of other scandals, like the magnates'
dinner or the Tabasco case discussed earlier. It is also likely that there was a perva-
sive fear of imminent infiltration by organized crime, or even that it had already
occurred. The government has recognized that the amounts appropriated were
extremely high but has defended its proposals, citing "reasons of state." President
Zedillo jumped into the controversy, defending the reform and the enormous
amount of government money given to the political parties by saying that it was a
priority to prevent them from resorting to illegal financing.

In a speech on November 18, 1996, Zedillo summed up the recently approved
electoral reform as follows:

An agreement was reached to expedite the new general law governing the means of electoral competition; and unanimously—and this is very important—the IFE general council
was created as well as an electoral court. In fact, there was agreement on the vast majority
of the substantive changes in the IFE. The main point of disagreement has been over
financing for parties and electoral campaigns. I want to stress—because there has been a
lot of confusion over this—that this was not a disagreement among the political parties: I
want to say it clearly, the disagreement was with the Federal Executive. As a principle, I
have considered this point as one in which the State's vision must prevail at the expense of
the necessary partiality of each political party. And the State's vision would lead Mexico,
like any nation, toward a system of preponderantly public and clearly adequate system of
financing with the goal of ensuring transparency and certainty about the finances of those
who hold power. This system is the best guarantee that a campaign or a party will not be

subject to undesirable pressures from particular interests, including shameful promises. We do not want Mexico, as has unfortunately occurred elsewhere, to be a place where parties or candidates become vassals of people or organizations which, in fact, could be criminal.[61]

One of the negotiators of the 1996 electoral reform, Porfirio Muñoz Ledo,[62] believes that the president's preference for public financing was clear from the beginning, and this is reflected very clearly in his speech. It is possible, judging from subsequent events, to suppose that Zedillo felt uncomfortable with how his own campaign had been financed. Not only did he have to listen to Roberto Madrazo say on television that huge sums of money had been spent in 1994 on all of the 1994 campaigns (not only on his own), but Zedillo also had to avoid speculation that the Cali cartel had infiltrated his presidential campaign.

The issue of financing for the 1994 presidential campaign was reopened by an article in the weekly *Proceso* by Pascal Beltrán del Río. The article was based on a conversation that he had with an American academic, Peter Lupsha, who told him about a conversation with a U.S. DEA agent named Sandy González. According to that information, in April and June 1994, two aircraft took off from Colombia's San Andrés Island carrying $40 million that belonged to the Cali cartel, and landed in Mexico. The destination of the funds was not known. In Beltrán del Río's bylined article, he notes that the funds could have been for the Zedillo campaign or for investments.[63] We should note that Lupsha has contested *Proceso*'s account of the conversation, writing in a letter to the weekly that it was clear

by a 70 or 80 percent probability that the previous summer (1994), the Cali cartel took about $40 million dollars from Colombia to Mexico on two flights. But I stressed that it was a hypothesis and a conjecture based on the timing. What I said was that it may have been used to corrupt the coming elections. It was equally likely that the money was used by Miguel Rodriguez Orejuela to buy a 707 or a 727 jet. Or to invest in developing ports or tourist resorts.[64]

It is possible that he was misquoted, but Lupsha himself wrote about the difficult subject as follows:

Usually reliable sources say that one of the major contributors from the foreign private sector to this campaign [the one in 1994] was the Cali drug trafficking cartel. During the late spring and summer of 1994, they report, Miguel Rodriguez Orejuela of the Cali group sent 40 million dollars (U.S.), in two shipments to Mexico. While this could have been for economic investment, they hypothesize it was for political corruption, to guarantee Cali a superior, favored and protected position in the new administration.[65]

Amid the quibbling, the subject has been catching the attention of influential sectors, which consider it a rumor but are keeping an eye on it. This is the case of the National Defense University's Strategic Assessment, which says the following: "Colombian organizations even are rumored to have contributed funds to the 1994 presidential campaigns of Ernesto Pérez Balladares in Panama and Ernesto Zedillo in Mexico."[66] Lupsha's backing down from information given to *Proceso* reduced the impact of what was said. It was very difficult to prove that there was a link between drug trafficking and the campaigns, but the ghost of a doubt hovered above the negotiations on political reform, and perhaps the legislation and the budgets appropriated were influenced by the same risk.

The way in which the president himself conceptualized his support for electoral reform indicates that he is not prepared to give up. A president inclined toward political consensus in electoral matters, as Zedillo has been, not so subtly broke with it and left no room for reconsideration. It is impossible to determine how worried the government was about the possibility that organized crime would get involved in the campaigns, but it is clear that the ghost of organized crime and its power to corrupt is a concern in Mexican political life.

Conclusion

The crisis of the Mexican political system that began in the mid-1980s paved the way for a transition to democracy. This process has been reflected in three fundamental areas: (1) pluralization of the political system; (2) increased demand for a genuine rule of law; and (3) demands for more accountability in management of public resources.

During the transition period that began in 1985 (the year of the controversial Chihuahua elections which called into question the legitimacy of the system) and stretched into 1997, the debate over the organization of the state focused on controls to guarantee a reasonable electoral system and on building and controlling judicial and accounting mechanisms to ensure that public resources are used legally.

New threats and conflicts have appeared in this gray zone of transition. The crisis in the traditional electoral system has cost the PRI positions in the territorial structure and federal legislature, lessening its margin to maneuver in decision making. Reform of the judicial system and the periodic house cleaning and re-structuring in the attorney general's office were aimed at reducing the margin of tolerance or complacency that existed with regard to organized crime. Finally, in-creased scrutiny by political parties, nongovernmental organizations, and society at large have increased the political costs of illicit enrichment via traditional cor-ruption.

In this scenario of displaced politicians—who in addition to remaining out-side the political game are seeing fewer opportunities to make deals via privatiza-tion—coupled with better social controls (at the governmental level there is a lot to do in this area), organized crime could find the political system easy to culti-vate. Concern about this possibility appears to be what underlies new legislation regarding the financing of political parties, which despite all the deserved criti-cism is a model that addresses the nature of the Mexican transition, attempting to meet two fundamental goals. The first is to break the ties that link the PRI to the government. The second is to ensure that the parties have sufficient resources to reduce the chance that organized crime may penetrate their structures, as other pressure groups have done.

Much still needs to be written about the relationship between crime and poli-tics in contemporary Mexico. More detailed works will follow, with evidence that will refute or confirm the hypotheses we have put forward in the final portion of the chapter. But one thing seems clear: Mexico's governability during this transi-tional period still depends on arrangements between the government and the pressure groups that have a proven capacity to destabilize an economy that ap-pears solid and a president who won 17 million votes. The exit from the gray zone would entail the consolidation of a state that is strong enough and anchored firmly enough in the law so that no pressure group would be able to put the stabil-ity of the nation at risk. But that is the topic for another discussion.

Chapter 5

Scope and Limits of an Act of Good Faith

The PAN's Experience at the Head of the Office of the Attorney General of the Republic

Sigrid Arzt

THE PURPOSE OF THIS CHAPTER is to identify the challenges that the PAN (National Action Party) administration confronted in the Office of the Attorney General of the Republic from December 1994 to December 1996. The chapter consists of three main sections. The first part provides a brief sketch of the country's political context in early 1995, in which there were expectations of change when, for the first time in Mexico's postrevolutionary history, a member of the opposition was appointed to a cabinet post. The job, however, was to head up the most discredited institution in the political system—the Office of the Attorney General of the Republic (PGR).

The second main part describes the juridical and legal instruments that PAN Attorney General Antonio Lozano Gracia had at his disposal at the beginning of his term of office. This section includes a description of the functions of the PGR, the body whose constitutional sphere of competence is to investigate and prevent crimes under federal law. The section also includes the reforms promoted by this administration and examines the groundwork that was laid to professionalize both the police and public prosecutors. Finally, a brief diagnosis is offered of the dysfunction that results when the army is assigned tasks that are the duty of the federal public prosecutor's office as a solution to the problem of organized crime and drug trafficking.

Political Context

Before dealing with the condition of the Office of the Attorney General at the outset of President Ernesto Zedillo's administration, we need to place in context the political moment that Mexico was living, specifically as regards law enforcement. By December 1, 1994, Mexico had already witnessed three horrific political assassinations that were replayed on television several times. During President Salinas' six-year term of office (1988–1994), Mexico saw the appointment of five attorneys general, accompanied by their respective changes in personnel and forms of organization.[1]

Moreover, the political atmosphere at the end of Salinas's term of office was complicated by the course of the investigations into the assassination of PRI Secretary General José Francisco Ruiz Massieu. Ruiz Massieu's brother, who held the post of principal deputy attorney general, began to accuse the incumbent attorney general of obstruction of justice and of protecting members of the PRI political class who might be responsible for the death of José Francisco. Finally, Mario Ruiz Massieu resigned and became an adviser to the Party of the Democratic Revolution (PRD). Later, in March 1995, he was arrested in the United States for making a false declaration about the amount of currency in his possession upon entering the country.[2]

This turmoil was compounded by accusations and statements discrediting the PGR, and by the continual leaks to the news media about the penetration and extent of drug trafficking. No less serious were the continual abuses committed by the federal judicial police. Experts have pointed out an image problem: Both the PGR and the police are viewed as the "sewage" of the public edifice.[3]

The attorney general's office totally lacked credibility and legitimacy, and was viewed by Mexican society as one more instrument of power for the president of the Republic. Furthermore, the PGR was sufficiently powerful for the police corps to be permeated by a culture of "unconditional obedience in exchange for impunity."[4] In a political gesture by Salinas, and with the aim of establishing the "independence" of the PGR in relation to the political system, Dr. Jorge Carpizo was appointed as the first attorney general who did not come from the ranks of the PRI and who, owing to his academic background, would dedicate himself to establishing the institution's credibility and promoting the rule of law.[5]

During the Salinas administration and up to mid-2000 the government has been unable to overcome the perception of the impunity that prevails in the police corps and in the administration of justice. The government has proved incompetent in reversing this image and, even worse, in sanctioning and prosecuting those who have abused their position as public servants.

A Member of the Opposition in the Cabinet

The political crisis seriously endangered President Ernesto Zedillo's capacity to govern, that is, to begin his administration given such uncertainties. In a bold move, the incoming president invited a member of the opposition to become part of his cabinet. Zedillo had already expressed his commitment to perform major surgery on the justice apparatus,[6] but, more than mere goodwill, this required granting total independence to the person undertaking the task. The first step would be to promote amendments to the Mexican Constitution so as to achieve greater autonomy for the performance of the office of the federal public prosecutor, and therefore of the attorney general himself.[7]

Forthwith, Antonio Lozano, a member of the center-right PAN, was invited to join the cabinet and undertake the necessary internal reforms to attain true rule of law. The appointment was welcomed by society in general and even applauded in international circles. It was undoubtedly a gesture of political commitment to changing things and promoting democracy. It did not, however, seem the most appropriate decision to all, and as soon as the PAN attorney general took office, he became the target of all the system's connivers. Expectations were very high. Society demanded unprecedented changes, and immediately.

One of the key obstacles in effecting reforms in the PGR was the isolation that Lozano encountered from the start. This meant that he did not have the support of the system's other political forces. The center-left Party of the Democratic Revolution (PRD), for example, undermined the credibility of this effort by accusing the PAN of negotiating an agreement with the PRI for the post. Hard-line PRI members, for their part, viewed what seemed a commitment to change as an act of betrayal on Zedillo's part, one contrary to the party's interests. Moreover, one could even speculate that more than one politician feared being targeted by a "witch hunt" resulting from a real internal cleanup in the institution or by the simple act of applying the letter of the law. Finally, even some members of the PAN expressed concern over acceptance of the post and criticized at length the different tasks being performed. Even with the intraparty tensions, however, the PAN leaders acknowledged that, having demanded so often that this institution should be in the hands of the opposition, "it would have been a contradiction, and even an act of cowardice, not to accept it now."[8]

During his inaugural address, President Zedillo acknowledged the degree of disintegration reached by the justice system and announced a series of reforms he would promote to change this situation. Among the first reforms were requiring Senate ratification of the attorney general's appointment and creating the Legal Counsel for the Presidency. These were the first pillars that granted greater independence to the office of the public prosecutor, and hence also to the functions and performance of the attorney general as head of that institution. This greater independence enabled the PGR to stop acting as judge in its own case in matters concerning the federal government.[9] It meant that the legal counsel would deal with the executive branch's legal affairs and even with the development of legislative bills without involving the PGR or the attorney general.

Regardless of the reforms, however, the political assassinations that took place during Salinas's six-year term and the dismay produced by the "December error" (the sudden devaluation of the peso at the end of 1994) had led the public to make its own judgment. So, to achieve a real change in law enforcement it was essential to do away with the ruling elite's impunity and abuse of power. This public sense of anxiety and frustration exerted enormous pressure on the PGR, placing it always at the center of the political debate.[10] Society expected the PGR to establish new rules on political practices and on coexistence between the different actors, but the agency was never really prepared to accomplish that.

Faced with attacks from various quarters, on several occasions President Zedillo had to express publicly his full support for Lozano's work and stated, in a republican gesture: "The Attorney General knows that he should perform his work with absolute freedom, with no other limit than the law, and without paying attention to pressures of any kind."[11] But such backing gave rise to contrary reactions and even indiscipline among members of the PRI. To illustrate this point, from the time Lozano took office, on every March 23 the PGR was invaded by Federal District PRI groups headed by Roberto Campa. For hours, they would use loudspeakers to demand an immediate solution to Luis Donaldo Colosio's assassination. Once Lozano was replaced by Jorge Madrazo (on December 3, 1996), there were no further demonstrations of this kind.

To reiterate, the PGR simply lacked credibility. Perhaps one of the most unfortunate incidents that occurred at the beginning of the PAN administration was the attempt on the life of the director of the Judicial Police, Juan Pablo de Tavira, on December 23, 1994. De Tavira had made it clear that he would do everything within his power to eliminate corruption and abuse in the police force and had declared that "the Federal Judicial Police was not incurable."[12] Later, in January 1996, Attorney General Lozano himself was the target of attempted murder.

Something unheard of in Mexico's history was the imprisonment of an ex-president's brother, in this case, Raúl Salinas.[13] This event, however, increased societal pressure on the PGR to investigate ex-president Carlos Salinas himself. Collective judgment held the ex-president responsible for the so-called December error. Therefore, in the public view, if justice was to be done, the ex-president himself should be arrested. Finally, in what appeared to be a political agreement between Zedillo and Salinas, the latter went into self-imposed exile in Ireland.[14]

Toward the end of 1996, a PGR team headed by the new Special Deputy Attorney General Luis Raúl González Pérez traveled to Ireland to interrogate ex-president Salinas de Gortari on the assassination of Luis Donaldo Colosio. Another interrogation was scheduled for a few weeks later, this time in connection with the assassination of José Francisco Ruiz Massieu, which the ex-president's brother was accused of plotting. In addition to these events there was a possible motion of unconstitutionality that Attorney General Lozano could file against the executive for a particular article in the Federal Electoral Law. The conjunction of these three factors appears to have led to Lozano's removal from office in December 1996. But one should not disregard the impending midterm elections in summer 1997 and public support for the PAN, which reached around 40 percent in the Federal District by December, and also may have been a factor in Zedillo's decision.

With this as a sketch of the political context, I shall describe the responsibilities and sphere of competence of the Office of the Federal Public Prosecutor (Ministerio Público), which is constitutionally responsible for carrying out the investigation of federal crimes with the assistance of the Federal Judicial Police (PJF) and the support of experts in investigations.

Office of the Attorney General of the Republic

This section describes the functions of the Office of the Public Prosecutor (MP) as the principal instrument of the attorney general's office. The law states that the MP will be assisted in its work by the Federal Judicial Police and by technical experts, who are subject to the MP's instructions. In reality this has occurred very little, largely because since the institution was created the PGR lacked both the necessary autonomy to act impartially and the professionalism in its police and experts. Along with this situation, the political regime that was established during the system's initial postrevolutionary stage converted the PGR into the natural niche of authoritarianism, abuse of power, arrogance, impunity, and disrespect for the rule of law. The PGR has acted in collusion with the political interests of the ruling elite.

The office of the MP is incorporated into the PGR and is the essential instrument of the federal justice system, representing individuals, society, and the state. The PGR is supposed to promote and monitor fulfillment of the constitutional order and enforce the law within its sphere of competence. It also participates in crime prevention to ensure public security.

Article 21 of Mexico's Constitution reads as follows:

The imposition of penalties is exclusive to the judicial authority. The investigation and prosecution of crimes is the duty of the Office of the Federal Public Prosecutor, which shall be assisted by a police force under its immediate authority and command. It is the duty of the administrative authority to apply sanctions for infringements of administrative and police regulations, which shall consist only of a fine or arrest for up to thirty-six hours . . . Decisions by the Office of the Public Prosecutor on non-exercise and discontinuance of penal action may be challenged jurisdictionally in the terms established by the law . . . public security is a function incumbent upon the Federation, the Federal District, the States and the Municipalities, in the respective spheres of competence indicated by this Constitution. The actions of police institutions shall be governed by the principles of legality, efficiency, professionalism and honesty.[15]

Federal Code of Penal Proceedings (CFPP)

The CFPP establishes the procedures to guide the public prosecutor's office with respect to initiating a penal action,[16, 17] in which case the MP[18] should carry out the investigation. The MP receives the report, accusation, or complaint, which may be presented orally or in writing, on the facts that might constitute a legal offense. The MP then should undertake all the pertinent actions for the verification of a crime. In such an event, the MP should demonstrate the probable responsibility of the accused. It is also the responsibility of the MP to arrest or detain suspects if necessary.

Article Three of the CFPP clearly states that the Federal Judicial Police (PJF) "will act under the authority and immediate command of the MP."[19] Therefore, the PJF is subject to the MP's instructions and orders. The PJF is disqualified from receiving statements from suspects or arresting persons other than cases of *flagrante delicto*. These restrictions resulted from the continual abuses committed by PJF agents with regard to human rights violations, a situation basically stemming from this police force's lack of adequate professionalization.

What Is a Public Prosecutor?

A public prosecutor (also called an MP) is a law graduate with a professional license who, after passing a competitive examination, joins the ranks of the attorney general's office. The MP is in charge of investigating, that is, of initiating a preliminary investigation, analyzing whether there are facts that prove the law has been broken, and submitting the evidence to a judge, who is responsible for imposing penalties for the offenses committed. It is important to point out that the office of the public prosecutor is where the complainant presents a complaint that can lead to an investigation.

What is the great handicap of the MPs who engage in the task of investigating and prosecuting federal offenses? MPs are recent graduates of law schools and lack training and professional skills when they join the PGR.[20] Even so, the agency leadership has failed to understand the importance of professionalizing the MP. This has meant the lack of a comprehensive system of specializations in each of the federal offenses that the PGR should prosecute. This professionalization can hardly be expected to be self-taught. A formal academic education does not equip MPs with a sense of governing authority in the application of law. Furthermore, they lack the training to maintain command and oversight of an investigation—as the law stipulates—and therefore lack awareness of the assistance they should receive from the judicial police and criminal experts.

Prior to the reestablishment of the National Institute of Penal Sciences

(INACIPE), the Training Institute (ICAP) was in charge of training and profession-alizing public prosecutors and police officers together. In the past, however, the entrance mechanism stipulated that persons wishing to gain access to the institution had to pass a competitive examination.[21] This was an oral exam presented before a five-person board, but in reality it took place after having entered the institution. This meant that a person interested in joining the PGR first chose what area of the agency he was going to join and what post he could occupy. Then, after joining, he took the competitive oral examination to match the required qualification as MP.

It was only in 1993 that the Regulations for the Career of Agent of the Federal Public Prosecutor's Office were issued, which made it obligatory for new members to participate in an initial training course for public prosecutors.[22] The regulations make up the juridical framework that establishes the legal responsibilities entrusted to MP agents and outlines procedures for selection, entry, reentry, training, tenure, promotion, benefits, and sanctions for MPs.

The reestablishment of the INACIPE and the development of a career civil service aimed to strengthen this institute as the sole means of entry into the PGR took place only in August 1996.[23] As of the 1996 restructuring, professionalization functions were divided. The INACIPE would train MP agents and the ICAP would train Federal Judicial Police officers.[24] As of July 2000, both institutes lacked innovative leadership capable of constructing the necessary curricula to professionalize these operational personnel. Moreover, training continues to be one of the most neglected areas in the budget of the attorney general's office.

This neglect stems from the lack of vision that exists in society as a whole with regard to the need to train, educate, and professionalize individuals as a sure investment that they will therefore perform their work properly, thus benefiting society. Mexico lacks a general acceptance of investing in forming a solid academic body for specialization; training generally stems from individual initiative, not from institutional support. There is therefore a lack of specialized personnel who can deal with basic tasks.

Restructuring of the PGR

The change toward consolidating democracy and the rule of law in Mexico still confronts some authoritarian vices. There is broad agreement that the cancer of corruption hinders the administration of justice as well as the progress in promoting efficiency in an institution such as the PGR. However, during the mid-1990s, the organizational bases for addressing the challenges of delinquency in Mexico were laid, and certain juridical reforms were introduced. This section begins with a brief description of the organization that existed in the PGR prior to these reforms.[25]

To achieve the 1996 reforms, the new leadership undertook a series of internal consultations with experts in the field of law enforcement and with PGR officials. These resulted in a new approach to the institution's organization and administration, as well as in the establishment of clear standards and regulations for the operating bodies, a fundamental step in monitoring and evaluating the performance of MP agents and PJF officers. Subsequently, the modernization of the statutes for the prosecution of federal crimes was carried out by passage of the Federal Law against Organized Crime.[26]

At the beginning of Antonio Lozano's tour of duty, an Administrative Modernization Commission was established that set about analyzing and diagnosing problem areas within the PGR's organizational structure. After almost a year, six major groups of obstacles were identified: (1) lack of coordination between areas; (2) absence of controls; (3) lack of institutional balance; (4) insufficient information and technological development; (5) deficient administration of material and human resources; and (6) lack of overall vision of the functions of the PGR.[27]

In order to address these severe internal institutional deficiencies, Attorney General Lozano and his team adopted the following actions: defining the institutional mission; undertaking a comprehensive change by establishing objectives and strategies; instilling a sense of commitment to the institution. To achieve the restructuring, the government amended the Organic Law of the PGR and its regulations.[28] The driving aim behind the process of restructuring was to attain the rule of law. The main goal was to make the attorney general's office a modern and honorable institution with the capacity to combat federal crimes, but also to recover society's confidence and recognition.[29] The definitive step in talking of a

Table 5.1 Reorganization of PGR, August 1996

Before the August 1996 reform	After the 1996 reform
General Office of the Deputy Attorney General[a]	Deputy Attorney General's Office for General Coordination and Development
General Directorate of the Federal Judicial Police[b]	General Directorate of Criminalistic Services
General Inspector's Office[c]	General Directorate of Planning and Technological Development
State Delegations	
	General Directorate of Coordination, Planning and Operation of the PJF
	General Directorate of Inter-institutional Coordination
	General Directorate of Promotion of Ministerial Security
	Training Institute
Deputy Attorney General's Office for Preliminary Investigations[d]	Deputy Attorney General's Office for Penal Proceedings "A"
Directorate of Preliminary Investigations	
General Directorate of Expert Services	
Deputy Attorney General's Office for Control of Proceedings[e]	Deputy Attorney General's Office for Penal Proceedings "B"
General Directorate of Control of Proceedings	Deputy Attorney General's Office for Penal Proceedings "C"
General Directorate of Amparo (Protective Injunction)	
Deputy Attorney General's Office for Juridical Affairs[f]	Deputy Attorney General's Office for International Juridical Affairs
General Directorate of Juridical Affairs	General Directorate of Amparo (Protective Injunction)
General Directorate of International Legal Affairs	General Directorate of Contentious and Consultative Matters
Attaché's Offices	General Directorate of Constitutionality
Special Deputy Attorney General's Office[g]	Special Deputy Attorney General's Office
Office of the Chief Administrative Officer[h]	Office of the Chief Administrative Officer
General Directorate of Human Resources	General Directorate of Human Resources
General Directorate of Programming	General Directorate of Programming
General Directorate of Control of Confiscated Goods	General Directorate of Control of Confiscated Goods
General Directorate of Information and Statistics Systems	General Directorate of Information and Statistics Systems
General Directorate of Air Services	General Directorate of Air Services
Office of the Internal Comptroller[i]	
General Directorate of Supervision and Audit	
General Directorate of Protection of Human Rights	
	Office of the Internal Comptroller
	General Directorate of Supervision
	General Directorate of Audit
	General Directorate of Complaints and Accusations
	General Directorate of Human Rights
	Performance Evaluation Unit
	General Inspector's Office
	General Directorate of Inspection
	General Directorate of Internal Inspection

Before the August 1996 reform	After the 1996 reform
General Directorate of Media Communication[j]	General Directorate of Media Communication
General Directorate of Crime Prevention and Community Services[k]	General Directorate of Crime Prevention and Community Services
National Institute for the Fight against Drugs (INCD)[l]	FEADS - Special Prosecutor's Office for Attention to Health Crimes
Training Institute (ICAP)[m]	Training Institute (ICAP)
Center Planning for Drug Control (CENDRO)	National Institute of Penal Sciences
Special Prosecutor's Office against Electoral Offenses	Special Prosecutor's Office against Electoral Offenses

Sources: Mexico, "Organic Law of the PGR," *Gaceta Oficial*, 1996. Also, organization chart in Antonio F. Lozano, *Compromisos con la Justicia, Informe de Gestión de Fernando Antonio Lozano Gracia, Procurador General de la República* (Mexico: Epessa, S.A. de C.V., 1998), 232.

Notes: a. The Federal Judicial Police was under the authority of the General Office of the Deputy Attorney General, as was the Inspector's Office, which could deal with any matter of its interest; it also had an area of Special Investigations. There was therefore an overlapping of functions and power at the level of internal command. See "Regulations of the Organic Law of the PGR," *Gaceta Oficial*, October 8, 1993. The office was held by Hiram Escudero Alvarez (PAN).

b. Prior to December 1994, the post was held by Commander Adrian Carrera, who has been linked to health crimes but is currently facing charges of money laundering only. Subsequently the post was held briefly by Juan Pablo de Tavira. See *Proceso*, July 16, 1995. On January 19, Commander Enrique Gándara Chacón was provisionally appointed to the position, which he held from December 1994 to January 1996. He was replaced by Américo Flores Nava, who purportedly left when he was unable to solve the murder of agent Isaac Sánchez, perpetrated in Mexico City in June 1996. He was followed by Commander Emilio Islas Rangel. See SUN, August 15, 1996.

c. Post was held by Tristán Sánchez Canales, into whose home a grenade was thrown. See *La Jornada* (Mexico City), July 24, 1996.

d. Post was held by Manuel Galán (PRI) from May 1994 to December 1996.

e. Post was held by Dr. Moisés Moreno (PRI) from December 1994 to 1996.

f. Post was held by Rafael Estrada Samano (PAN).

g. After the entry of Pablo Chapa Benzanilla, it became a Special Deputy Attorney General's Office with three prosecutor's offices to deal with the cases of Cardinal Posadas and the assassinations of presidential candidate Luis Donaldo Colosio and PRI Secretary General José Francisco Ruiz Massieu.

h. José Antonio Gándara Terrazas (PAN) was appointed to the post.

i. According to regulations, this area came under the authority of the office of the chief administrative officer, but it operated directly with Attorney General Lozano. The head of the area was Leticia de Anda Munguía.

j. Juan Ignacio Zavala (PAN) was in charge of this office.

k. This directorate was headed by Guillermo León Ramírez Pérez (no party affiliation).

l. The head of this institute was René Paz Horta, who was replaced in May 1996 by the ex-attorney general of the state of Chihuahua, Francisco Molina (PAN).

m. At the beginning of the PAN administration, General Rodolfo Alvarado (retired army officer, with no party affiliation) headed this institute. He was succeeded by Norma Guido, and when the restructuring was set in motion, it was headed by Dr. Marco Antonio Besares (PRI).

consolidation of democracy in Mexico's case requires, as a *sine qua non*, respect for the law in the fullest sense of the word. This means its impartial enforcement under the existing regulations without detriment to anyone and without excluding anyone.[30]

Professionalization

One of the first findings from the internal diagnosis in the PGR was the lack of a comprehensive system of professionalization for its operational bodies, the MP,

PJF, and investigative experts. Training programs for professionals were far below the minimum acceptable standards as regards the performance of the office of the federal public prosecutor and its subsidiary bodies.[31] There was undoubtedly a need to place priority on furthering professionalization and specialization in order to improve the capacity to investigate crimes and carry out preliminary investigations, streamline follow-up of judicial proceedings, and eradicate corruption. But, similarly, the course of penal proceedings had to be restructured, since the preliminary investigation was typically handled by one MP while the final stages of the same investigation were handled by another one. The investigative process was fragmented at various stages, and this typically caused evidence, statements, and case records to be lost.

Perhaps the clearest example of concentration of power and lack of checks was the general office of the deputy attorney general, which toward the end of the Salinas administration had become a mini-attorney general's office within the PGR itself.[32] This concentration of authority was the result of the division between the different chains of command in the operational bodies. In other words, the attorney general had authority over the public prosecutors and in theory also over the judicial police, but in fact the latter reported directly to the principal deputy attorney general.[33]

The restructuring effort became the most far-reaching internal process that the institution had ever faced. Nevertheless, the backlogs and day-to-day inertia in many areas slowed the pace of reform to such an extent that the urgent institutional change was not fully consolidated by the time of Lozano's departure. To modernize the PGR and make it more efficient, twelve strategic objectives were established, the most important being to reduce the crime rate, do away with impunity, professionalize public servants, combat drug trafficking and organized crime, and eliminate corruption. Below we take a closer look at the areas targeted for reform.

The restructuring model selected required the elimination of the deputy attorney general's offices for preliminary investigations and for control of proceedings and brought about the creation of three deputy attorney general's offices for penal proceedings ("A," "B," and "C"). The main function of the deputy attorney general's offices was to concentrate the entire criminal action proceedings under a single command. This meant that the MP in charge of a case would supervise it at every stage, without losing control of the preliminary investigation, the follow-up on the proceedings, and the holding of the accused for trial if so ruled by the judge.

The changes in responsibilities grew out of an effort to balance the workload as fairly as possible. Certainly one of the most innovative aspects concerned the oversight of the PGR's field offices. Each of the states and the Federal District has a PGR delegation (field office) with a subdelegate in charge of the judicial police. In the new scheme each of the deputy attorney general's offices would have direct control over a specific group of state delegations.[34] The distribution of field offices among the states aims to closely monitor each delegation's performance in order to avoid abuses of authority or other shortcomings in handling investigations. The former general office of the deputy attorney general became the deputy attorney general's office for general coordination and development in the new scheme, with the aim of taking away the absolute control it had exercised over the institution's operations.[35] This area would also handle coordination and linkage with state attorney generals' offices.

Until November 1996, the Federal Judicial Police were directed by a technical council for planning and coordination of operations whose main function was to organize and supervise the planning of operations to be carried out by PJF units under the command of the respective MPs.[36] Two areas of counterbalance, control, and internal supervision were strengthened: the General Inspector's Office and the Internal Comptroller's Office. The General Inspector's Office acts as a technical means for supervision and control of the operational bodies, a sort of "internal affairs" office. The General Inspector's Office became hierarchically dependent on the attorney general, which allowed the head of the MP to have first-hand information on the PGR officials' performance enforcing the law. Of special interest was the follow-up on Federal Judicial Police officers. Furthermore, the inspector would be in charge of a specialized unit dealing in crimes committed by the PGR's public servants.

The Comptroller's Office was strengthened in order to audit and supervise the different internal units and bodies of the PGR. This office is responsible for the Ongoing Program for Detection of Narcotics and Psychotropic Drug Consumption.[37] It is also responsible for supervising drug incineration, in addition to responding to the recommendations issued by the National Human Rights Commission. The poor operation and lack of resources and trained personnel to carry out the tasks of supervision and monitoring that these areas are responsible for contributed to the weakening and corruption of the performance of personnel. It was essential to provide resources and transparent supervision mechanisms to achieve the internal counterbalances that are required for the functions of the public prosecutor's office.

The deputy attorney general's Office for Juridical Affairs was redesignated as International Juridical Affairs, with the main objective of maintaining close relations with similar bodies in the fields of cooperation and extradition treaties and personnel training at the international level.[38] This area also has the responsibility for monitoring the constitutional provisions that assist the attorney general in examining the disputes that arise in the Federation.[39] The National Institute to Combat Drugs (INCD)[40] was recast in order to undertake specialized work in the broader fight against organized crime. The INCD sought to strengthen its operational areas and reduce the administrative work it carried out. With the reorganization, the INCD would have an MP specializing in the fight against organized crime, specifically against drug trafficking.

It should be emphasized that the INCD was created in June 1993 with a serious defect.[41] The person initially appointed to head the institution was not a lawyer, as required under PGR statutes. The figure of "commissioner" was therefore created to satisfy this formality.[42] This juridical deficiency resulted in the creation of a specific directorate of preliminary investigations to deal with health crime investigations initiated in the INCD. This adjustment involved two issues: First, although the commissioner might be informed about an investigation, he was unable to act on it *de jure.* Since the commissioner was not a lawyer, he could not act as a public prosecutor, and therefore, according to law, he could not investigate. Second, the creation of the INCD seemed more of a political gesture in response to U.S. pressures than an effective professionalization project in the fight against drug trafficking.

Prior to the scandal that prompted the removal in 1997 of General Jesús Gutiérrez Rebollo as INCD commissioner, Attorney General Jorge Madrazo had to issue an amendment whereby command decision making by the public prosecutor in the INCD was newly eliminated, an adjustment that had already been rectified by the PAN administration. Once again, since the commissioner was not a lawyer, his investigation and prosecution of crimes as a public prosecutor were illegal. However, the modification did not last long, since in February 1997 General Gutiérrez Rebollo was accused of providing protection for the Juárez Cartel, headed by Amado Carrillo.

Some months later the INCD was renamed the Special Prosecutor's Office for Health Crimes (FEADS). As of 2000, the FEADS operates through three major areas: first, the Border Task Forces (BTFs) comprised of Mexican and American law enforcement authorities operating in the Mexican border states; second, the Organized Crime Unit (UCO); and third, an anti–money laundering unit, which was created in January 1998. All of these units focus on anti–drug trafficking operations. The FEADS and UCO develop operations that range from eradication efforts, to drug interdiction (land, air, and sea), to the application of the Federal Law against Organized Crime.[43]

The UCO owes its regulatory and operational framework to the implementation of the Federal Law against Organized Crime (LFvsCO). Article 8 of the law establishes the creation of a specialized unit to investigate and prosecute organized crimes.[44] This specialized unit should also have a technical group made up of experts in methods of interception of private communications. This unit should have the training to evaluate the intercepted information. The initial effort to launch this unit was led by Dr. Samuel Gonzalez Ruiz, who also participated closely in drafting the LFvsCO. Dr. Gonzalez headed the UCO until December 1998, when he accepted an appointment as a consular official in Spain. Gonzalez was succeeded at the UCO by José Trinidad Larrieta.

FEADS has a Confidence Control Center, an area in charge of investigating in depth the background of the staff that operate within it. This center works in close coordination with the FBI and DEA, owing to continued evidence of penetration by the drug cartels in the structure of the attorney general's office.[45] Unfortunately, this personnel verification appears to have been implemented so far only in this department. Not surprisingly, it is the area that has the most contact with U.S. authorities.[46]

The UCO should be an elite unit. One of the main reasons for this is to have close control over the officials administering the LFvsCO. The core of these is a small group of well-trained public prosecutors. Also, the selective recruitment permits the vetting of the members of the UCO at least every six years by DEA and FBI authorities in conjunction with their Mexican counterparts.

Finally, it is important to emphasize that the special investigative tools such as undercover agents, the witness protection program, and wiretapping can be responsibly applied only by the public prosecutors who have passed the Control Center's tests and the vetting process mentioned above.

The restructuring of the PGR marked the beginning of a new stage in one part of the justice apparatus in which the rule of law should prevail above all else. It should also be pointed out that it is not enough to have the regulatory framework, or the expression of goodwill,[47] to implement the changes required, but rather a change must be effected in the bureaucratic culture to make it professional. The political leadership should also provide sufficient financial resources and transparent monitoring mechanisms for the proper functioning of the institution.

Federal Judicial Police

As mentioned earlier, one of the most serious matters for the PGR is the lack of adequate professionalization of the Federal Judicial Police (PJF). This police force combines corruption and impunity with a lack of professionalism, a lack of control over the use of resources, and a lack of clear objectives. Efforts have been made to regulate the PJF's operations and functions, the first of these coming in March 1993 when the Regulations for the Career of Federal Judicial Police Officer were created.[48] Subsequently, during Attorney General Lozano's reorganization, he stated on several occasions that what he found was a force of almost 4,000 agents with incomplete or nonexistent records (Table 5.2) and without the proper training to perform the functions of police officers.

The task of professionalizing this force would be enormous. Formal regulations were drafted to clearly define the functioning and responsibilities of the PJF,[49] and from that time onward agents would be closely supervised and trained to deal with crimes in a professional manner.[50] The institution charged exclusively with per-

Table 5.2 Number of Judicial Police, 1988–1998

1988	1991	1992	1993	1995	1997	1998
900	2900	2200	1500	4500	3200	2900

Source: For the period 1988–1994, see S. González et al., *Seguridad Pública en México*, 103. PGR records.

forming this function is the Training Institute (ICAP) mentioned above. However, weeding out problem agents, training, and enforcing internal regulations did not appear to be the only tasks required. Parallel to this effort, a redefinition of the image of the PGR and of the judicial police had to be undertaken. Up to that time, many of those who joined the PJF did so because they shared the values of abuse of power and illicit enrichment with their predecessors. Thus, the new recruits were willingly socialized into the existing, corrupt value structure. Having discovered this enormous deficiency as a result of applying axiological examinations, Attorney General Lozano set about strengthening and applying training courses in ethics.[51] Owing to the factors described above, it appeared that the transformation of the police would entail an investment of at least ten to twelve years.

As the last step in the appointment process for applicants selected by the PJF, the PGR should carry out, with the scarce resources and personnel at its disposal, an in-depth verification of the candidates' documents and records. This verification effort requires at a minimum efficient coordination among the Ministry of Defense, the Ministry of Education—to check the authenticity of the certificate of studies—and the Ministry of the Interior.[52] The lack of automated data banks and the bureaucratic inertia of each of these institutions make it almost impossible, or at least very slow, to clear potential full-time PGR employees. This has provided opportunities for the entry of unreliable candidates or even ones who are already colluding with organized crime.

Once the training course has been completed, the PJF agent goes on to form part of the General Directorate of the Federal Judicial Police, which became the General Directorate of Planning and Operation of the PJF.[53] Its director is currently (July 2000) a military officer who performs the following functions: monitoring the police; supervising the quality of the formal procedures carried out during the preliminary investigation; executing writs of attachment, searches, and other writs issued by the judicial authority, as well as warrants of arrest; and supervising and evaluating operational results.[54]

Certainly the above description suggests that at least the basic instruments of operation, command, coordination, and regulatory framework are in place. Nevertheless, I will suggest a basic issue that is working against strengthening the rule of law. Having a military officer as head of the judicial police breaks the basic functional principle of the backbone of the attorney general's office. There are two reasons for this: First, the military officer does not subordinate himself to the civilian authority,[55] and second, he is not trained for the tasks that the law imposes on the PJF. I won't go into further detail, but the presence of military officers in key posts leaves the current attorney general without essential support in performing the tasks assigned to him by the Constitution. Therefore, once again we have a situation that violates the law. Now, the logic appears to be that the crisis of rampant criminality and the penetration and corruption of the police apparatus leave no alternative. A military officer is appointed under the logic that because of his training and discipline, he will impose order and resist corruption. But reality has proven the contrary.[56] Members of the army are currently offered large sums of money to "turn a blind eye" to drug traffickers' operations.

In addition, and given the increase in drug trafficking for some time now, the most coveted positions have been those in the north of the country. To obtain them it is necessary for aspirants to a certain state field office to take part in a *polla*.[57] The *polla* can collect sums as high as $30 million. Contributions for the *polla* can range from US$10,000 to US$400,000, depending on the post one wishes to occupy—that is, delegate, commander, judicial police agent, etc.—and on the delegation or office one wishes to join.[58] Obviously the money is of illicit origin, and it is the first link in the chain of collusion between drug traffickers, public prosecutors, and police agents. Commanders tend to have a select group of agents in their confidence who are in charge of collecting the money and transmitting it to the appropriate authorities to ensure an appointment to a particular position. Recently these positions have been filled by military officers, which has exposed them to huge sums of money.

Moreover, the rigorous training of army personnel does not include training in skills for dealing with society. The military are trained to kill in order to safeguard the state; police officers should be trained to protect society. If the appropriate reorientation does not occur soon, we will continue to lack adequate operation and training of the PJF.

Weeding Out the Federal Judicial Police—What Do We Gain?

Toward mid-1996, and in response to the results of the axiological examinations, it was decided to operate on two fronts in the PJF: first, to reformulate the study plans and requirements for entry into the PJF, and second, to weed out undesirable officers. In the exercise of his authority, Attorney General Lozano dismissed a total of 826 PJF agents, among them 22 of the 33 subdelegates,[59] reaching an overall total of 1,200 during his term of office. This was done because the drug traffickers had infiltrated the police force. The action involved joint efforts throughout the country during which agents' PJF insignia or badge were collected. The operation aimed to remove the key instrument of their impunity—the badge, undoubtedly a symbol of power—which, together with their weapon, enabled them to act with total impunity.

The basis for weeding out was to identify the agents who lacked the ethical characteristics required to perform their functions. The dismissals also resulted from reports issued by the Ministry of the Comptroller General and Administrative Development, the Ministry of National Defense, and the Ministry of the Interior; these ministries worked together to remove those agents most in collusion with organized crime and drug trafficking. For example, there were delegations in which all the agents were removed and the army took over because of the degree of contamination that existed.[60] However, the army's stay was temporary in view of the antecedent of the Chihuahua experiment, where they had shown signs of being corruptible.[61] The special forces positioned in Chihuahua had served there for almost a year, after which they were removed because they were just as contaminated as the civilian police by the narco-corruption.

Unfortunately, the PJF's internal weeding out measures enjoyed little support and were insufficient in the face of penetration by drug traffickers. In fact, society viewed the measures as theatrics to divert attention, and even as a mechanism to sidetrack and confuse public opinion so as to forget the overwhelming failures registered by the administration.[62] Incredible as it may seem, the clean-up of the police forces, together with the measure to take an internal census, led to the introduction for the first time of a reliable automated data bank within the institution, containing information on the members of the PJF. Before this time, such information was incomplete, inaccurate, or simply did not exist. Along with these actions, the first steps were taken to establish a civilian career model in the operational forces. This model had three basic elements: training public prosecutors and police officers; supervising and closely monitoring their performance; and above all, instilling a sense of pride in belonging to the PGR, which would be accompanied by expectations of professional development. Furthermore, the police training model brought to bear national and international norms regulating the functions that a police officer should perform in society.[63]

As of 1996, the institutional bases consisted of at least the following elements: a system of comprehensive academic training accompanied by social recognition; clear standards of competence and operation; basic principles of behavior, ethical conduct, and transparent rules on the use of force; and systems of administration, control, supervision, and evaluation which differentiated the operational command from the authority for administrative control. Society also had to be informed about these measures and demand their strict application in order to share the responsibility for the changes and to monitor the actions undertaken.

The Professionalization Council of the Office of the Federal Public Prosecutor was established as a result of the restructuring and weeding-out process. The purpose of this collegiate body was to authorize the guidelines for supervision, control, and evaluation of a civil service career program. As a priority, it would deal with the area of the Federal Judicial Police. However, the three operational forces that made up the functions of the PGR were included. The council began its work in August 1996 and as of mid-2000 its results, and the progress made in applying the regulations and strengthening the civil service career, are unknown.

Federal Law against Organized Crime

A third step undertaken by the PAN administration was that of modernizing the legal framework to attack organized crime, particularly that associated with drug trafficking. The Federal Law against Organized Crime was passed in November 1996; its incorporation into Mexican law meant a radical change in the legal framework to combat organized crime.[64] However, at the outset the preliminary draft encountered enormous resistance from constitutional experts, lawyers, academics, and the public in general.[65] The first bill, introduced on October 2, 1996, underwent modifications to forty-eight of its fifty-four articles prior to its first reading before the Senate on October 26 of that same year.

At present organized crime is accurately perceived as the main cause of public insecurity, as well as a national security problem. The State has shown itself incapable of effectively enforcing the law and, even worse, appears to be a victim of the phenomenon. Attorney General Jorge Madrazo recently declared: "The enemy is within."[66] Criminal organizations play a significant role in relations with diverse actors in public life. The press tells of their penetration and the State's deficiencies in combating them, as well as of their power.[67]

Two positions were adopted with the creation of the Federal Law against Organized Crime: (1) those who opposed the changes because they believed that the changes violated civil liberties;[68] and (2) those who promoted the reforms under the essential premise of acquiring a modern, sophisticated legal framework to attack the phenomenon of criminality that had developed in Mexico. The central features of the Federal Law against Organized Crime are: a definition of organized crime as a concept and techniques to investigate those who carry out this activity—with emphasis on the right to tap private communications, rewards, the use of undercover agents, and protection for persons who take part in penal proceedings, that is, a witness protection program.[69]

As of mid-2000, the investigative activities carried out by the Unit against Organized Crime suffer from a lack of strong leadership, lack of professionalization, and insufficient will to take on challenging investigations. A number of internal rivalries within the Unit and the departure of key personnel have further hampered effectiveness. Progress is being made in dismantling criminal organizations, but—with one or two exceptions—we have yet to see stiff sentences being handed down by the Judiciary for this illicit activity. Also, the Executive or Legislative Branch should promote regulations for the proper enforcement of the Federal Law against Organized Crime.

Challenges Faced in Modernizing the Attorney General's Office

I shall sum up some of the points and concepts concerning the operations of the PGR. First, it should be understood that the attorney general is head of the federal public prosecutor's office and that the latter is in charge of carrying out investigations with the assistance of the PJF and crime experts. Second, neither of the two institutes responsible for training civilian personnel to carry out the functions of criminal investigation and prosecution (INACIPE and ICAP) has sufficient material or human resources available to meet the challenge of professionalizing

**Table 5.3 Budget of the Office of the Attorney
General of the Republic (in pesos)**

1995	1996	1997	1998
960 million	1.6 billion	2.4 billion	3.556 billion

Source: Lozano, *La Jornada* (1998), 85.

the PGR's operational bodies. It is not enough to count on technical and training support from similar agencies of other countries such as the United States, France, and Israel; it is necessary to establish a permanent, professional technical body, modern curricula, and a comprehensive training program with real economic resources. Table 5.3 provides an overview of the attorney general's budget from 1995 through 1998.

Third, there is no overall vision of the operations and professional administration of the attorney general's office in the federal government and society as a whole. The discredit, poor image, lack of professionalism, bureaucratic culture, and vested interests within the system of justice—partly the result of the economic power acquired by drug traffickers—are still the main obstacles to moving forward with institutional reform. Furthermore, the use of the army to combat crime has created an impasse in the proper training of the PJF.[70] Prosecutors do not have proper assistance in carrying out investigations. The army has committed numerous human rights violations. Curiously, Attorney General Madrazo stated before the National Human Rights Commission that "the Army cannot carry out police functions."[71] He, like his predecessor, speaks of a temporary army presence. Society seems to place more trust in the military institution,[72] but this may also reflect its despair at the rise in crime and the defenseless state in which it finds itself. We should note that other experiences show us how the incorporation of army personnel into police functions leaves a wake of impunity and abuses,[73] and their involvement does not therefore contribute to strengthening the rule of law. Their long-term involvement serves as a palliative that acts to the detriment of the army, because more often than not they do not solve the underlying problem.

The main challenge is undoubtedly to develop a strategic overall vision to combat public insecurity and strengthen the administration of justice and the rule of law. Above all, this implies removing the prevailing antidemocratic culture in the exercise of law. The modernization of the attorney general's office should be kept separate from political interests in order to avoid the vestiges of Mexican authoritarianism.

It is urgent to eradicate the culture of corruption and impunity, but this requires the participation of society in building transparent mechanisms to monitor the institutions in charge of providing security.[74] The absence of a step of this magnitude endangers not only the progress of Mexican democracy but even the very survival of the State. On the threshold of the twenty-first century, Mexico must ensure a democratic and impartial system of security and justice based on law that is capable of protecting society and the State from rampant organized crime and drug trafficking.

Chapter 6

Containing Armed Groups, Drug Trafficking, and Organized Crime in Mexico

The Role of the Military

Raúl Benítez Manaut

THE MEXICAN TRANSITION taking place at the end of the twentieth century and into the new millennium has deeply altered economic, social, political, and international relations at all levels. Both in civil society and in state and government structures, these changes have shifted the position of key actors in national life. In civil society, businesspeople, union leaders, merchants, intellectuals, and journalists have a new role. Some are becoming stronger in society and in relation to the state; others are seeing their position diminished. Within the state and the political system, the actors who traditionally played key roles in the years of full hegemony of the institutionalized Mexican revolution (from the 1930s to the 1980s) are witnessing the deterioration of their image.

Similarly, the emergence of highly influential transnational forces at the end of the century have had an impact on political change in Mexico. Many of these actors are considered to be new threats to international security, such as the large drug trafficking mafias. All of this creates a difficult scenario for Mexico and its core state structures. The military, as set forth in the Constitution, must act as the arm that exercises legitimate violence to face the risk that negative factors, both internal and external, can endanger the nation and its security.

This chapter analyzes the changes in the civilian-military relationship that stem from the new conditions in the country at the end of the twentieth century. It further examines the missions being given to the armed forces because of ungovernability and instability (both real and potential) in the country. Certain phenomena are reappearing on the social and political scenes in Mexico, including the growth in drug trafficking and organized crime, the emergence of armed groups such as the Ejército Zapatista de Liberación Nacional (EZLN, the Zapatista National Liberation Army) and the Ejército Popular Revolucionario (EPR, the People's Revolutionary Army), the increase in public insecurity, and the great crisis in the country's judicial institutions, which are being overwhelmed by these actors.

The Military: History, Doctrine, and Missions

The successful demilitarization of Mexico's political life coincided with the installation of its postrevolutionary political system, which is monopolized by a product of the army—the Institutional Revolutionary Party (PRI).[1] An implicit relationship of cooperation was established between the PRI and the army, in which the military was officially subordinated, as set forth in the Constitution of 1917, to the commander in chief of the military, the president of the Republic.[2] The military has ceased to be pivotal for political control and governability and only acts in times of serious political crisis, when the police forces are overwhelmed. This has occurred in rural areas with high social and political violence (such as the State of Guerrero, where guerrillas emerged in the 1970s) and at times of great political crisis, such as to contain the student movement of 1968:

The Mexican army has the grave responsibility of maintaining domestic peace and order, as set forth in the Constitution, so that our institutions may function, Mexicans may enjoy the liberty guaranteed by the law, and the country may continue making progress. The way the army fulfilled its commitments [with regard to the student movement of September and October 1968—RBM] is clear proof that we can trust in its patriotism and its civil and institutional conviction to reestablish order and immediately return to its normal activities.[3]

In terms of military doctrine, the Constitution grants the Mexican military two missions: defending sovereignty (defending the country from foreigners) under Defense War Plan 1 (DN-I) and maintaining domestic order under Defense

War Plan 2 (DN-II).[4] Similarly, the Constitution provides for the establishment of a national guard for DN-II.[5] However, that force does not exist because the legislature has not created it under the corresponding law, which leaves the security forces to maintain domestic security. Only when those forces are overtaken do the army and navy take action under plan DN-II. A third war plan was incorporated into the Organic Law of the Army in the 1970s: Defense War Plan 3 (DN-III), which consists of assisting the civilian population in support and rescue activities in times of natural disaster.[6]

For our purposes, it is the DN-II plan that truly defines the structure, organization, and territorial organization of the army. It dates back to the Mexican Revolution, when the revolutionary armies were gradually disarmed and subordinated to centralized civilian leadership, but the army was still deployed to prevent rebellions. Subsequently, owing to the lack of security forces in the countryside, the army began to act as a rural police: "The rural defense corps concept has been ongoing for many years and primarily provides the army and the government additional loyal eyes and ears in the countryside. Indications are that plans are being made to streamline and improve the effectiveness of these forces, which reinforce the military presence provided by the *partida* system. These rural defense forces are drawn from Mexico's *ejido* (communal farm) system."[7]

Similarly, because of the make-up and structure of the military (see Figure 6.1 and Table 6.1) and its "social" nature, and because of the shortcomings in the institutional coverage of other units of the federal government, the army uses its deployment in rural areas to carry out civic action programs. In this way it allows the government to have an institutional presence.

The Mexican army has a rich tradition of rendering assistance to the civilian population, the foundations of which date back to the early 1920s. The army engaged in such tasks as building roads, constructing irrigation works, and repairing railroad and telegraph lines. The 1926 organic law of the armed forces formally made civic action a part of the army's overall mission. Article 81 of the law provided for the use of military resources in the construction of communications networks and public works that had some correlation with the overall needs of the military.[8]

Up to the present, the army (not the Ministry of Health) has been responsible for vaccination campaigns in some of the poorest regions in the country and on many occasions has even been responsible for distributing food staples. These so-

Figure 6.1. Organization of the Mexican Army, 1997

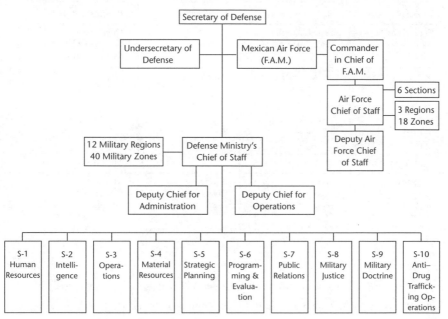

Elaboración: Raúl Benítez Manuat

cial duties also serve to conduct "preventive intelligence," although originally they were not part of any counterinsurgency activities:

Civic action, generally composed of a variety of developmental-type projects, brings the officer corps in contact with rural poverty and ordinary Mexicans. . . . The military is the entity representative of the federal government in the hinterland, and in that sense performs a political function for the political leadership. . . . Military civic action did not originate as counterinsurgency measures but as a component of the armed forces revolutionary tradition.[9]

The rural counterinsurgency aspect of the modern Mexican army began with the fight against the *Cristeros* (1926–1928) in the center of the country and, subsequently, in the 1960s and 1970s, to combat leftist guerillas, primarily in the state of Guerrero.[10] In this way, the army went from social action that originated in revolutionary ideology (institutional presence, building infrastructure to communicate with the countryside, and support for marginalized rural populations) to a labor of pacification (rural guard) and containing outbreaks of violence, which at

Table 6.1 Military Regions, 1997

I. Military Region	II. Military Region	III. Military Region	IV. Military Region
Federal District State of Mexico Morelos	Baja California Baja California Sur	Sonora Sinaloa	Nuevo León Tamaulipas San Luis Potosí
V. Military Region	VI. Military Region	VII. Military Region	VIII. Military Region
Jalisco Nayarit Zacatecas Colima Aguascalientes	Puebla Hidalgoíí Tlaxcala Veracruz	Chiapas	Oaxaca
IX. Military Region	X. Military Region	XI. Military Region	XII. Military Region
Guerrero	Yucatan Campeche Quintana Roo	Coahuila Chihuahua Durango	Michoacán Guanajuato Querétaro

Source: Secretaria de la Defensa Nacional, Mexico, 1997.

their worst were organized into rural leftist guerilla groups in the early 1970s. Put another way, the first postrevolutionary mission was to project the presence of the federal government, to neutralize the power of local *caciques*, to integrate the nation's territory, to carry out work where there was no state infrastructure, and to integrate the population politically.

Originally, the military's presence in the war on drug trafficking in the 1940s was also part of the civic action programs, and it supported and/or replaced the Office of the Attorney General (PGR) because of its institutional incapacity. From the 1940s to the 1970s, the war on drugs was not an issue of national security but was focused on destroying marijuana and opium crops.[11]

Until the 1970s, the military played a functional role for the Mexican state at various levels; although the political system was demilitarized, in rural areas the army continued to perform political and police functions (supporting the system against outbreaks of dissent and maintaining order). In addition, the military collaborated with governmental structures that could not cover the entire territory, in order to fulfill their missions (replacing the Ministries of Communications and Transportation, Education, Health, and Food Distribution [CONASUPO], municipal police forces, etc.). In this way, the army continuously performed nonmilitary missions, many of which were linked to the state's obligations. In political terms, this was to benefit and consolidate the regime:

The army has served as a major constitutional instrument for political enforcement during conflicts. Zone commanders remain an important presidential agent for replacing state governors during crises. The army is frequently used to separate and prevent violence between rival political factions in provincial areas, while civilian officials seek to resolve the conflict. Electoral defense for the PRI and suppression of political rebels and radicals are other uses that the army has served. . . . The army has also helped the government to secure control over isolated, unruly rural areas. In this respect, the expansion of a government's politico-administrative control often follows from the extension of economic and social services to needy peasant populations in isolated areas. Such developments may disturb the traditional forms of local politics, and thus in high conflict areas such as Guerrero the army may become an indispensable participant in the process.[12]

In this sense, the Mexican army was modernized but not depoliticized.[13] That process began later, in the 1980s, when the partisan opposition emerged. Nonetheless, it is difficult to claim that this entire time the army was the armed force of the PRI (as it was in the 1930s). The order of loyalty in the military is to the Constitution and the commander in chief (the president), who is the head of state, head of government, and, unofficially, the top leader in the PRI. Therefore, it was up to the president, not the army, to fulfill missions to support the PRI; of course the army applies the standard of "due obedience," which states that an order from a superior is not to be questioned, even if it is unconstitutional.[14]

In Mexico, due obedience is related to impunity. Historically, as one goes up the chain of command, it is more difficult to punish a person for an illegal order since that order is linked to the interests of the political authorities, who are themselves unaccountable.[15] Therefore, in the Mexican army the Code of Military Justice punishes persons for not following an order,[16] without taking into account whether or not it was unconstitutional or violated a civil law.[17]

With regard to military missions, the importance of the DN-II plan with respect to the real operation of the military (primarily the army) is such that, historically, the Mexican military functions throughout the territory of the country, and is in reality carrying out nonmilitary, civic action missions such as the integration of rural areas, as well as police and political duties. The military's sole domestic security mission provided for in the Constitution is the use of the army against armed groups organized explicitly to challenge the military, with the goal of seizing the state, or when the police forces are unable to exercise containment. In such cases an executive order is used to reestablish order. These missions are not intended to be permanent:

However, there is also the obligation of supporting the authorities when necessary, primarily in cases of serious upheavals in law and order. . . . This subject has been the cause of serious controversy, since it is argued that the country's military should never intervene to suppress the actions of groups of dissenters that in some way alter the proper law and order that must prevail, since this activity is the sole and exclusive responsibility of civilian authorities, through the preventive police forces, but is never that of federal forces, i.e., the army, navy, or air force.[18]

In the 1980s, the political mission of protecting the political leadership of the government (by supporting the party in power, when necessary) stopped being an operational mission of the military; however, its territorial deployment continued unchanged. Therefore, modernization and professionalization occurred at the same time as gradual depoliticization, and thus the military serves the state and not the short-term (or partisan) interests of high-level government officials. Since the emergence of the political opposition in elections, roughly between 1982 and 1988, an unsuccessful attempt was made to revert to using the army in the traditional manner. Writing in 1990, Cornelius and Craig observed:

Since 1985, civilian authorities have called on the military to provide highly visible "security" for elections. Formerly, troops were deployed only in response to election-related disturbances if they occurred. Now they can be seen before, during, and after the elections, particularly in states that are strongholds of the opposition parties. The opposition charges that the huge military presence in these places is intended to intimidate their supporters from going to the polls and from taking to the streets to protest fraudulent election practices.[19]

The continuous growth of the political opposition silently influenced the army to cease executing this traditional police function, primarily in rural areas. The prevention-police-political function was gradually abandoned in the 1990s, and the army became the strategic force of the state and not of the government. Therefore, subordination to the principles of the Constitution also translated into respect for the sovereignty of the people to elect political authorities (as stated in articles 39, 40, and 41).

However, other missions that had been secondary became essential to the military's operations, primarily because of the crisis in the political system, potential ungovernability, and the growing inefficiency of civilian government structures. At the start of the twenty-first century, the military has three missions:

1. Drug trafficking has increased capacity to destabilize law and order, the economy, and political stability, confronting a weak state that can be easily penetrated. Military action against trafficking is not new, but different strategies must be used. Therefore, the military must allocate more human and economic resources, as well as the use of military combat facilities, to this task.

2. In 1994, the eruption of the Zapatista National Liberation Army (EZLN) led the army to deploy resources to contain it.[20] Although leftist armed revolutionary groups are not new in Mexico, the EZLN and, since 1996, the People's Revolutionary Army (EPR),[21] have called into question the capacity of the government and the army to handle the situation.

3. The crisis in the public security system, both prevention and investigations, throughout the country is causing the army and its members (retired or active) to assume leadership of the police in the most important cities.

These three problems, which the state and key sectors of society view as issues of national security, and the fact that the Mexican government lacks efficient civilian structures for resolving them, are pushing political leaders to order the use of the military. This has unleashed a great controversy over the dangers of using the military to deal with these problems and has sparked a debate on the militarization of the country.

Part of this debate concerns constitutional issues. Article 89, subparagraph VI, of the Constitution states that the president may "dispose of all the permanent armed forces, army, navy, and air force, for the domestic safety and foreign defense of the federation."[22] This constitutional provision justifies deployment for the DN-II plan. However, this could contradict article 129 of the Constitution, which states that "in times of peace none of the military authorities shall exercise functions other than those bearing direct relation to military discipline. No permanent military posts shall be established other than in castles, forts, and arsenals dependent directly upon the federal government, or in camps, barracks, or depots established outside of inhabited places for the stationing of troops."[23]

The possible contradiction between articles 89 and 129 of the Constitution lies in what is understood as "time of peace" or "time of war." In addition, the concept of "space" must be considered. There are rural regions in the country with a high incidence of drug trafficking and armed groups where the presence of the army is almost permanent; they would therefore have to be considered war zones in order to deploy the army in fulfillment of the DN-II plan. Logically, politically, no one wants to assume the risk of considering a region of the country as being at war or under martial law; therefore, this situation does not legally exist in any region of the country. But in reality, since the 1980s, the army has had a semipermanent presence in extensive rural areas, such as Guerrero, Chiapas, Sinaloa, regions of Hidalgo, Tamaulipas, Sonora, Tabasco, mountainous areas of Veracruz, Jalisco, and Michoacán.

In the case of the Mexican navy, its missions are focused to a greater extent on the DN-I plan, and it has important responsibility for controlling illegal fishing and protecting the environment. Nonetheless, it has prominent functions in the war against drug trafficking;[24] and similar to the army and air force, collaboration with the United States is key.[25]

Political Transition: Between Governability and Chaos

Political transition is a process that runs parallel to the modernization of the state and the economic reforms implemented to orient the economy under market rules; however, this change process is not balanced.[26, 27] There is progress at some levels of the state structure, but there are also large setbacks (the extent of modernization of the state in the executive, legislature, and judiciary is very unequal). This inequality also occurs at the three levels of government (federal, state, municipal) as well as in the economic structure. Some sectors of the economy are very well suited for participation in globalized markets and the Free Trade Agreement with the United States and Canada, but some very backward, traditional economic structures are being reproduced as well. There are similar gaps in culture and society. Therefore, this is a "dysfunctional" transition.[28]

The foregoing leads us to affirm that the lag in modernizing the state along with the existence of great regional, economic, political, cultural, and social differences combine to produce conditions that are conducive to criminal activity, particularly to drug trafficking.

Political change in Mexico is leading the country toward a democratic system of government. However, the nature of the political system is such that traditional elements continue to be important, thus enabling illegal criminal activity to be part of the operation of the system: "Our political democracy is not yet born and is already being combated by very powerful enemies, including, most notably, state-level *caciques*, drug trafficking cartels, and those persons that have both big money and political influence. . . . There was a time when the police more or less kept the underworld in check. Today, that very same police force, without leadership, is one of the main sources of criminality."[29]

As in any comprehensive transition, the danger lies in the state's losing control of the political, economic, social, or international actors conducting these activities, resulting in conditions of instability or ungovernability. When interpreting the situation in Mexico in the 1990s, chaos has been mentioned as a trend to be curbed through militarization.[30] Others mention that the degree to which crime has penetrated state structures has reached levels similar to those in Colombia; therefore, one can speak of "narcodemocracy."[31] In other words, in the Mexican transition of the 1990s, there are functional actors for modernization and democratization, and there are dysfunctional and disruptive actors that threaten domestic stability, create ungovernability, conduct illegal activities, and even have substantial capacity to cause international instability, such as organized crime and drug trafficking. These actors also threaten the future of NAFTA, since much of the criminal activity is either committed outside Mexico or originates domestically and quickly has an impact abroad, thus decreasing the possibility of free trade and positive, transnational economic activities.

Many of the actors that are negative or dysfunctional for the process of democratization and modernization are in the state machinery, owing to the reproduction of traditional activities such as "corruption" (which served the single-party political system) and resistance to losing power.[32] At the time of crisis in the political system, corruption became linked to criminal activity since state institutions have more controls on the handling of resources. Better administration helps purify and improve controls on the administration of public money, but this improvement leads public employees to conduct parallel, illegal activities to generate income.

For example, when traditional segments of the political system begin to be affected by democratization (traditional politicians lose public posts) and modernization (control of public money, emergence of accountability), they turn to criminal groups for backing to fund political campaigns or to retain substantial personal income, in keeping with the standard of living of the elite during the nondemocratic era of the political system.[33] Therefore, because of the increased obstacles to robbing money from the government, and in order to survive, the link between current and former government officials and criminal activity was strengthened: "A Mexican tradition of accepting money for governmental services rendered (known in the U.S. and Canada as 'corruption') contributes to the ease of laundering illegal profits, facilitates drug smuggling, and adds to the difficulty of maintaining cordial relations."[34]

In short, the challenge is for the leadership of the Mexican state to carry out the transition without creating ungovernability or instability. Therefore, in order to neutralize the negative agents and to make effective the positive agents of transition, the state faces hurdles at two levels: internally, the easy penetration of the state by mafias due to historical corruption, and externally, the limited capacity of the judicial system and security forces to contain organized crime and drug trafficking activities. In reality, it can be said that the country is in a gray area ("where governments are unable to govern")[35] and the state does not have the credibility to lead change.

Since the 1990s, Mexican politics has faced the crisis of the corporatist-authoritarian-clientelist system that determined the mechanisms of stability, returning to the starting point of the political system in the 1920s and 1930s. The government turns to the strongest state institution—the army—because of its own weakness, crisis of inefficiency, and inability to achieve governability. The revaluation of the military stemmed from crisis, as a last resort of upper-level state leaders and not as an institutional project. In this way, the army's missions are expanded (the missions of the DN-II spread out) despite the fact that the army may be taking a detour on its path toward modernization and professionalization (DN-I), with the resulting risk either of inefficiency (since its missions are civilian in nature) or of politicization (using the armed forces for political purposes).

In the Mexican transition we are witnessing a weakening of the president's power, with a rebalancing in favor of the legislature and an unprecedented crisis in the judiciary. Meanwhile, in the federal system there are proposals to strengthen state and municipal levels in various ways. One of these is to strengthen the responsibility of the judicial system and the preventive security forces. This phenomenon, called "new federalism," may be contradictory, since what is healthy at the political level (for example, the growing autonomy of municipalities) may endanger public security and contribute to drug trafficking and other criminal activities. This is because the municipal police in rural areas and small cities, as well as the judicial systems (the Office of the Attorney General), are much more susceptible to corruption and often act in the interest of local groups *(caciques)* and not with the necessary impartiality and professionalism. What is good for political democratization (decentralization) is bad for justice and public safety.

Given the above, the mafias take advantage of this state-local autonomy and the weakness of the judicial systems in carrying out their activities, since they are more likely to be successful if the systems are decentralized. Making a comparison with Colombia and Russia, in the case of the former, the strength of the local-rural powers is the basis for the action and reproduction of the large cartels.[36] The breakdown of centralized Soviet power, disintegrated state mechanisms for controlling the border, and illegal groups—including the largest mafias—have created an environment of almost total anarchy in Russia.[37] This should serve as an example of precisely what to avoid in Mexico. If this phenomenon were to occur, the modernization of Mexico would take a step backward, and there would follow the feudalization of power, the privatization of security, and a dismantling of the state's capacity to conduct security policies. This would leave public order in the hands of the *caciques,* as is occurring in parts of Chiapas, Guerrero, Sinaloa, Hidalgo, Oaxaca, and some northern states.

In the Mexican transition, the dismantling of the nationalist-revolutionary state is occurring in an unbalanced manner. It is a process in which a modern democratic state is being born that can impose the rule of law and where the old oligarchies still exist; therefore, modern structures coexist with traditional ones. In many parts of the country, this process has produced a vacuum of power that is often filled by the mafias. In other words, the traditional classes have not been displaced entirely (for example, the *caciques*), and modern actors have not been able to hold public office. This exemplifies the concept of dual power in the political structure, in which federal institutions and state and municipal governments are divided between the traditional "dinosaurs" or *caciques*—who are generally supported in the backward structures of the PRI, and the "modern actors,"—who are anchored in the urban and progressive sectors of the PRI and the opposition, essentially in the PAN and PRD.

This dual power is bolstered by a free-market economy and open international borders. In other words, in a country with weak governmental structures, international organized crime takes advantage of globalization. That is to say, the state (following Max Weber) has a monopoly on the exercise of legitimate violence, but it does not have governmental structures to really impose that monopoly, and private actors with specific, illegal goals replace the state. The government is penetrated by these private actors and the officials who support them. Instead of acting for the common good, they pursue personal benefit: "The police stem from order and disorder that coexist at a particular moment in society. Bandits and police officers exchange roles and are interchangeable, depending on the circumstances."[38]

Given the above, the increase or effective containment of crime depends on two circumstances—the success of the economic, social, and political transition (structural factors), and the success and generalization of reform, the democratization, modernization, and professionalization of all the arms of the Mexican state. Success depends on the process of "institution destruction" of the parts of the state belonging to the authoritarian model, which generated corruption and inefficiency and must be accompanied by a process of "institution building." Such institution building is urgent in the judicial and crime prevention systems and in the security forces.

To date, the processes of institution destruction/reconstruction are not under way in a comprehensive manner; therefore, the old institutions, with their heritage and structures, are being incorporated into modern structures. This contradiction foments organized crime. One notable example is the institutional decomposition of the PGR and the thirty-two offices of the attorney general in each state of the country, as well as of the respective Federal Judicial Police forces. These are considered to be the structures most commonly infiltrated by organized crime. In the absence of the political resolve necessary to proceed with institution destruction/reconstruction, the state turns to the military because of the magnitude of the growth in organized crime, violence, and lack of public security, which is considered to be a matter of "national security." Therefore, according to the key national planning document:

To guarantee the national security of Mexico, it is necessary to:

1. Preserve, according to the law and the international treaties and agreements signed by Mexico, the integrity of the land, air space, and the territorial seas and those that are the public domain of the country, in dealing with other states, the threats of international criminal organizations, the illegal trafficking in arms and persons, and the illegal exploitation of the resources of our seas;

2. Ensure at all times the effective exercise of the rule of law in the national territory and monitor our borders, always respectful of individuals' human rights;

3. Update the strategic planning of the Mexican army, air force, and navy; modernize and consolidate their military, operational, intelligence, and technical capacity and their ability to immediately respond to emergencies and disasters; strengthen the protection of vital installations in the country and update the laws thereon to the new circumstances and challenges;

4. Coordinate the units and entities of the federal public administration and the states in the federation in their relations with other nations; in particular, ensure unity in the criteria for combating modern threats to national security—drug trafficking, money laundering, illegal arms trafficking, and terrorism;

5. Take advantage of international cooperation in the exchange of information on drug trafficking, criminals, and terrorism.[39]

Since the 1970s, many armed groups have emerged in Mexico, influenced partly by the trend of guerrilla movements throughout Latin America. These groups have included both rural and urban movements: rural ones, in states such as Guerrero, rising in defense of peasant interests against corrupt local authorities,[40] and the urban ones, primarily clandestine groups with little popular support.[41] The army could successfully control the rural movements using traditional counterinsurgency tactics, and the security forces of the Interior Ministry contained the urban ones.

In 1977, when the government of José López Portillo introduced an amnesty, many of the groups from the 1960s and 1970s lost their military capacity and merged with newly legalized political parties of the Left, many of which were linked to the popular movements of the PRI. Other former guerrillas went to Central American countries, primarily Nicaragua and El Salvador, to join guerrilla groups there. Although most analysts claimed that the era of guerrilla movements had ended in Mexico, on January 1, 1994, the EZLN, descendent of the FLN,[42] emerged in the state of Chiapas. This was the first time in the history of contemporary Mexico that a guerrilla group garnered substantial support and leadership from important sectors of the population; estimates place sympathizers and combatants at more than 2,000 and the range of influence over more than 200,000 indigenous persons. The Mexican army estimated approximately 5,000 combatants at the start of the conflict.

The rise of the EZLN can be traced to two principal coinciding factors. First, the closed political, social, and economic structures, increasing tensions over land disputes, and dwindling state capacities prompted peasants to mobilize in order to protect their interests. As the local authorities and elites reacted with repressive measures, the mobilization gained even further momentum with the appearance of radical political leaders. Initial peasant movements, led by groups such as liberation theologists with their ideals of alternative power against the local elites, coalesced into the EZLN. Hence, a process of feudalization occurred in Chiapas, and a situation of extreme violence ensued as the EZLN confronted the local and state structures of the PRI.

At the outset, the EZLN declared war on the government and the federal army: "We issue the present (declaration of war) to the Federal Mexican Army, pillar of support for the dictatorship under which we suffer, monopolized by the party in power and headed by the federal executive that today is held by the chief illegitimate leader, Carlos Salinas de Gortari." The EZLN ordered its military forces to Mexico City to "advance toward the capital of the country defeating the Federal Mexican Army."[43] These original demands, initially projected on a national level, quickly changed, with the ensuing focus on the needs of the indigenous population of Chiapas.

The six-year crisis in Chiapas (1994–2000) has been characterized by zig-zagging between the EZLN and the government. This has resulted in the unsuccessful search for a political solution since military strategies have not been viable for either side. We can identify five distinct phases of the conflict in Chiapas. First came the war from January 1 to 11, 1994, in which the army reacted—active military containment—to the EZLN offensive, which resulted in 152 deaths. A cease-fire and first dialogue followed, from January 12, 1994, to February 8, 1995. This second phase can be subdivided into a period of official dialogue from January to June 1994, and then an informal cease-fire between the government and the EZLN until February 1995. The next military phase of the conflict, from February 9, 1995, through March 6, 1995, focused on the capture of Subcomandante Marcos (identified by the government as Rafael Sebastián Guillén Vicente) with the "Operación Arco Iris" of the military. A renewed dialogue culminated in the Larráinzar Accords of February 16, 1996.[44] The principal channels of mediation were the National Commission of Intermediation (CONAI) and the Commission for Peace of the Congress (COCOPA). The dialogue cooled off and negotiations continued without military conflict as the two sides engaged in a political and philosophical debate over the Larráinzar Accords and reform of the Constitution.[45] On December 22, 1997, when forty-five indigenous people were killed in Acteal by a group of paramilitaries under the direction of extremists of the PRI, the conflict escalated to another phase.

After the incident at Acteal, the federal government abandoned the political initiative and transferred the responsibility of "containment" of the EZLN to the local political elites (what we have established as the feudalization of society).[46] This strategy is based primarily on the harassment of Zapatista sympathizers by paramilitary groups. Various sources claim that seven of these existing paramilitary groups (the Chiapan version of the Guatemalan and Salvadoran death squads of the 1970s and early 1980s) have caused more than 1,500 deaths and 10,000 forced relocations of indigenous persons since 1995. The feudalization strategy means that contradictions flourish in the indigenous communities, causing community members to fight against each other on grounds of religious differences, land problems, heritage, and so on. Logically, this situation leads to an increased level of violence, a weakened rule of law and, in the end, a debilitated federal government.

The army has only taken an active role in containing the EZLN on two occasions: during the initial war phase and then from February 9 to March 5, 1995. Even though the military has been only a passive force of containment the rest of the time, it retains approximately 20 percent of its forces (30,000 to 40,000 soldiers) in Chiapas on a semipermanent basis. Because of both domestic and international pressure, both sides in the conflict have largely resisted the use of military force, opting instead for the dialogue that legitimizes the government strategy.

Precisely because of its discourse, based on "moral force," representation of the indigenous, and the fight for a good and noble cause, the EZLN cannot take direct armed action easily. Instead of military action, the group relies on its international "invisible army of militants" or "net of guerrillas" for political force and influence. Organized to combat conventional enemies, the Mexican army cannot respond to this new kind of opponent. Nevertheless, for the first time since the 1970s, the military has been accused of human rights violations against the civilian population.[47] In political terms, since both the army and the EZLN benefit from not engaging in armed fighting (the former gaining national and international legitimacy for being subordinate to civil authorities and the latter demonstrating that it is not a fundamentalist group), weapons are used more for dissuasion than for combat.

In June 1996, the Popular Revolutionary Army (EPR) emerged in the state of Guerrero. The EPR takes action in the most violent states in Mexico, primarily Guerrero and Oaxaca, where local *caciques,* integrated through "families," control the economic, social, and political structures.[48] The EPR was formed from fourteen clandestine groups (principally from the PROCUP) which date back to the 1970s. The group has both urban and rural forces but much less popular support than the EZLN, with no support from civil society. The government is employing the same counterinsurgency tactics against the EPR that it used against guerrilla groups in the 1970s: using the army in rural areas and security forces in urban zones. There is no sign of any dialogue or negotiation between the government and the EPR.

There is vast speculation in Mexico about the existence of more armed groups. Since the explosion of the crisis in Chiapas, there has been talk of numerous groups that are secretly organizing. One group of ex-guerrillas from the 1970s, which form the Center for Historic Research of Armed Movements (CIHMA), claim that there are "at least" fourteen armed movements operating principally in Puebla, Hidalgo, Chiapas, Oaxaca, Veracruz, and Guerrero. Likewise, the CIHMA maintains that there were "500 casualties among government officials, soldiers and guerrillas between 1994 and 1997."[49] Given the dispersion of these groups and the uncertainty regarding their existence, the army's action is defensive, preventative, and intelligence-based.

Drug Trafficking and Organized Crime

The increasing participation of the Mexican drug mafias in the trade and production of illegal drugs gives them increased wealth and more opportunities to take advantage of the ingrained corruption of the government. Increasingly, they are taking advantage of Mexico's largely unregulated financial sector as a means of laundering illegal profits. Already a strong influence, the mafias are a major threat to Mexico's national security through the easily corruptible government. Narco-corruption is becoming a serious impediment to stemming the flow of narcodollars, and remains Mexico's major challenge, as money laundering is not yet a criminal offense.[50]

Since the mid-1980s in the United States, this subject began to be considered a matter of national security and was included in the new doctrine of containment: low-intensity warfare, which involves "militarizing" the fight against drugs and considering it a "war."[51] This new conception began with the participation of the military as an experiment in the Andean countries.[52] For the United States, the main weakness in employing this strategy in Mexico is corruption.[53] However, there are American analysts who believe that Mexico's stance of adopting almost 100 percent of the United States' antidrug policies contributes to corruption, in addition to "infecting" the United States with this phenomenon: "It is also true that the costs of current policies—violence and corruption—fall most heavily on the Latin American countries, Mexico in particular, even as they infect the United States as well."[54] The foregoing leads to a pessimistic diagnosis on drug trafficking as the main activity of organized crime in Mexico. Since the 1980s, the increase in drug trafficking has been one of the main sources of strife between the governments of the United States and Mexico.[55] This friction worsened with the assassination of DEA agent Enrique Camarena in Guadalajara in 1985.[56] At that point, Mexico began to view the problem as a matter of national security.[57] The government first classified it as such in 1987.[58]

During the administration of Carlos Salinas de Gortari (December 1988–November 1994) all the institutional and coordination strategies for combating drugs were reformulated. Unprecedented cooperation also began with the U.S. government. Mexico's strategy, in the words of one of its main authors, was not one of elimination, but rather containment. "The goal of this war is not to destroy the enemy, because that is impossible, but rather to keep it under control."[59] Recognizing the main vulnerability of the forces of the Mexican government, that official stated that "the wars on drugs expose national institutions to increasingly greater risk of corruption. One of the most frustrating lessons of these campaigns conducted throughout the world is seeing the institutions responsible for the law being exposed to corruption by drug barons. Increased contact with traffickers, even as enemies, always increases corruption."[60]

Since 1990, the collaboration between governments and armies has been covered by the mass media. In June of that year, it was stated that a tactical unit of the U.S. army had detected aircraft in Mexican air space.[61] During President Salinas' second trip to the United States, in June 1990, agreements were established on the presence of DEA agents in Mexico and, in November of that year, frameworks of action for U.S. activities with surveillance aircraft and satellites in the war on drugs were established.

Among the most important actions carried out during the Salinas administration were the establishment of the Center for Drug Control Planning (CENDRO) in 1992, which exercised basic intelligence functions; the establishment in that year of the National Drug Control Program; and, following the assassination of Cardinal Posadas in Guadalajara on May 24, 1993, the establishment of the National Counternarcotics Institute (INCD) as a unit of the PGR.[62] The INCD was founded on June 17, 1993 to replace the General Office on Crimes against Health. The INCD had operational functions with agents of the Federal Judicial Police assigned to it.

The outcome of the fight against drugs is contradictory. Official reports indicate very significant progress in the war; however, numerous studies claim that the war is being lost. Between January 1989 and December 1992, 178.91 tons of cocaine were intercepted (an average of 45 tons per year).[63] During Ernesto Zedillo's administration, between December 1994 and December 1996, 47 tons were seized; that is half the amount seized per year during Salinas' six-year term.[64] Cocaine seizures have also declined in the United States, although not to the same extent as in Mexico. In 1993, 118 tons of cocaine were seized; 120 in 1994; and 98 in 1995.[65]

As for other drugs, such as marijuana, during Salinas's six-year term, an average of 500 tons were intercepted annually, whereas during the Zedillo administration, from September 1994 to August 1995, that figure rose to 600 tons; and from September 1995 to August 1996, 878 tons were intercepted. The interception of heroin also increased in the Zedillo administration, rising from an average of 160 kilos per year during the Salinas administration to 166 kilos in 1994–1995 and 215 kilos in 1995–1996.[66]

The war on drugs in the Zedillo administration is guided by the 1995–2000 National Drug Control Program. In this administration, cooperation with the United States has become closer, beginning with the establishment of the U.S.-Mexico High Level Contact Group for Drug Control in March 1996.[67] This cooperation was strengthened by President Clinton's visit to Mexico in May 1997, during which the two presidents signed the Declaration of the Mexican-U.S. Alliance Against Drugs, which notes shared responsibility in the fight, through a comprehensive approach and the establishment of extradition agreements. This document states that cooperation "will improve our capacity to interrupt drug shipments by air, land and sea" (with the clear participation of the armed forces of both countries); training and technical cooperation programs will be established, and institutional systems for the exchange of information (i.e., intelligence) will be developed.[68]

President Clinton subsequently traveled to Central America where he signed a similar agreement with all the presidents of the Isthmus, following the guidelines of the strategy for hemispheric cooperation to combat drugs, drawn up by his administration:[69] "Security issues do arise. Among them are illicit drugs that poison communities, threaten societies, and undermine national security. Working cooperatively on such challenges is an effective and efficient use of our resources. In the process, nations and militaries can learn from one another."[70]

In the U.S. strategy for containing narcotics shipments to its territory, Mexico is the top priority with regard to interception, and Colombia is the priority with regard to eliminating production. According to General Barry McCaffrey, the U.S. Drug "Czar," 70 percent of all cocaine enters the United States through Mexico, and, according to Mexico's PGR, profits from narcotics exceed $30 billion.[71] Likewise, 80 percent of marijuana and 20–30 percent of heroin enters the U.S. through Mexico.[72] In the militarization of the war on drugs, assistance is being channeled directly to the Mexican army, out of mistrust of the PGR forces.[73] There has been a marked increase in educating and training Mexican soldiers in the United States. Under the International Military Education and Training (IMET) and Foreign Military Sales (FMS) programs, 293 Mexican soldiers were trained between 1983 and 1988; 821 between 1988 and 1994; and that number rose to 1,910 between 1994 and 1997.[74]

In 1995, when drug trafficker Héctor Palma was captured, there was evidence that he had been "protected." Andres Oppenheimer reported that "the spectacular circumstances of the June 1995 capture of Sinaloa drug cartel baron Héctor 'El Guero' Palma confirmed what most Mexicans had long known—in Mexico, the police are for sale, and the criminals are buying. . . . Most members of his heavily armed entourage were agents of the Federal Judicial Police."[75]

U.S. assistance and cooperation have focused on strengthening the information systems on aircraft coming from Colombia, supporting the inflow of equipment (seventy-three UH-1H helicopters and four C-26 airplanes), and training personnel (300 soldiers in fiscal year 1996 and 1,500 in fiscal year 1997) who basically belong to the Special Forces Air Groups (GAFEs).[76] With regard to cooperation with the PGR, efforts are being concentrated on institution building (Counterdrug Institution Building–Law Enforcement Training) through support for the establishment of the Organized Crime Unit of the PGR, founded on February 1, 1997; through the training of its members; the establishment of Border Task Forces; and funding for a new intelligence unit on organized crime in the PGR.[77]

In Mexico, the war on drugs in its various forms (destruction of plots of marijuana and poppy and the interception of cocaine) is focusing increasingly on the military. Even equipment belonging to the PGR was transferred to the army; for example, eighteen of the PGR's Bell 206 helicopters were handed over to the Ministry of Defense (SEDENA). In addition to the seventy-three UH-1H helicopters donated by the United States, in 1997 the army purchased sixteen MI-8 and MI-17 helicopters manufactured in Russia. The reform of the structure of the military regions and areas focused on the establishment of a general headquarters and 51 GAFEs. According to the 1996–1997 report on the work of SEDENA, a daily average of 9,714 persons participated in eradication activities and 10,738 in intercepting drugs, with three civilian casualties, and seven injured, and twenty-one civilian casualties and ten injured, respectively.[78]

The Paris-based *Observatoire géopolitique des drogues* notes that Mexico is one of the axes of the *continentalización* of drug trafficking activity. In 1996, it was home to six large cartels—the Gulf Cartel in Veracruz and Tamaulipas; the Sinaloa Cartel in Sinaloa and Guerrero; the Tijuana Cartel in Baja California and Sinaloa; the

Juárez Cartel, with actions extending to Chihuahua, Tamaulipas, and Chiapas; the Clemente Coto Cartel in Sonora; and the Emiliano Quintero Cartel in Jalisco. According to the *Observatoire*, these cartels owe their success to their political and business ties, connections which are the main hurdle to winning the war on drugs.[79]

The largest shake-up to date in the war on drugs in Mexico occurred on February 23, 1997, when it was discovered that the Commissioner of the INCD, the former commander of the Fifth Military Region (headquartered in Guadalajara), General Jesús Gutiérrez Rebollo, was conducting activities to support the Juárez Cartel (headed by Amado Carrillo).[80] The myth of the incorruptibility of the military broke down, and a conflict broke out with the United States. The U.S. Department of State was on the verge of not certifying Mexico in the annual spring certification process. This myth was refuted even by the Minister of Defense: "The risk of contamination within the army has always existed. What is new is the willingness to combat those who become involved, regardless of their prestige, rank, or position held."[81] The Gutiérrez Rebollo case led to a purging of the military, in which thirty-four soldiers involved in supporting drug cartels were jailed in 1997.[82] As for the navy, in 1997, it accused fourteen sailors of drug trafficking activities.[83]

The binational report on the war on drugs published by the High-Level Contact Group made a direct allusion to the Gutiérrez Rebollo case, when it stated:

Recently, drug-related corruption was discovered at the highest levels of main anti-narcotics unit in Mexico. The charges of corruption made by the government of Mexico against high-level officials, including the former director of the INCD, are very serious. These officials have been accused of involvement with a large transnational organization of drug-traffickers that operates in the United States and Mexico. These cases, in addition to the Office of the Attorney General of Mexico's dismissal of 1,200 police officers in 1996, show that corruption has extended to the judicial systems. This problem undermines the effectiveness of the efforts made to respect the law and decreases the society's confidence and the credibility of the organizations responsible for protecting public safety and upholding the law.[84]

Drug trafficking is the main activity of organized crime in the world and is bolstered by two trends, one of which is sociocultural and the other economic. These are, respectively, the expansion of alternative culture through the mass media and the opening of borders, which is the result of the expansion of commerce.

Nonetheless, organized, random, and street crime increased markedly in the 1990s in Mexico. This is what is known as increased public insecurity, or social violence, which has led to the problem being considered an issue of national security.

Lack of Public Security

Andres Oppenheimer has written that "according to an internal Interior Ministry report, there were an estimated nine hundred armed criminal bands in Mexico, of which more than 50 percent were made up of current or retired members of law enforcement agencies. And some of the bloodiest gun battles in Mexico's war on drugs pitted these law enforcement–related gangs against each other."[85]

The actions of these gangs have created a widespread sense of insecurity among the population. The increase in crime can be observed in the increase in the number of "accused" and "convicted" criminals. Between 1974 and 1981, there was almost no increase. In 1974, 66,992 persons were considered accused criminals, of whom 54,725 were convicted; in 1981, there were 76,184 accused criminals, of whom 65,456 were convicted.[86] If we take population growth into account, there was no increase in crime in relation to the number of inhabitants. However, in 1994, the number of accused criminals rose to 165,927, with 142,365 convicted.[87] In 1997, the figures for Mexico City show that 189,000 crimes were committed (as reported to the Office of the Attorney General), which is 8,000 more than in 1996, despite the militarization of the Ministry of Public Safety (SSP-DDF) of the Federal District.[88] These crimes are a combination of organized crime and common crime. Figures show the following incidence of cases of: (a) violent home burglary—553; (b) nonviolent home burglary—5,871; (c) violent burglary of a business—4,535; (d) nonviolent burglary of a business—9,432; (e) armed bank robbery—59; (f) muggings—24,533; (g) theft from delivery trucks—17,148; (h) violent auto theft—15,074; and (i) nonviolent auto theft—28,110. Also, there were 713 homicides; 1,127 rapes; 18,374 assaults; and 2,082 robberies.[89] In addition, one of the new crimes in the 1990s that merges drug trafficking with organized and common crime is arms trafficking.

One should also note that the types of crime are proliferating, with the addition of two types that were almost nonexistent prior to the 1990s—political crimes and the crimes resulting from organized criminal activities (kidnapping, drug trafficking, car theft, bank robbery, kidnapping children, organ trafficking, and the like). With regard to political crimes, murders and violence have been manifest since the democratization of the country began at the end of the 1980s. Between 1989 and 1994, over 400 political leaders died in conflicts between the PRD and the PRI in the state of Michoacán alone. There are also the previously mentioned deaths of indigenous persons in Chiapas; the increase in political violence in the state of Guerrero (which culminated in the murder of *campesinos* in Aguas Blancas); the increase in numbers of journalists murdered (in 1971–1987, forty-eight journalists were murdered, or 2.82 per year, whereas between 1988 and 1994, forty were murdered, or 6.6 per year); there were 592 kidnappings in 1995; and bank robberies rose from 220 in 1981 to 485 in 1996 (from 0.6 to 1.13 per day).[90] Undoubtedly the two political assassinations that had the greatest impact were those of Luis Donaldo Colosio, the PRI candidate for president, on March 23, 1994, and José Francisco Ruiz Massieu, the national leader of the PRI, on September 28 of the same year.[91]

The government of Mexico itself recognizes the erosion of its image and its lack of credibility with the people: "One of the clearest and most widespread expressions of social reaction has been specifically the lack of credibility of governmental actions in this area, a phenomenon that has been bolstered by the emergence of specific cases related to acts of corruption or inefficiency in the justice system."[92]

In an effort to address this problem, since 1994 the government has developed different options for institutional reform, the majority of which have not had the success anticipated. Reform began with the establishment of the Mexican Public Safety Office in April 1994.[93] The promulgation of the law establishing the Public Security System was an effort that culminated in changes in criminal laws and strengthened measures for curbing crime, including the militarization of the police.[94] At the end of 1996, the Federal Law on Organized Crime was passed.[95]

In the 1990s, the presence of military personnel (the majority of whom are retired or on leave) in federal, state, and municipal security forces increased throughout the country. The presence of members of the armed forces responds to a perception that the problem of security should be approached by: (1) stopping corruption, toward which civilians are "more inclined" while the military has more "immunological" mechanisms; (2) restructuring the leadership hierarchy; (3) strengthening police containment of crime; and (4) professionalizing police activity. The employment of soldiers is a nonpartisan matter in the federal, state, and municipal governments.

This can be observed, for example, in Baja California Norte where the security forces are made up entirely of military personnel, and where the PAN has governed for the longest period of time, beginning in 1989. Even the Federal District, governed by the PRD since December 5, 1997, appointed retired military personnel to head the Ministry of Public Security, despite the leaders of the PRD's very emphatic criticism of militarization during their 1997 campaign. Statistics also show that crime does not decrease when there is an opposition government. Of the four least secure states in the country, three are governed by the PAN—Baja California, Chihuahua, and Jalisco. Sinaloa, the fourth state, is governed by the PRI. Drug trafficking activities, which are a direct factor in increasing public insecurity, have not declined in those states either. In other words, the "lack of security" and militarization do not depend on the political party in power, and they reflect a trend that is determined by national factors, not local, state, or regional ones.[96]

In 1997, the most important positions in public safety, police, and investigative institutions were the following: State agents and officials of the Federal Judical Police of the PGR; INCD agents—Special Inspector's Office on Narcotics;[97] State Judicial Police; Municipal Police (with the most important positions in the state capitals and large cities); and airport and port control. In 1997, in Baja California, Tamaulipas, and the Federal District, there were soldiers in five such units; in Chihuahua, Nuevo León, Estado de México, and Quintana Roo, they were in four units; in Baja California Sur, Sonora, Sinaloa, Coahuila, Jalisco, Hidalgo, and Oaxaca, they were in three; in Durango, Nayarit, Aguascalientes, San Luis Potosí, Veracruz, Tlaxcala, Tabasco, and Yucatán, they were in two; in Zacatecas, Colima, Michoacán, Guerrero, Morelos, Puebla, Chiapas, and Campeche, they were in one; and there were no soldiers in these institutions in Guanajuato and Querétaro.[98]

At the end of the 1990s, there were approximately 400,000 preventive police in the country, organized in the 2,395 municipalities. Of these municipalities, 1,990 have fewer than 100 police officers on the police force (82.53 percent); in 318 the police force is made up of between 100 and 1,000 officers (13.18 percent); and

87 have 1,000 officers or more (4.29 percent).[99] In addition, the various federal police forces total approximately 7,000 members. These include Highway, Tax, Immigration, Forest, and Environmental police. The police forces that investigate crimes are grouped together under the Federal Judicial Police Force which is 7,000 strong, and the State Judicial Police Forces which have 21,000 officers.[100]

The greatest challenge for the military in fighting crime was collaborating with the Department of the Federal District to assume responsibility for the Ministry of Public Security, beginning on June 8, 1996.[101] The most important qualitative difference wrought by the presence of military personnel in the rest of the institutions in the country is that they took their positions on an individual, rather than an institutional, basis. However, the appointment of General Enrique Salgado and fifteen generals, fifty field officers, eighteen officers, and nineteen sergeants, as well as the transfer of 2,000 soldiers to replace the police in the Iztapalapa district *(delegación)* and the training of civilian police officers in Military Camp No. 1 (3,500 officers were trained), is a policy of institutional cooperation.[102] The person ultimately responsible is the president, with active-duty military personnel remaining in SEDENA.

The purpose of participation in greater police cooperation in the country is to banish corruption—which should increase the effectiveness in the fight against crime—and to launch an all-out war on crime. The strategy outlined was to locate criminal groups (bands) and carry out commando raids, using rapid response groups or special police forces, primarily the Jaguares and Zorros (units especially trained for urban police functions). This strategy has been criticized for focusing on street crime, leaving organized crime virtually untouched.

The outcome of the war on crime is contradictory. The Minister of Defense has stated that one significant achievement is that nobody "can accuse the soldiers that participated in the police force in the Federal District of being dishonest."[103] Nonetheless, the harshness of these raids called their legality into question, based on the events in the Buenos Aires neighborhood *(colonia)* where a group of six young criminals captured on September 8, 1997, were later found murdered on the outskirts of Mexico City. This event led to a serious erosion of the military's image and criticism from numerous sectors about human rights violations.[104] The results of the investigation led to the arrest of three soldiers (a general, a colonel, and a lieutenant colonel) and twenty-six police officers (nineteen Jaguares and seven Zorros).[105] Because of these actions, the Jaguares were broken up.[106] The defense of the Jaguares in the statements made by members who participated in the raid maintained that "we are corrupt, but we are not bullies."[107]

The change in government in the Federal District on December 5, 1997, did not bring about a radical transformation in the strategy for confronting crime, since retired soldiers were again used to head up the SSP.[108] This pattern leads us to suggest that the opposition parties do not have an alternative strategy for transforming the security forces. Rather, they focus on trying to make the institutions more efficient by simply eradicating corruption and applying tough policies, but without a different program for modernization or professionalization.

With regard to the militarization of the security forces, one must bear in mind that Mexico has a crime prevention system similar to that of the United States (decentralized police at the municipal level), but this does not take into account the different social, economic, political, and even cultural conditions in the two countries. Therefore, the Mexican constitutional system of the "free municipality," which includes the capacity of municipalities to have their own police forces, has led to the deformation of the police forces to such an extent that it is impossible to professionalize and modernize them. Furthermore, the police respond to political interests, since they are under the "personal" leadership of the municipal authority. When that municipal authority is linked to economic power groups (legal or illegal) the police typically protect those interests instead of those of the population. That is to say, "persons in authority in Mexico have tended to abuse rather than govern and steal rather than manage."[109] This has caused a crisis in all the municipalities in the country, from the most backwards and rural ones with one or two police officers (for example, in Oaxaca), to Mexico City, which has the largest police force in the country—the SSP—made up of 27,000 officers.

The lack of democracy in the political system causes inefficiency and corruption to spread because of the way in which the government manages the administration of justice. In an authoritarian and vertical political system, public office is owed to higher authorities, not to the population; therefore, government and justice are administered to protect the interests of the elite, not of the population. With the democratization of public office, officials are already corrupted by practices carried out in the past, which makes the problem endemic:

However, the main component of the criminality from which we suffer is its organization and the protection of its interests, which are intricately linked to those of the government and police; therefore, there will not be a reduction in serious crimes even if the economy improves markedly. . . . There is a solution to the lack of security, but it requires the elimination of impunity, thus making the full exercise of the rule of law indispensable, which has never occurred in the country. Now that the era of the PRI is starting to wind down, the possibility of moving forward in this direction is conceivable.[110]

Another development that has occurred in the cities—and that goes hand in hand with the feudalization of security in the countryside—is the population's extreme distrust of the security forces. This has led to the privatization of security, which is endangering the state's capacity to provide "security to the population" (as defined by Hobbes). In Mexico, in 1997 there were some 917 private security companies, 587 of which operate in the Federal District. These employ almost 40,000 security guards in the country.[111]

The limits of the strategy of militarization are clear, since it is a partial action, and not a comprehensive one. Rather than solving the problem, it merely attacks visible facets thereof (fighting street crime). It is not able to attack the root of the problem of common crime and it leaves criminal organizations intact. The danger lies in enlisting a strategic security force—the army—in a mission that is impossible if there is no comprehensive strategy aimed at political institutional factors and not simply at eradicating corruption.

Conclusion

It is important to note that the reemergence of armed groups since 1994 has reaffirmed the army's actions as one of the federal government's main forces for containment and dissuasion. The military is improving its position as a state institution, and counterinsurgency is once again becoming one of its main missions. This weakens the path toward modernization aimed at strengthening the DN-I plan and channels the purchase of equipment, the budget, training, and deployment throughout the country to the DN-II plan.[112]

Armed groups can only be neutralized in the long term if political democratization can effectively contain the power of traditional, basically rural groups, and if the *caciques* cease to determine the balance of power; in other words, when the state's power can be extended throughout the country through modern institutions (political-electoral, social, and judicial institutions). If this does not occur, rural structural violence will continue, always with the specter of Colombianization and the army as an institution of containment-dissuasion.

If the economic, social, and political structures (primarily the rural ones) are not modernized, the state will continue to be weak and the *caciques's* inclination to conduct illegal and even criminal activities will continue to be very strong. In other words, maintaining the political system and its traditional mechanisms is one of the main factors favoring the emergence of armed groups with diverse purposes, ranging from promoting campesino self-defense to protecting the *caciques* who conduct criminal activities.

As for drug trafficking, the criticisms of the strategy implemented include evidence that the strategy developed by the United States and adopted in general by Mexico is not successful. In the United States, some are indicating that the war on drugs is being lost: "The United States is losing the 'War on Drugs.' Since 1989, when the U.S. military first became involved, the harvest of coca, the production of cocaine, its delivery to the United States, and the use of cocaine within the U.S. have all gone up. Clearly, the present use of military force is not weakening the drug industry."[113]

Other analyses lead to the conclusion that in addition to the war being lost, the spread of corruption includes U.S. governmental structures. There is increased drug consumption and an overall change in the crime prevention and judicial forces; therefore, containment and militarization must be radically revised. The risk is that the Latin American states will become "narco-states" and "narco-nations," with the following characteristics: economies in which the dynamism (capital flows for investment) increasingly comes from drug trafficking; the weakness of the states, which is a result of corruption, begins to produce narco-corruption. More specifically, narco-corruption would lead to narco-politics, whereby groups with political power are linked to drug traffickers; narco-society, wherein vast sectors of society (businesspeople, politicians, judges, military personnel, clergy, union leaders, campesinos, and professionals) benefit from drug trafficking and are employed as operatives for cartels; narco-justice, through which court officials sell out and traffickers are protected in their structures, and also where anti-system groups emerge that further weaken the effective exercise of the rule of law, such as narco-guerrillas or narco-terrorism.[114] In Mexico, some of these trends have emerged in certain regions of the country and have developed links with some business and political power groups.

Overall, the most radical proposal is the regulated legalization of the consumption and marketing of some drugs in order to prevent this trend. This proposal comes from analysts in Colombia, where the phenomena of the narco-state have developed to the greatest extent.[115]

Mexico's main weakness in its antidrug strategy is that there is no link between the identification of the problem and its medium- and long-term solution. The state recognizes the corruption and lack of efficiency in the administration of justice and the actions of the security forces, but addresses the problems with short-term strategies and tactics. The state employs the most solid state institutions—the armed forces—overloading them with too many missions and distorting their true functions (DN-I and DN-III). In other words, the fact that the Mexican military outlines its essential military operations in the DN-II plan responds to a backwards state, with weak civil structures, no professionalization, and a distortion of the possibility of modernizing justice and public security structures. As for the population, it is silently challenging the state and is diminishing the state's basic mission of providing security, since in practice it does not provide it, and citizens and businesses must seek out alternative mechanisms to secure their property, family, and economic livelihood.

In the 1990s, the military was strengthened in terms of personnel and budget (see tables 6.2, 6.3, and 6.4) despite cutbacks in the rest of government. Therefore, many analysts are speaking of militarization.

In this way, the country is witnessing a quantitative growth in armed persons but a qualitative distortion of their functions because of the aforementioned problems. If the 435,000 members of the security forces are added to the number of soldiers, which in 1997 totaled almost 230,000 in the army, air force, and navy, the total number of armed persons employed by the state is 665,000. With a total population in the country of approximately 95 million inhabitants, that is one armed person for every 143 inhabitants. One must also add to this about 40,000 private guards and citizens with arms, whose number is difficult to discern.

For the military, facing these missions poses a serious risk ranging from the danger of its becoming politicized and falling under the leadership of politicians

Table 6.2 Gross Domestic Product, Government Expenditures, and Military Expenditures, 1990–1995 (millions of pesos)

	1990	1991	1992	1993	1994	1995
GDP	738,897.5	949,147.6	1,125,334.3	1,256,196.0	1,420,150.5	1,792,694.7
GDP ($millions)	250,898.9	309,067.9	361,263.0	404,571.9	267,954.6	234,645.9
Total Budgeted Government Expenditure	180,744.0	186,565.3	195,253.2	206,987.2	230,360.6	199,329.9
Armed Forces Budget	3,547.0	4,770.0	5,876.1	7,162.6	9,633.5	10,367.8
Armed Forces Budget ($ millions)	1,206.4	1,553.2	1,886.1	2,310.5	1,810.8	1,357.0
% of Armed Forces Budget with respect to GDP	0.48%	0.50%	0.52%	0.57%	0.67%	0.57%
% of Armed Forces Budget with respect to Government Expenditure	1.96%	2.55%	3.00%	3.46%	4.18%	5.20%
Exchange rate Pesos per dollar	2.94	3.07	3.11	3.10	5.32	7.64

Sources: President of Mexico, *Segundo Informe de Gobierno* (Mexico: Poder Ejecutivo Federal, 1996), Ernesto Zedillo Ponce de León, 1996, Anexo; Secretaría de Hacienda y Credito Público, *Cuenta de la Hacienda Pública Federal 1995* (Mexico: SHyCP, 1996).

(in an institutional way) to the personnel's (when retired soldiers or those on leave are employed) not necessarily serving the interests of the state, the nation, or the population.

This danger is constant in the three main missions. In counterinsurgency, there is the danger of meeting the interests of individuals. In Chiapas, Guerrero, and Oaxaca, the army's operations are dangerous, since obeying orders may mean meeting the interests of the local *caciques* or political forces. In the war against drug trafficking, the risks range from inefficient functioning to the greatest danger—protecting political groups or *caciques* linked to the cartels or going directly on the payroll of the capos. As for public security, as was the case with the SSP-DDF, there is considerable danger when the strategies are toughened or militarized without objectively weighing the consequences and their long-term effectiveness.

In the three wars, the outcome for the army has been negative. There is social,

Table 6.3 Size of the Armed Forces, 1986–1995

	1986	1987	1988	1989	1990	1991	1992	1993	1994	1995	Increase 1986–1995
Total Federal Government	2,242,554	2,219,600	2,752,060	2,783,393	2,301,486	2,405,300	2,275,754	1,549,318	1,609,761	1,601,324	
Total Armed Forces	169,746	175,960	179,305	184,095	192,994	198,955	203,829	210,241	217,859	225,200	32.6%
Army and Air Forces	129,695	133,435	137,350	142,961	151,178	155,218	157,142	162,169	169,689	172,072	32.6%
Navy	40,051	42,525	41,955	41,134	41,816	43,737	46,687	48,072	48,170	53,128	32.8%
% Armed Forces to Total Government Employees	7.56	7.92	6.51	6.61	8.3	8.27	8.95	13.56	13.53	14.06	

Source: President of Mexico, *Segundo Informe de Gobierno* (Mexico: Poder Ejecutivo Federal, 1996), Ernesto Zedillo Ponce de Leon, 1996, Anexo.
Note: Includes Federal Government and Other Government Agencies. After 1992, government decentralization, especially of the Ministry of Education, drastically decreased the number of people employed by the government.

**Table 6.4 Members of the Armed Forces, 1990–1995
(Percentage of Total Population)**

	1990	1995	Percentage Change
Population (thousands)	84,249.6	91,120.4	12.12
Total Armed Forces	192.994	225.200	16.68
Percentage	.23%	.24%	

Source: President of Mexico, *Segundo Informe de Gobierno* (Mexico: Poder Ejecutivo Federal, 1996), Ernesto Zedillo Ponce de León, 1996, Anexo.

political, and even international questioning, and accusations of human rights violations are beginning to spread (in Chiapas in January 1994; in Mexico City, with the raid in the Buenos Aires *colonia* in September 1997). Focusing the military's actions in the three end-of-the-century wars in Mexico corresponding to the DN-II plan even jeopardizes the plan to modernize the military, which seeks to concentrate its basic constitutional mission (DN-I) and to develop the operational capacity of its structure, which has wide social and political recognition (DN-III).

Part II

Crime and Governability in the U.S.-Mexican Borderlands

The Historical Dynamics of Smuggling in the U.S.-Mexican Border Region, 1550–1998

Reflections on Markets, Cultures, and Bureaucracies

Louis R. Sadler

SMUGGLING ALONG THE BORDERS of the sovereign nations of the world is an ancient and almost honorable occupation. Indeed, if prostitution is the world's oldest profession, then smuggling and espionage most certainly run a close race for second place. From the cigarette smugglers of Andorra—with their backpacks loaded with cartons of cigarettes, humping their loads over the Pyrenees Mountains and evading Spanish customs guards—who are virtually legendary;[1] to the famed rumrunners of the Prohibition era evading U.S. Coast Guard cutters to bring hard liquor to thirsty Americans;[2] to gunrunners like the legendary "Earthquake McGoon" (real name: Captain James McGovern) and his less well known cohort Allen Lawrence Pope in 1954, flying ammunition into the doomed French fortress of Dien Bien Phu in Vietnam for a then-obscure charter airline called Civil Air Transport for the ubiquitous Central Intelligence Agency;[3] to the Mexican truck drivers in northeastern Mexico, who for decades clandestinely transported hundreds of thousands of tons of chemicals from the United States across the Rio Grande to the huge industrial complexes in Monterrey, Nuevo León;[4] smuggling has, to a significant degree, a patina of romanticism attached to it, with the significant exception of one commodity—drugs.

Unfortunately, there is a relationship between smuggling and drugs that has grown enormously in recent decades. This chapter will attempt to sketch the broad outlines of this relationship and the sometimes obscure circumstances that brought the United States of America and Los Estados Unidos de México (the United States of Mexico) to a difficult juncture in 1998.

Therefore, as historians are wont to do, I shall begin in the beginning—the latter part of the sixteenth century. From approximately 1550 forward, what is today Mexico—then the central core of what was Imperial Spain's incredibly wealthy Viceroyalty of Nuevó España (New Spain)—grappled with the rigidities of Spanish mercantilism. Mercantilism (which was initially developed by the French minister Colbert in the seventeenth century) essentially required that Spain's colonies not trade with another country except through the mother country. Given the distance between Spain and the east coast of Mexico in the days of sail, coupled with the scarcity of goods produced in the mother country, Spanish mercantilism was patently unworkable. As a result, smuggling as early as the late sixteenth century became endemic along the east coast of what is now Mexico. By the time two centuries had passed (the beginning of the nineteenth century), smuggling had become entrenched in the Viceroyalty.[5] More important, the economy and fiscal system of New Spain had been substantially affected by the loss of revenue to a smuggling industry that had evolved as early as the late seventeenth century not only in Mexico but throughout Spanish America.

By the dawn of the nineteenth century, the newly independent United States of America had begun to probe the northernmost outposts of what was euphemistically called the Spanish borderlands. In actuality the first U.S. government official to visit was a young U.S. Army captain who arrived in 1806 in what is now known as Santa Fe . The Spanish officials quite rightly viewed Captain Zebulon M. Pike as a spy, which of course he was. As a result he was arrested and transported to Chihuahua City, where he ultimately was able to win his release.[6] But Captain Pike was only the first of a long line of U.S. citizens (some official, some unofficial) who arrived on the border of northern New Spain (the later ones bearing merchandise they wished to trade). By the time Mexico acquired its independence in 1821, smuggling along both its northern and southern borders (plus both coastlines) had become commonplace—indeed virtually customary. This was particularly true both in Santa Fe and Tejas (Texas).

Following the war with Texas in 1835–1836 and the war with the United States in 1846–1847, smuggling accelerated in Mexico's northeastern states (Coahuila, Tamaulipas, and Nuevo León). By the beginning of the 1850s, it was estimated that fully two-thirds of the merchandise sold in northeastern Mexico had been smuggled across the border from the United States. Indeed, by 1850 the situation had become so serious that the Mexican government, in an attempt to stem the flood of imported and smuggled goods, created a new customs enforcement bureau—the *Contraresguardo de Gendarmería Fiscal*. But despite the best efforts of the new customs agents, local Mexican officials up to and including the governor of Coahuila, operating in league with Texas merchants (and smugglers), succeeded rather easily in thwarting the enforcement efforts at the highest levels of the Mexican government.[7] From then until the present, the smuggling that began along the northeastern Mexican and Texas frontiers continues along the entire U.S.-Mexican border (some 1,951 miles).

There have been peaks and lulls in the volume of smuggling. Nor has it been simply a north-south operation; indeed, smugglers in both the Mexican and U.S. border states have historically adapted to "changing market conditions." For example, during the late 1850s, the so-called Guerra de la Reforma (War of the Reform), gunrunning became the premium "activity" as weapons were smuggled across the Mexican-U.S. border to both sides during this Mexican civil war.

The same thing happened beginning in 1861 with the outbreak of the American Civil War, except in this case smuggling and gunrunning ran both ways. The Confederates smuggled cotton into Mexico to be transshipped to Europe and on occasion received weapons in return. In addition, with the beginning of the so-called French Intervention, weapons from the United States were smuggled into Mexico for President Benito Juárez's troops until 1867, when Emperor Maximilian I was overthrown.[8]

During the 1870s, the smuggling of munitions from Texas into northeastern Mexico was a major industry in furtherance of General Porfirio Díaz's attempts (finally crowned with success) to overthrow the Sebastián Lerdo de Tejada administration.[9] By the early 1890s two pre-precursor rebellions occurred in northern Mexico (the so-called Catarino Garza rebellion which was spawned out of south Texas and northeastern Mexico,[10] and the Santa Teresa outbreak in northwestern Chihuahua).[11] Both led to a sizable traffic in the smuggling of guns and ammunition from the United States into Mexico.

But more important, in the late nineteenth century a new product was introduced into the smuggling mix: narcotics. Ironically, it was an import from the Pacific Rim and was the result of U.S. immigration policy. In the 1880s, the U.S. Congress slammed the door on Chinese immigration into the United States. But the Chinese had earlier brought a taste for opium to both Mexico and the United States. By 1909, the U.S. government had banned the importation of opium. Subsequently opium was smuggled into Mexico and then transsmuggled into the U.S. border states.[12]

Coincident with the outbreak of the Mexican Revolution in 1910, opium smuggling began to accelerate from the northern tier of Mexican states into the United States. However, gunrunning became the smugglers' choice for obvious reasons. By 1912, one prominent smuggler was musing publicly about using aircraft to smuggle arms across the border. In the same year, a notorious smuggler and murderer named Victor Ochoa added a new wrinkle to smuggling across the border. Ochoa, who was responsible for acquiring ammunition for the revolutionary forces of General Pascual Orozco, Jr., used large black rubber bladders to float tens of thousands of rounds of ammunition across the Río Grande from El Paso to Ciudad Juárez during the night.[13] And given the length of the border it was virtually impossible to seal it completely. Even in June 1916, when war with Mexico seemed imminent and the entire National Guard of the United States (some 112,000 strong) was called to active duty and sent to the border to back up approximately 40,000 U.S. Army regulars (including 10,500 troops inside Chihuahua chasing Pancho Villa and his guerrillas) who were deployed from southern California to the lower Río Grande valley of Texas, it was not possible to protect the border completely. Although these thousands of troops slowed the smuggling of guns and ammunition considerably, it was never completely stopped.[14]

Before the Mexican Revolution, the smuggling of alcohol (tequila, pulque, mescal, and rum) from Mexico to the United States without paying for a tax stamp had been a staple for the smugglers. And it had been comparatively easy during the Revolution to shift from smuggling alcohol to 7-mm Mauser ammunition. The Revolution came to an end in the summer of 1920 (although there were sporadic outbreaks as late as 1929), and the smugglers quickly shifted back to smuggling alcohol from breweries and distilleries in Mexico into the American border states.[15] With Prohibition in full swing, Federal Prohibition Agents and

Texas Rangers in particular tried in vain to stem the flow of alcohol into the United States.[16] Furthermore, by 1924 the U.S. Congress passed the first comprehensive immigration statute and created the U.S. Border Patrol within the Department of Justice.[17] Thus, the trafficking in human beings began in Mexico. Some of the same smugglers in both Mexico and the United States who had smuggled ammunition during the Mexican Revolution now smuggled people.

In 1934, Prohibition in the United States finally came to an end, and the smugglers again shifted products. Smuggling of various consumer durables began. Automobiles, refrigerators, and stoves became the smugglers' items of choice, and the rise in smuggling of such consumer items began to accelerate. In the coming decades, the smuggling of small arms from the United States into Mexico became a staple not for overthrowing governments but for self-protection. In addition, another crop, marijuana, whose popularity had increased during the Mexican Revolution and soon became the drug of choice in the United States during the 1930s, began to be smuggled across the border in increasing quantities during the 1930s and 1940s.[18] However, from the 1940s forward it was unquestionably the smuggling of consumer goods that occupied the attention of the Mexican-U.S. smuggling industry. High tariffs imposed by the Mexican government on items such as television and radio sets and microwave ovens (by the 1960s) made smuggling a large and increasingly profitable industry throughout the post–World War II decades.[19]

There was one World War II program that had significant impact on the U.S.-Mexican border. In 1943, in the midst of the war, the U.S. and Mexican governments agreed on the terms of the so-called *Bracero* program in which several hundred thousand Mexican workers would travel to the United States for limited periods of time to harvest crops. The program was so popular in the U.S. agricultural sector that following the war the program was extended until 1964 (with a one-year extension to 1965).[20] With the termination of the program, the smuggling of *indocumentados* accelerated at a substantial pace. And during the past third of a century, so-called *coyotes* (smugglers who smuggle people) established networks and safe houses to expedite the smuggling of illegal aliens into the United States.[21]

At virtually the same time (the decade of the 1960s) there was an explosion (particularly percentagewise) in the population of the Mexican border states (Tamaulipas, Nuevo León, Coahuila, Chihuahua, Sonora, and Baja California).[22]

Although some scholars have suggested that the development of the *maquiladora* (or twin-plant industry), which was designed in part to provide employment for *bracero* workers now unable to come to the United States, accelerated this population buildup, in truth the number of *maquila* plants grew very slowly throughout the latter part of the 1960s and early 1970s.[23] What is indisputable is that year-by-year apprehensions by the U.S. Border Patrol increased significantly beginning in 1966—the first year after the close of the *Bracero* program.[24]

By 1969, the drug smuggling from Mexico to the United States was also increasing. Scholars of the period will remember that in the fall of 1969, the Nixon administration launched "Operation Intercept," which attained much publicity but very little success. It should be noted parenthetically that the U.S. Department of Justice official responsible for Operation Intercept in what was then the El Paso Customs District was G. Gordon Liddy, which may explain in part why Operation Intercept was such an abysmal failure.[25]

It was during this period that both Washington and Mexico City suddenly discovered the border. For almost one-half of a century (1930–1975), a kind of modus vivendi was in place on both sides of the border. On the U.S. side, U.S. customs, backed up by the U.S. Customs Agency Service, had a well-deserved reputation for eliminating corruption in the Customs Service. Furthermore, U.S. customs administrators (particularly district directors and their deputies, along with senior supervisory customs inspectors) were usually left in place for lengthy tours, sometimes five years or more, ensuring that they learned the terrain, the people on both sides of the border, and who the players were. Consequently, customs officials developed a quid pro quo as a matter of policy and practice.

Was this a quid pro quo with U.S. customs winking at Mexican customs illegalities? Not at all! U.S. customs officials usually were aware of payoffs (including, in some cases, the specific sums acquired). Without being specific (for obvious reasons), one of the smaller of the forty-two ports of entry along the U.S.-Mexico border yielded to the *administrador de aduana* during the 1970s–1980s an estimated $70,000 per annum in kickbacks for granting permits for imports. Although U.S. customs was aware of this, it was viewed pragmatically as a Mexican matter and one that the U.S. government could not and should not be involved in. In reality, these payoffs were viewed more in the context of "tips" and a throwback to Spanish custom in Latin America. As a rule, Spanish officials not only in what is now

Mexico but throughout Latin America were paid, in most cases, only a pittance in salaries. As a result, the custom of bribing officials (tipping them) became almost customary.[26] This was particularly true for Mexican *aduana* officials.

Nonetheless, ranking *aduana* officials (for example port directors who carried the title of *Administrador de Aduana*) usually knew that the U.S. officials had knowledge of the "tips" but seldom commented on the fact. What U.S. customs officials (district directors and their deputies, along with port directors at small ports of entry) did do was develop relationships with their Mexican counterparts. Usually this consisted of a luncheon, perhaps weekly, alternating sides at the favorite restaurant of the host. For example, for years the favorite luncheon location for Mexican *aduana* officials in Ciudad Juárez was La Fogata, a traditional restaurant/bar located adjacent to the Juarez Hospital, not far from the international bridges separating the cities of El Paso and Ciudad Juárez.[27]

Usually, the ranking Mexican and U.S. customs officials would exchange home and private office telephone numbers so that they would be able to communicate in case of an emergency.[28] When there was a change in personnel at the top (a new U.S. district director/port director/Mexican *administrador*, etc.) there usually would be a hand-over. The outgoing district director would host a luncheon to which the *administrador* would be invited. The new U.S. customs official would be formally introduced. Oftentimes there would be a farewell luncheon or dinner for the outgoing Mexican/U.S. official by their counterpart. In addition, it was something akin to custom that a farewell party by U.S. customs for the outgoing official would result in an invitation to the Mexican counterpart and that official would present a gift (perhaps an expensive bottle of tequila or a box of cigars, depending on the preferences of the recipient). The same party and exchange of gifts were generally followed by U.S. officials for their Mexican colleagues.[29]

This relationship in most cases was not corrupt but highly useful for both sides. The U.S. customs officials almost always spoke at least basic, sometimes excellent Spanish and made a habit of speaking Spanish whenever they were in Mexico. Oftentimes their Mexican *aduana* colleagues would speak English at the U.S. meetings with customs officials.[30]

There also was a clear understanding of the quid pro quo relationship. If a U.S. customs official requested something unusual from his Mexican counterpart, it was understood that the favor would at some point in the future be reciprocated.[31]

A couple of anecdotes will perhaps illustrate the point. A senior U.S. Customs Agency Service officer had over a period of several decades developed excellent relationships with a variety of Mexican *aduana* officials. Although this customs investigator was fairly senior, he was not a ranking official. But he had accumulated a fairly extensive collection of veritable "I.O.U.s" with his *aduana* colleagues.

What triggered the quid pro quo was a frantic phone call U.S. customs received at the Laredo Port of Entry. Apparently someone at the U.S Army's Fort Sam Houston, in San Antonio, had surplused a Bell (UH-1) helicopter after the last U.S. Marine had been picked up from the roof of the U.S. Embassy in Saigon in April 1975.[32] But what initiated a frantic hunt for the helicopter was the belated discovery that the helicopter had not been stripped of some highly classified electronics gear.

When the Customs Agency Service officer (who shall remain unnamed) received a panicked call inquiring whether he had seen a U.S. Army helicopter on a flatbed truck crossing the bridge over the Río Grande, his reply was, "Yes, a couple of hours ago." When asked if he could somehow get the helicopter back from Mexico, his response was a laconic, "Perhaps." The officer called in one of his "I.O.U.s" by contacting one of his friends (a very senior Mexican *aduana* official across the river).

Reminding his friend (very gently) that he owed him one, he asked if he could obtain the return of the U.S. Army surplus helicopter. The Mexican official said he would see what he could do. The protocol was to never ask something that was impossible or would get the Mexican official in real trouble. The *aduana* official called the checkpoint south of Nuevo Laredo to see if the truck hauling the helicopter had passed, which it had a short time earlier. The customs official ordered an *aduana* vehicle to drive south, stop the truck, turn it around, and bring it back to the Nuevo Laredo *aduana* facility. It was done in a very short time; according to the U.S. customs agent, in a couple of hours. When the helicopter on the flatbed truck arrived back at Mexican customs in Nuevo Laredo, the driver was ordered to drive it back north across the river to the U.S. customs facility in Laredo. The *aduana* official called his friend in U.S. customs to inform him that the helicopter and the truck would arrive momentarily.

The protocol was observed. The U.S. customs investigator thanked his Mexican official friend who reminded him that he owed him a drink, or two, or three.

The U.S. customs officer agreed that he did and arranged to buy his friend a drink. When the helicopter on the truck arrived, the U.S. customs agent called his contact at Fort Sam Houston and assured him that the helicopter appeared to be intact and could be picked up in Laredo at U.S. customs, which would guard same until it could be retrieved.[33]

Another war story which illustrates the same point, but at another level, occurred a couple of decades ago in Texas. Ever since the Republic of Texas was formed, many Texans and particularly Texas law enforcement officials have never forgotten that Texas was once a sovereign nation, and to this day still think that it is. This is particularly true insofar as Mexico is concerned. And although Texas and Texans generally speaking are hardly revered in Mexico, there is a grudging respect among many Mexican officials who operate along the Texas border.

This respect extends even to the fabled Texas Rangers, a Texas law enforcement organization that is not particularly beloved either by Mexicans or Mexican-Americans. A senior Texas Ranger captain related this particular anecdote to me a few years after the incident had occurred, and he himself was a principal actor in it. This captain had dealt for a number of years with a senior Mexican customs official based in northeastern Mexico. The Ranger captain had learned over time that some of the so-called *grupos*—the family-based industrial combines that control Monterrey, the capital of the state of Nuevo León—had been smuggling hundreds of thousands of tons of industrial chemicals from plants in Texas to industrial plants in Monterrey, evading Mexican customs. These evasions deprived the Mexican government of tens of millions of pesos in customs revenue.

In a conversation with the Mexican customs official, the Ranger captain said, in essence, "It's none of my business, but do you know about the 18-wheel trucks that evade your customs en route to Monterrey from Texas chemical plants?" The Ranger provided details of their routes and timetables in case the Mexican customs officer was interested. The *aduana* official was very interested; he followed up on the tip and made a major seizure of a convoy loaded with chemicals. At the time, Mexican *aduana* officers received a significant percentage of the value of the shipment as an incentive to seize illegal shipments. The value of the seized shipment exceeded $250,000 (U.S.) and the very happy Mexican customs official called his Texas Ranger friend. Informing him of the seizure, he told the Ranger captain that he would split the reward with him. However, the Ranger explained

that although he would love to be able to take his share of the reward being prof-
fered, his organization would not allow him to do so. But he was grateful for the
offer and he did have an I.O.U. with his friend the Mexican customs official.

Several months later, the Ranger captain indeed had a pressing reason to call
the Mexican customs official. A boyhood friend and private employee of a very
senior Texas state government official had been murdered at a ranch along the
border. It was suspected that a Mexican citizen was responsible for the killing and
the Ranger captain informed his friend that the Rangers were under great pressure to find the murderer. He informed the customs official that they had identified a suspect who was believed to have fled back to his home in northeastern
Mexico. The Ranger captain asked his friend if he could help locate the suspect
and have him arrested, so that he could be extradited to Texas to stand trial. The
Mexican customs official said he would do what he could.

Two days later, an unmarked black four-door sedan bearing Nuevo León state
plates pulled up in front of the Texas Department of Public Safety (DPS) headquarters in Austin. Two men jumped out of the vehicle and opened the trunk.
They removed the murder suspect, who was bound and gagged, and laid him on
the front steps of the DPS building.[34] There were no lengthy, involved extradition
proceedings between the Mexican Foreign Ministry and the U.S. Department of
State. The matter had been handled unofficially as matters between the two sovereign nations were sometimes handled at the border. The I.O.U. had been paid.

To be sure, these two anecdotes illustrate a relationship that existed two decades ago, but they nonetheless depict a reality that worked, in spite of its shortcomings. Frankly, I believe it is much more desirable than the current situation.

Generally speaking, problems along the U.S.-Mexican border, at least through
the 1970s, were seldom referred to either Mexico City or Washington. Usually they
were solved at the district director or *administrador de aduana* level, although on
the U.S. side, the regional commissioner of U.S. customs in Houston or Los Angeles would nominally be consulted or reassured that the problem was being solved
at the local level.[35]

Referrals to the U.S. Commissioner of Customs or to the U.S. Department of
State or the Ministry of Foreign Relations in Mexico City were almost never made.
In a sense, both state and foreign relations seldom wanted to know what was hap-
pening on the U.S.-Mexican border. Generally speaking, the local political estab-

lishments played a major role in the operations of customs/*aduana* on both sides of the border. In the case of the United States, the two U.S. senators in each border state (but particularly in Texas) were usually consulted, and they often influenced the selection of district directors of the U.S. customs districts along the border. To a somewhat lesser degree, depending upon seniority and committee assignments, members of the U.S. Congress with districts on the border also played a role in determining personnel selection and policy. There are a number of Texas customs districts in which U.S. senators virtually picked the district directors and had some influence in the selection of the regional commissioner based in Houston.[36]

Institutional politics as always played a role. Historically on the U.S. side of the border, U.S. Customs was the lead agency, with the Immigration and Naturalization Service and Border Patrol being the poor country cousins. In the mid-1970s, the Drug Enforcement Administration (DEA) worked its way into the border game and acquired drug enforcement primacy over U.S. Customs/Customs Agency Service. In addition, the Border Patrol in the 1980s moved aggressively into the drug enforcement arena, moving U.S. customs into a distant back seat.[37]

On the Mexican side of the frontier, the *aduana* took the visible front seat with the most powerful Mexican cabinet-level department, *Gobernación*, supervising matters from a discreet distance. The state and federal *Policía Judicial* at various times played a significant role, yet that role tended to ebb and flow depending upon the politics of a given situation.[38]

How could U.S. customs suddenly lose primacy at the border? Several things coincided. First, the border in a sense "blew up" beginning in the 1960s and early 1970s with the explosive population growth in cities like Ciudad Juárez and Tijuana.[39] But even border villages like Palomas (technically General Rodrigo Quevedo), Chihuahua, across the border from Columbus, New Mexico, grew from a population of a few hundred to a few thousand in a span of a decade.[40] The same thing happened in Nogales, Sonora (across the border from Nogales, Arizona).[41] But in particular, the cataclysmic growth of Ciudad Juárez and Tijuana, the two largest Mexican border cities, unhinged local and state control. Not only did the local officials lose a handle on their respective *municipios*, but they could not provide the necessary social infrastructure—streets, schools, hospitals, sewer and water facilities—as the two cities doubled in population in less than two decades.[42]

Suddenly, the border had become red hot. The word "border" itself had become "sexy," and it was—from the U.S. side at least—where the action was. If you were an upwardly mobile U.S. customs official or perhaps a Border Patrol supervisor or a DEA agent with aspirations for advancement, the border was the place to be. Recall actor Jack Nicholson, whose portrayal of corruption in the U.S. Border Patrol played out along the west Texas/El Paso border with Juárez was a poor imitation of reality, but it reflected at least a perception as seen by Hollywood.[43]

By the mid-1980s, U.S. customs had lost its way. To be fair, at the working level even upper-level customs officials were hardly decision makers. Now that the border was hot, Washington cowboys and Mexico City *chilangos* were deciding who did what and where. Senior officials (district directors) who did not know Spanish (and had no inclination to learn even a few courtesy terms—*buenos días, con mucho gusto, muy bien, gracias*) and hated Mexico, Mexicans in general, and Mexican officials in particular, suddenly populated most of the major U.S. customs districts. No longer were there Hispanic district directors, whose Spanish was fluent and who developed excellent relations with their Mexican counterparts.[44]

In addition, corruption in the U.S. Customs Service, which had previously been negligible, accelerated during the 1980s. Supervisors no longer understood who the players were, the language they spoke, the terrain, or for that matter almost anything about the border. They were there to get promoted—just like officers going to Vietnam to "get their tickets punched" so they would receive their next promotion. To be sure, the stunning sums offered by Colombian cocaine smugglers when they shifted from smuggling into south Florida to the U.S.-Mexico border were extraordinarily tempting, even to the most incorruptible customs inspectors.[45]

But that would come in the future. By the 1970s, the driving factor was the smuggling of consumer goods from the U.S. border region into Mexico. Light planes loaded with television sets, microwave ovens, and small refrigerators made virtually daily flights to small airstrips in Coahuila, Sonora, and Chihuahua. The economic impact of this smuggling in the Arizona/Texas border counties was so substantial that sales tax revenues were of a volume similar to cities much larger than Laredo and Nogales.[46]

By the mid-1970s, the scale of smuggling of consumer goods had become so large that it was virtually an industry. It included personnel from both the United

States and Mexico: department store owners in the United States; ex-Air America pilots who flew the television sets and similar items into Mexico; the friendly Mexican neighborhood smugglers who handled the surface smuggling from cities like El Paso into the interior of Chihuahua; and the Mexican customs officials who were "on the take."

Two anecdotes will illustrate the situation in the late 1970s. I was standing on the tarmac at Laredo Municipal Airport (a former U.S. Air Force base) watching a single-engine light plane packed with microwaves, television sets, and small portable refrigerators taxiing out on the runway. The pilot was literally flying with the stick in his stomach because the small plane was so loaded. A U.S. Customs Air Support pilot was asked where the pilot was heading. He explained that he was making his daily flight for a large Laredo department store south into the interior of Coahuila. He also stated that the pilot was suspected of not deadheading back to Laredo but was believed to be flying drugs into Texas on his return flights. Indeed, the previous year he had been arrested in Mexico on a smuggling flight and jailed for some weeks for evading Mexican customs before he was finally released (apparently the proper authorities had not received the appropriate payment).[47]

If arrangements to smuggle capital goods from cities like Laredo and Nogales were efficient, the system in Chihuahua was the most urbane. A native of Chihuahua, who was a member of a wealthy and politically powerful family, described how *el sistema*, as it was sometimes called, worked. Imagine the wife of an upper-middle-class family living in Chihuahua City who drives to El Paso for a monthly shopping trip. She heads for her favorite department store ("The Popular"—long the favorite of Chihuahuans)[48] and purchases several thousand dollars worth of merchandise. It was routine to request that the store deliver the purchases to a nearby hotel (the Hotel Plaza). At the Plaza a Chihuahuan smuggler would pick up the packages and make the proper arrangements with the Mexican *aduana* inspectors on the so-called free bridge (the Bridge of the Americas) and with the inspectors at the customs checkpoint seventeen kilometers south of Ciudad Juárez.

By the time the shopper had returned to her residence in Chihuahua City, her purchases would have already arrived at the family residence, where a "reasonable" fee (including of course the bribes) would have been paid by a family re-

tainer. In this way wives did not have to engage in the distasteful business of negotiating bribes with Mexican customs officials. The system, particularly in Chihuahua, had evolved since the 1940s and lasted almost four decades.[49] Similar
scenes with variations were played out throughout the border region. Both the
U.S. and Mexican governments winked at this irregular exporting business which
grew at an enormous rate, particularly during the decade of the 1970s until the
time of the 1982 peso devaluation.[50]

From the U.S. point of view, this trade was highly lucrative and assisted the
U.S. balance of payments. The matter of bribes was one for the Mexican government, not the U.S. government. From the standpoint of the Mexican government,
the smuggling was viewed rather gently. At the time, the Mexican manufacturers
could not satisfy the demand for TV sets, refrigerators, and microwaves, and
smuggling handled a problem the Mexican government had not been able to
solve. Furthermore, the bribes paid supplemented the meager salaries of the customs inspectors and could simply be ignored.[51]

No one was unhappy with the status quo; yes, bribes were paid, but American
manufacturers could hardly be unhappy, and neither could the department store
owners in U.S. border towns. The problem of course was that a system that had
lasted for decades would be swept away by the impact of the events of the 1970s
and 1980s.[52]

The Yom Kippur War of 1973, the Organization of Petroleum Exporting Countries (OPEC) embargo against the United States, and the explosion of crude oil
prices beginning in the fall of 1973 had profound effects on Mexico. The discovery
of the great Tabasco heavy crude fields in the mid-1970s enabled Mexico to begin
exporting crude oil in huge quantities (1.5 million barrels daily) by 1980 and resulted in a huge financial windfall (an estimated U.S.$15 billion) for the Mexican
government. However, subsequent oil overproduction coupled with the introduction of oil conservation measures, particularly in the United States, caused a precipitous decline in the price of crude oil. By 1982, the administration of President
José López Portillo was forced to devalue the peso. And, by December 1982, when
López Portillo's chosen successor Miguel de la Madrid assumed the presidency, he
had inherited what could only be characterized as a "godawful mess."[53]

President de la Madrid stepped into office with the Mexican economy in free
fall. Three years later de la Madrid, who had allowed the peso to float downward

to more than one thousand pesos to the dollar, was able by early 1985 to cobble together a pact between labor and the Mexican private sector, which limited wage and price increases. He also made a decision in 1986, which in many respects was more important to the Mexican economy than the later decision to establish the North American Free Trade Agreement (NAFTA).

President de la Madrid persuaded the economic elites in Mexico (almost all of whom opposed his decision) that the nation must join GATT (the General Agreement on Tariffs and Trade). In so doing Mexico effectively joined the twentieth century economically. Economists and friends of Mexico applauded de la Madrid's political courage in forcing his country into the ranks of GATT.[54]

Unfortunately, there was an unexpected and unintended consequence of the president's decision, one that is barely known even today. By joining GATT, Mexico unconsciously destroyed the smuggling industry on the northern border. Although the import duties on a number of items were phased in over a period of years, smugglers, who had made at the very least a comfortable living, and the Mexican customs inspectors, who had their salaries supplemented by bribes paid by the smugglers importing consumer goods, now faced the reality that their standard of living had just been reduced in a very substantial way.

In the early 1980s, Mexicans tightened their belts as a result of the precipitous fall of crude oil prices and a concomitant 60 percent devaluation of the peso. These combined events forced Mexican customs officials and smugglers to adjust to "changing market conditions" virtually overnight. These events occurred at precisely the same time as the shift by the Colombian drug cartels from smuggling cocaine through Florida to the U.S.-Mexican border.

The combination of these factors—an economy in free fall, Mexican and U.S. smugglers (some of whom had been involved to a limited degree in drug running) who had lost their source of income as a result of President de la Madrid's decision to join GATT, and literally hundreds of Mexican *aduana* inspectors who had lost a significant percentage of their income from both the devaluation of the peso and the bribes they had received for allowing capital goods to be imported without paying duty—had an extraordinary impact.

The results of this unlikely combination were a disaster for Mexico, a windfall for the Colombian cocaine smugglers, and a crack cocaine epidemic in most American inner cities.[55] Obviously, the Mexican customs inspectors, who knew portions of the border like their own backyard and whose legal and illegal income had been more than cut in half, were a fertile recruiting ground for the Colombian traffickers and their new Mexican partners. Not only did they know the physical terrain of the border, but they also knew the ins and outs of smuggling drugs across the border. Furthermore, they knew the routines—shift changes, rotations, lane assignments, etc.—and in some cases they knew U.S. customs inspectors. Some of these officials also knew individuals who were quite close to U.S. customs officials and who might be open to a bribe. They also knew which inspectors were in financial trouble or which married inspectors had a mistress or lover on the side, and thus could be blackmailed.[56]

As a result, corruption among both Mexican *aduana* inspectors and U.S. customs inspectors accelerated to an alarming level beginning in the late 1980s. This continued through the mid-1990s. Ironically, with some 70 percent of the cocaine entering the United States in the mid-1990s via the U.S.-Mexican border, the situation changed dramatically by 1998. By the summer of 1998, DEA officials were estimating that only 50 percent of cocaine was being imported via the Mexican border. It seems the Mexican traffickers were demanding too much of a cut. As a result, the Colombian cartels have begun shifting their operations back to the Caribbean and Florida.[57] Given the volatility of cocaine smuggling, as traffickers shift routes to thwart U.S. law enforcement, the cocaine cartels will undoubtedly, at some point in the very near future, be back at full strength on the U.S.-Mexico border.

What we can be sure of is that the smugglers who operate cooperatively on both sides of the border will continue, as they have for centuries, to "adjust to changing market conditions."

Chapter 8

Organized Crime and Democratic Governability at the U.S.-Mexico Border

Border Zone Dynamics

Francisco Javier Molina Ruiz

PROBABLY NOWHERE in the world do two countries as different as Mexico and the United States live side by side. As one crosses the border into Mexico from, say, El Paso, the contrast is shocking—from wealth to poverty, from organization to improvisation, from artificial flavoring to pungent spices. But the physical differences are least important. Probably nowhere in the world do two neighbors understand each other so little, with differences in language, religion, race, philosophy, and history. The United States is barely two hundred years old and jumping wholeheartedly into the twenty-first century. Mexico is several thousand years old and is still held back by its past.[1]

If Riding's reference to the remarkable differences between the cultures of Mexico and the United States is correct, it is no less true that the border region has created a distinctive Mexican-American character. This is particularly evident on the Mexican side of the border, which is remarkably different from the rest of Mexico. The culture, education, and instruction, which are strongly influenced by American television and lifestyle; the relaxed morality of northern Mexico versus the conservative South; the constant search for opportunities in the hopes of receiving a penny rather than a peso; and a language intermixed with anglicisms and pochismos have all contributed to the creation of a society that expresses its ironic gratitude by saying "So far from God, but so close to the United States."

This perception of the border as a place underlined by liberal sentiments and a sense of freedom from all the evils suffered in Mexico is added to a feeling of pride border residents feel because they believe they are admired by other Mexicans for being citizens of the border. In most cases, they show a distinct tendency of feeling, living, speaking, and dressing like Americans. For these reasons, the region's inhabitants—at least those of the middle class—seek ways in which their descendants can enjoy American medical facilities, and, fundamentally, the right to be citizens of the United States, not by blood, but by birth. In other words, they strive to have their children born in the neighboring country.

However, this separation from the essence of Mexican culture (mexicanness) and the liberalism sought by border inhabitants stands in stark contrast with the norms of southern Mexico: disorder, improvisation, lack of culture, lack of discipline, cynicism, tardiness, and the lackadaisical attitude toward fulfilling obligations. Border inhabitants consider themselves privileged because, by living on the Mexican side of the border, they enjoy flexibility in discipline and social behavior while having instant access to the opportunities and satisfactions offered by the United States.

On the other hand, for border Americans the situation is the same but exactly the opposite: that is to say, they tend to respect law, work, and discipline. It is an exception when they cross the border to feel free, to relax.

These are the reasons why the economies on both sides of the border zone belong to different worlds. The goods and services offered on the Mexican side are strongly influenced by the desire to exploit these liberal values or, in many cases, these anti-values. Bars, cabarets, and discotheques offer an opportunity for these prejudices, chained to American conventions, to bloom. On the other hand, crossing illegally into the United States and earning dollars or being hired as a substitute employee, without social security or even the assurance of a stable job, affirm the Mexicans' conviction that it is better to live in the border zone than anywhere else, because the border combines the advantages and conveniences of both sides, which would not be available anywhere else. The same pattern is repeated across the border zone, in cities, towns, or ranches, regardless of how far they are from their respective capital centers. Worldwide, the Mexican-American border is unique, as its society is also unique.

Culture and Economy

Mexico's northern border, which corresponds to the southern border of the United States, is a vast region that extends over 3,000 kilometers—from Imperial Beach, California, on the Pacific to Brownsville, Texas, on the Gulf of Mexico on the American side, and from Tijuana, Baja California, to Matamoros, Tamaulipas, on the Mexican side—and constitutes a *sui generis* spatial dimension, full of contrasts and contradictions. The border runs from densely populated areas, where the economy, culture, and development have had unprecedented growth levels for more than twenty years, to places made uninhabitable by the desert, drought, or rough terrain. It extends from trenched spaces denoting a mental and political battle against clandestine migration, where walls, fences, and columns are erected to prevent people from seeking food and wages in exchange for labor, to places where the demarcation line is so imperceptible that the chance crosser loses the sense of being in one country or the other.

All along the border between the United States and Mexico, there are cities that have a counterpart in the other country, on the other side of the dividing line. Since the conquest of both countries had different origins and consequently spawned different cultures and languages, a subculture has developed along the border resulting from the combination or *mestizaje* of these two ways of life. A clear example of this is pochismo, also called "Spanglish," as it is the combination of the English and Spanish languages, which permits the use of words in English and Spanish within the same phrase or sentence. Spanglish creates new anglicized words, like "parkear" instead of "estacionar," which is derived from the English "to park." This manner of speech is most prominent among persons of Mexican origin who have moved to the United States, also known as Mexican-Americans. Similarly, there are innumerable elements that constitute the border subculture, which encompass not only people's customs but also invade the political, social, and economic spheres.

Another important element of the border phenomenon is the type of familial relations that exist among the inhabitants of both sides of the border, usually Mexicans or Mexican-Americans. One could almost assert that there is not an inhabitant of a Mexican border town who does not have relatives in its twin U.S. city. Moreover, one could say that there is not a border Mexican who does not have a relative in Los Angeles, California. As a result, American border states are populated, in a high percentage, by Mexican-Americans. In fact, the population of U.S. border cities consists mainly of inhabitants originally from Mexico.

It is practically impossible for a Mexican-American to lose his or her Mexican customs, including language, which has been spoken jointly with English, even though there is a clear tendency of late to speak both languages correctly and separately from the other so as to make the Mexican-Americans completely bilingual. This effort has been generated by the mass media, who have more recently been transmitting programs in Spanish.

These factors have given rise to a special economy on the border. The twin cities along the different settlements on either side of the border share unique characteristics that are not found at any other border urban settlement. Each pair of communities is a true set of "twin cities." For example, the twin-city dynamics are not the same in Mexicali-Calexico as in Ciudad Juárez-El Paso. In general, though, the common denominator between the two sister communities is an economic interrelationship that would not exist if this twin-city situation did not exist.

At the beginning of the century, specifically during the 1920s and 1930s—basically during Prohibition—the main generators of wealth in Ciudad Juárez, Chihuahua, Tijuana, Baja California, and Laredo, Tamaulipas, were casino gambling and horse- and dog-track racing, the sale and open consumption of alcohol, and organized prostitution. The main consumers were Americans. Simultaneously, the Mexicans would cross the border to purchase the necessary goods for the maintenance of these commercial establishments. The source of income was, precisely, commerce.

With time and policy changes in both countries, Prohibition was abolished in the United States, while in Mexico gambling was prohibited. These circumstances changed the sources of wealth for the Mexican population and the dynamics of American consumption: Prostitution remained legal, while bars and restaurants frequented by Americans remained open. These locales multiplied in the 1940s and 1950s as a result of the increasing number of young military men who would cross the border to Ciudad Juárez or Tijuana from the military installations located in El Paso, Texas (Fort Bliss and Biggs Field), and the naval bases in the San Diego area, in search of amusement and other distractions.

Another source of income for the Mexicans was quick divorces for foreign couples, which turned the border into a new attraction. Married couples would travel from all parts of the United States to the border to obtain a divorce decree in a matter of hours. In many cases, the divorcing parties would come accompanied by their new partners, to be remarried with equal speed.

In time, "divorces on the run" were prohibited. In the beginning of the 1960s, prostitution went out of style as a result of the relaxation of moral values in the United States. In its place, free love was practiced more generally. The bars and restaurants also faced very aggressive competition from comparable establishments on the American side of the border. The Mexican side of the border suffered a serious economic collapse. However, the *maquiladora* industry displaced this amoral market, bringing a newfound source of wealth to the Mexican border cities.

Therefore, the border zone, fundamentally in the urban centers, has become a strong region of accelerated economic growth—more on the Mexican side than on the American side—where a unique society has developed. This society is shaped by rigid as well as flexible value systems, and is full of ample contradictions and ambiguities, going from the modern to the traditional, from opulence to poverty, from legitimacy to illegality, from propriety to delinquency, from dignity to denigration. In this "new nation," communities arise, developing their own identities, perhaps more independent because of their distance from the capitals of their respective nations, or perhaps because of their daily struggles to survive in the neglect of their own capitals.

Border Criminality

In the surreal border zone between Mexico and the United States, as a result of time and circumstances, in the same fashion that economic and cultural interrelations have been shaped, so too have criminal relations developed in this wide region. The years of Prohibition left a deep impression that has marked the development of crime in this region. We could say that this was the first experience with organized crime in both countries. Given that in Mexico the production or sale of alcohol was not prohibited, large centers like Ciudad Juárez turned into important alcohol producers—legally and clandestinely. For the most part, this merchandise was sold in the black market in the United States. This activity permitted the accumulation of great capital, since the producers knew that these products would violate U.S. law and would be sold illegally in the United States. Of course, in order to carry out these illicit activities, it was necessary to count on the participation of corrupt authorities, who were easily bribed with the great quantities of money handled by the criminal organizations.

In contrast, organized crime in Mexico evolved around the contraband of innumerable goods that were not only aimed for border consumption, but also for sale in other regions in Mexico. Many warehouses were built in El Paso, San Diego, San Ysidro, Brownsville, Nogales, and Laredo to wholesale goods bought by contraband salesmen, belonging to well-structured criminal organizations, who with the aid of corrupt authorities—this time on the Mexican side—managed to carry out these types of activities.

Later on, in a more direct manner, seduced by the easy earnings and with a high degree of impunity, the American merchants themselves started participating in these exchanges. Mexican consumers from all over the country would come to certain American establishments to purchase the goods they needed. They would indicate their address in Mexico, and in three or four days, without having to pay import taxes—instead they bribed the border authorities—they would receive the requested goods in their homes in Mexico.

Contraband became so institutionalized that the American retail stores had special departments to serve Mexican clients. Evidently everything was done de facto since compliance with American laws concerning the receipts and taxes was documented with precision. One cannot deny the role that contraband played in promoting the alliance and participation of the merchants and the authorities, mainly those who had the jurisdiction to prevent the illegal introduction of foreign goods into Mexico, without proper permits and payment of import taxes. To understand this phenomenon, which constitutes the immediate precedent of today's cross-border criminal organizations, one must point out certain mechanisms that have been in place in the border region and that have allowed huge profits from the business of illicit contraband, going back to the years of Prohibition.

In Mexico, the Resguardo Aduanal (Customs Guard) is in charge of controlling and supervising the trade of goods across the border, as a department of the Administración General de Aduanas (General Customs Administration, formerly General Customs Department), under the auspices of the Secretaría de Hacienda y Crédito Público (Ministry of Finance). Since customs officers have earned ridiculously low salaries for decades, it has not been difficult to bribe them in order to avoid paying the taxes corresponding to the merchandise crossing the border. In many cases, illegal traffic was not solely practiced by professional traffickers but also by the customs officers themselves when they went through the customs procedures.

Even so, corruption in the Mexican customs system was not without rules. An example of one of those rules is the so-called *polla,* which designated that all the money received by each of the officers at a certain checkpoint had to be put in one basket, and from there it was redistributed, according to hierarchies. The officers who received the largest portions were the Customs Administrator and then the tenured officers of the Administración General de Aduanas (General Customs Administration) in Mexico City.

Similarly, severe punishment was meted out to the merchant who tried to cross without previously coming to an agreement with the customs authorities. Once the contraband was discovered, it was impossible for the trafficker to arrive at an understanding with the customs authorities to avoid the confiscation of the goods and to prevent his consignment to the prison authorities. This punishment was a deterrent for those who wanted to cross the border without previous arrangements with the border officials and who thought that in case of discovery they only had to bribe the customs officers. This was a very beneficial rule for the customs officers, especially because only those ignorant of the rules would fall, and because the strict adherence to this unwritten rule allowed the illicit accumulation of wealth by many.

To date, contraband is still a huge illicit business, tolerated and encouraged by the Mexican authorities. The vested interests created from the illegal traffic of goods and the lack of will to enforce the law make eradication a difficult task. One contraband case tells of a customs officer in the north-center border who lasted six years in his post (the longest tenure for that position). He became so wealthy that he permitted himself to finance the campaign of the ruling party's presidential candidate. In exchange, or as a reward, he was allowed to be the gubernatorial candidate for the state of Jalisco, in central Mexico. During that time, it was not difficult for him (or anyone in the ruling party) to win the elections and he was allowed to govern that state for six years, thus adding to his fortune.

Up to the early years of the Salinas de Gortari administration (1988–1994), the officers of the Customs Guard were, in general, middle-aged, completely corrupt and cynical, and they were members of an impenetrable union. Faced with this situation, President Salinas decided to erase the image and put an end to the practices of this entity by hiring a younger force, mainly from the center and south of the country, and training them in customs service. He was largely successful at the beginning of this endeavor. Afterwards, on the president's orders, the Customs Guard was eliminated, the customs union was dissolved and, in its place, the Policía Fiscal Federal (Federal Fiscal Police) was created and manned by the same aforementioned youth.

In the beginning, the project worked pretty well. However, the low salaries and insufficient training meant that the members of the new Federal Fiscal Police fell into the same vices as the old Customs Guard. Unfortunately, contraband continues at this time, as if nothing had changed. Currently, the contraband of American goods has spread throughout the entire country. The substantial profits, the impunity in which delinquents thrive, corrupt authorities, and the lax laws have implicated other departments, police organizations, and various officials at different levels, not only in terms of border corruption but also for the transportation and custody of the goods. Thus, we see how bribes, gifts, and other agreements in general cast the aura of corruption over the agents of the Policía Judicial Federal (Federal Police), the Policía Federal de Caminos (Highway Police), and the State and Municipal police forces.

With the passage of international economic treaties like GATT and NAFTA, border economic activities started evolving. Similarly, organized crime activities have undergone a comparable metamorphosis, creating, in the last twenty years, huge, multimillion-dollar criminal organizations, whose principal objective is drug production and trafficking. This illicit trade has made them different from the previous criminal organizations, because, as has been mentioned, previously illegality was prominent only on one side of the border.

These criminal organizations constitute another phenomenon of the border zone, and they find their distant origins in two fundamental factors:

1. The opportunity for growth inherent in the turmoil of the border zone;

2. The entrenched and proliferating presence of gangs, bands, and delinquent groups, engendered and multiplied by the daily settlement of scores of frustrated immigrants who have to settle for living on the border. Because of the speed with which this phenomenon has occurred, the Mexican State lacks the capacity to offer services or jobs to these settlements, and the inhabitants of the border eventually become marginalized and, inevitably, delinquent. This inexorable flaw, although not on the same scale or with the same impact, permeates the culture and environment on the American side and serves as fertile ground for the illegal activities of criminal organizations.

The international community no longer perceives organized crime as an occasional or regional delinquency, but rather as a global threat whose dimensions can jeopardize national security if it is not attended to firmly and adequately.[2] Since the criminal organizations of the border zone between Mexico and the United States are not concerned with geographic demarcations, and because their activities and operations are so dynamic and their penetration in the social fabric so uncontrolled, it is difficult to disassemble them with traditional and orthodox police methods.

Structure of Border Criminal Organizations

The first and best-known structure of criminal organization that develops in the border cities is based on the old model of "gangs." They are defined as a group of people, normally minors, who, as a result of their proximity to the neighborhood or "the hood," share the same prejudices, the same rejection by society, and suffer the same inability of the State to address their problems. Unemployment, drug addiction, promiscuity, unhygienic lifestyle, and systematic and constant family problems shape the character and personality of the members of these groups. They do not have a clear vision of the future, nor have they defined their goals in life. They lack interest in progress, and they suffer from a deep cultural ignorance, lacking values and religion. The gang is the seed that has the potential to sprout delinquent fruit. Its only teachings relate to the formation, strengths, and weaknesses of the group; and the search for easy rewards and the practice of criminal activities. Curiously, middle-class values are also adopted by these types of organizations; treachery, disloyalty, and cowardice are severely punished.

Another type of criminal organization characteristic of the border zone, although more complex, emulates the Mafia organizations in the United States. In order to understand how these Mexican criminal organizations operate, we must understand the origins and development of the American models. Criminal organizations in the United States whose structures have been emulated by the Mexicans originate in Italian criminal organizations, mainly the Sicilian Mafia. In Italy, different criminal organizations developed from the middle of the nineteenth century, especially the Sicilian Mafia, the Neapolitan Camorra, the Calabrian 'Ndrangheta, the Apulean Unified Sacred Crown. The Sicilian Mafia gave rise to the Cosa Nostra in the United States, which justified its existence in the massive immigration of Sicilian Italians toward the end of the nineteenth century.[3]

Some people believe that "mafia" means in Arabic "place of refuge." The word was adopted into the Sicilian dialect when the Muslims controlled the island of Sicily in the tenth century. The people of Sicily had been under unforgiving oppression by the Romans. They were dominated subsequently by the Normans, the Germans, the Spanish, and the French. The different foreign rulers enslaved the poor, exploited the work force, abused the women, and assassinated the leaders. In addition, the Spanish Inquisition called the Sicilians heretics and took their wealth away.

The Mafia arose as a vindictive secret society. For them, the highest virtue was the so-called *omerta*, or the rule of silence, because treachery was punishable by death. In the United States, the protection afforded to newly immigrated Italians by the Mafia was of such magnitude that the Mafia controlled the sphere of criminal organizations from the beginning of the century until the 1960s.

It is important to know this type of organization to understand the widespread delinquency at the border. It helps to understand how the border organizations think and evolve. The Mafia and Cosa Nostra were organized in the following manner:

1. The "family," composed of the "men of honor," is at the base.

2. At an intermediate level, one can find the *jefe decena*, who controls the armed members of the family.

3. The head of the family is called the "representative," chosen by a "false" democratic election, but whose position is really determined by the power relations he may have.

4. The representative is aided by "counselors."

5. The association of several "family representatives" is called a "commission."

Knowing this structure helps us understand how the border criminal organizations engendered and developed in imitation of the Mafia:

1. In the Mexican organizations, the "head" of the "family" is colloquially called "el capo."

2. The armed members are called "lieutenants."

3. Border criminal organizations exist to care for their territory and to form associations with international delinquents to increase their own power.

Activities of Some Border Criminal Organizations

Imagining the scenario in which border criminal organizations develop, we can discern the following structures of delinquent organizations that inhabit the various parts of northern Mexico and the southern United States. Starting in the United States, according to data reported in the official analysis of the Grupo de Contacto de Alto Nivel México-Estados Unidos (U.S.-Mexico High Level Contact Group), criminal organizations are composed of small nuclei called "cells," which inhabit the border and extend their illicit operations to various regions of the United States.[4] These cells are composed of small units, specialized in the execution of several illegal activities, which together help the survival of the criminal organization as a whole. Thus, while some specialize in car theft, assaults, abductions—fund-raising activities for the organization—others focus on arms trafficking, drug trafficking, or the transportation, storage, distribution, and laundering of money.

Each unit has only minimal contact with the other units. Units are directed by a supervisor, who reports to a director. Each cell director, in turn, reports to a regional director, who is responsible for the activities and operations of several cells. The regional director is in charge of contacting international criminal organizations in Colombia for the purchase and sale of drugs, in China for the traffic of arms and document falsification, and in Europe for currency smuggling and laundering. The rigorous enforcement of this method of operations isolates the heads of other cells in case of police raids.

Well-known criminal organizations that have operated in the United States since the 1970s include the following:[5]

1. Gangster Disciples, an organization that operates along the Mississippi River Valley, from Wisconsin to the Gulf of Mexico. This organization operates with no less than 100 members.

2. Logan Street Gang, who reside in the center of San Diego, California, and who constitute the foreign armed branch of the criminal organization that operates in the peninsula of Baja California, headed by the Arellano Félix brothers.

3. Urban gangs like the Crips and the Bloods, motorcycle gangs like Hell's Angels, and the Sarah Bernhard organization, which operate throughout southern California, and whose size is as yet unknown.

4. In Texas we find the Jimmy Jimenez organization, whose reach extends to Chicago, Detroit, and northern California.

5. Given its level of violence and militancy, we cannot ignore the Universal Zulu Nation in Philadelphia.

These criminal organizations that are embedded in the social fabric of the American society engender terror, drugs, murder, and in general criminal activities that torment the peaceful lifestyle of the most powerful country in the world. Their criminal doings and their addiction to crime are greater than their fear of the law or their respect for human life.

On the Mexican side, the criminal gangs embedded in border life are no less frightening. The inhabitants of the main urban centers like Tijuana, Ciudad Juárez, Laredo, and Matamoros live under a permanent state of siege and fear of the frequent public episodes, where the main characters kill, kidnap, and steal without mercy. For example, as of 1997 more than 287 gangs coexist in Ciudad

Juárez, thirteen of which are especially dangerous because of the degree of violence they promote, the type of weapons they carry, and the cruelty with which they punish their adversaries. Ninety gangs are extremely conflictive and are persistently and permanently in opposition to authorities—beyond the assumed disdain for authority that characterizes any gang. Their names and nicknames are arrogant and defiant, adopted from the streets or the distinctive criminal behavioral patterns. Some of the group names are: Camel, K-15, Cadena 16 (Chain 16), Bruno Traven, El Barrio López (the Lopez Hood), Chaveña Park, Vagos 27, Raza Unida (United Race), etc.

However, the drug trafficking organizations working for the past fifteen years in the border zone are more sophisticated and certainly more dangerous, violent, and powerful than these smaller defiant gangs. These economically powerful and internationally linked structures grow and move, leaving terror, violence, and corruption along their path. The common characteristics of all these organizations are their high capacity for corruption, the immeasurable amounts of money they handle, and the violence with which they repress any adversaries. They do not fear authorities, they are insensitive to the threat of incarceration, and they resist social re-adaptation.

These organizations owe their existence to Colombian suppliers. Through their structural and organizational capacity (similar to a legitimate business) and the cruelty with which they eliminate their enemies, they guarantee handling, transit, and delivery of the goods. Thus, the Mexican drug trafficking organizations have such intense, detailed, and sophisticated commercial links with Colombian drug trafficking organizations that would be the envy of legal commerce anywhere. Of course, the greatest difference is that these sorts of commercial transactions need not meet the bureaucratic requirements of legal imports and exports.

Some of the Colombian organizations with detected and recognized links to the border traffickers are as follows:[6]

Valle del Cauca Cartel
 Henao Montoya brothers

Cali Cartel
 Helmer "Pancho" Herrera
 Rodríguez Orejuela brothers

José Santacruz Londoño

brothers Jario y Julio Urdiñola Grajales

Medellín Cartel

Juan David and Jorge Luis Ochoa Vásquez brothers

In Mexico, the following are well-known organizations with centers of operation at the border, although this is not their only sphere of action.[7]

In the West

The brothers Benjamín and Ramón Arellano Félix operate in the Pacific Rim. Originally from Sinaloa, the Arellano Félix brothers have extended their vast drug trafficking empire to cover the states of Baja California, Baja California Sur, Sonora, Sinaloa, Chihuahua, Zacatecas, Nayarit, Jalisco, Michoacán, Chiapas, Quintana Roo, Puebla, México, and the Federal District. In each of these cities, the Arellano Félix brothers have a lieutenant who supplies the necessary vehicles and armed men for the brothers' secure transit. Usually, the brothers move within a convoy of four to five vehicles, one or two of which are armored vehicles, accompanied by eighteen to twenty armed men. With a majority of young men (mostly in their mid-twenties), the organization carries out its activities using two control mechanisms: (1) generalized violence, regardless of the publicity; and (2) the corruption of different police structures, including the military and the navy.

Upon the incarceration of the "capo mayor" (head) of the Guadalajara Cartel, the Arellano Félix brothers inherited the territory including the control and traffic rights from their uncle Jesús Labra Aviles. With a well-trained and armed paramilitary force, with training from Lebanese mercenaries, the brothers have committed collective and spectacular murders using car bombs.

The Arellano Félix brothers are usually received and escorted by authorities. They transport drugs by land, sea, and air. Drugs are stored in border cities like Tijuana, Ensenada, Mexicali and San Luis Río Colorado. Finally, the "merchandise" is transported into the United States. The drugs they transport into the United States reach far beyond Arizona and California, to New York, New Jersey, Florida, and Illinois. The brothers pay their associates and even the members of their organization with those same drugs, making alliances and complicities that are difficult to break.

The Arellano Félix brothers have formed ties with professionals, merchants, socially renowned families, and businesspeople in the cities where they work to cover their illicit earnings. They have recruited as partners young men from wealthy families who are interested and willing to participate in a high-profit business. They own the latest electronic equipment, which can intercept conventional telephones, cellular phones, faxes, sky-tel phones and others. Even in government offices and hotels, they have accomplices capable of installing sophisticated hidden microphones to keep them apprised of all activities against them.

In the Center

Just as one can say that the organization of the Arellano Félix brothers is the most violent, official reports highlight the Amado Carrillo group as the most powerful organization in Mexico. Amado Carrillo himself died under mysterious circumstances related to a plastic surgery operation in July 1997. Recently, Mexican authorities discovered that the Amado Carrillo group had bought off high-ranking members of the Mexican Army. The mechanisms to obtain the protection of such a governmental structure indicate the strength or control that this organization has throughout the country.

Amado Carrillo, born in Badiraguato, Sinaloa, on December 17, 1954, started his criminal life in Ojinaga, Chihuahua, under the tutelage of contrabandist Pablo Acosta Villarreal. Carrillo joined a group led by former head of the Dirección Federal de Seguridad del Gobierno de México (Federal Security Directorate), Rafael Aguilar Guajardo, eventually succeeding the latter upon his death in 1993.

Carrillo had direct links with several Colombian "heads," to whom he catered lavishly because their satisfaction guaranteed the flow of goods. Since he used planes of various sizes, capacity, and speed, he was internationally known as "el señor de los cielos" (the lord of the skies) or "cielito lindo" (pretty heaven) or "cuervito" (little crow). Carrillo's organization had developed several methods for transporting drugs from Colombia to Mexico, using high-capacity turbo-commander planes that can take off and land on short runways and at night, or 727 Boeing planes purchased in San Diego, fit for only one flight. He had the flexibility to change both his methods of transportation and his routes. In some cases, he would unload the drug cargo in Belize or Guatemala and transport it by land to Oaxaca or Puebla. From there, he used small Cessna planes, which fly short distances from one clandestine runway to another. Carrillo's organization moved the drug shipments using direct routes, stopover routes, and zig-zagging routes.

Carrillo's informants and corruption permeated the army, police forces, and even the administrative structures that supplied his planes with fuel and guaranteed the success of his business. From 1986 to 1989, Carrillo's organization alone introduced more than seventy tons of cocaine into the United States.[8] Sources say that until his death in 1997, 60 percent of the drugs entering the United States through the southern border could be credited to Amado Carrillo.

The suspicious conditions under which the news of the death of Carrillo was given at the beginning of 1997 unleashed multiple hypotheses over the fate that his organization would suffer. Time has clarified some of the circumstances. Looking back, we can see that the events that occurred from August 1997 to late 1998, in fact, confirmed that Amado Carrillo ceased to be the director-in-chief of the organization of the Ciudad Juárez Cartel. Nevertheless, it is not known, as of 2000, who may be capable of replacing him, but beyond that, it is undeniable that Amado Carrillo's organization won't disappear and, moreover, defends its territory against other organizations that are trying to take over the Juárez Cartel.

An important number of deaths and confrontations have occurred since May of 1997. At that time, the criminal organizations took over the streets of Ciudad Juárez, Chihuahua, and used them as battlefields with tragic outcomes that to date include several dozen dead in exchange for control of the zone and the extermination of their adversaries.

Judging from the characteristics of the dead and their known links to drug trafficking, the conflict for control of Ciudad Juárez is concentrated between two criminal forces: that which expands the Arellano Félix brothers' organization and the remainder of the killers that Amado Carrillo controlled. The Arellanos for many years had worked through a prominent courier of the zone (Rafael Muñoz Talavera) who played the key role in their relations in this territory; upon his death (September 10, 1998) the fate of the Ciudad Juárez Cartel and of the control of drug traffic across the center and southeast of the United States became uncertain, but the odds are in favor of the "heirs" of Amado Carrillo regrouping.

The changes brought by the 1998 elections to the state government of Chihuahua and the weak presence of federal police forces in the state offer little hope that the authorities will prevail or even will stop the advance of narco-trafficking in the area.

In the East

Juan García Abrego's now extinct organization began with his relative and predecessor, Juan Nepomuceno Guerra, and died, apparently, with the apprehension of Oscar Malherbe de Leon. García Abrego's organization, also known as the Gulf Cartel, at its peak was perhaps the most powerful in terms of trafficking and introducing drugs into the United States. Testimonies from different sources claim that, until 1995, García Abrego introduced into the United States between forty and fifty tons of cocaine per year.

García Abrego, currently in a U.S. prison, engaged in business transactions with the Colombian cartels through a lieutenant known as "el gringo," who knew the Colombian mafia because of his Colombian wife. The "gringo" paid with his life for the many mistakes he made. In one year alone he lost five tons of drugs, the authorities confiscated $12 million from him, and eighteen of his lieutenants were killed in a prison riot in Tamaulipas.

International networks of repression and the fight against drug trafficking succeeded in outmaneuvering the *capo*, who controlled the territory between the Yucatán Peninsula and Veracruz in Mexico up to parts of eastern United States, including New York, Chicago, and Florida. Striking the bottom ranks of the organization, anti-drug trafficking maneuvers included arresting the bodyguards, the lieutenants, money launderers, partners, and front organizations for various crimes.

After García Abrego's capture in February 1996, and the apprehension and disappearance of high-ranking members of the organization, the cartel found itself in dire straits. Toward the end of 1995, the cartel had not been able to introduce more than a ton and a half of cocaine to the United States. Oscar Malherbe de León, García Abrego's successor, tried to form an alliance with Amado Carrillo Fuentes, allowing the latter to introduce several drug shipments into the former's territory. However, this temporary partnership was not sufficient to foster the reorganization of the cartel. In fact, Oscar Malherbe de León, who was acute, astute, and street-smart, was exposed by Amado Carrillo. The National Defense Ministry arrested Malherbe de León, ending his short-lived career, on the afternoon of Thursday, February 27, 1997, in Mexico City.

Alternatives to Law Enforcement and the Fight against Criminal Organizations

The open coexistence of healthy social structures with criminal organizations at the border is shocking and difficult to understand. Perhaps the healthy social structures, focused on work, family, and the search for a better future, tolerate but do not participate in crime and the occasional violence it generates. In other words, there exists a live-and-let-live attitude. Perhaps the border inhabitants live in fear, captive to a situation that renders them impotent, leading to a life of limited social and economic progress, where social and family circles as well as daily activities are perfectly defined in an attempt to prevent contamination or instability.

Even if this is difficult to understand, whatever the origins of such coexistence, the inhabitants of the border, owners of a unique culture, live and develop within a social, political, and economic dynamic of unprecedented speed and growth. This environment, where winning or losing does not have the same impact as in other regions given the speedy ability to recoup losses, makes the border inhabitant tolerant of "minor vices," such as lesser corruption, influential relations, favoritism, street extortions, and generally all other vices that speed the process of personal advancement.

The special relevance acquired by authorities becomes clear. Similarly, we understand the desire to be close to the authorities for licit and illicit activities. This is particularly evident in the border region, given the legal ambiguities and the distance from the control and vigilance centers. Authorities and the organizations cannot refrain from joining in a sort of partnership, because their association fosters shared and leveled growth in the vast and highly unstable goods and services market.

We mentioned earlier that in previous decades, contraband, organized prostitution, and quick divorces enacted without regard to nationality or just cause occurred on a daily basis, and were accepted by the border culture as necessary for "daily survival." However, behind this framework of venal crimes, immoralities of greater and deeper roots than the ones visible were brewing. The phenomenon of corruption, through either gift or association, became institutionalized, absorbing licit activities through the daily motions of corrupting and becoming corrupt.

One of the weapons of delinquents and criminal organizations, one that strengthens their illicit activities, is the problem of corruption at all levels of the police forces, from the administrative authorities to mere inspectors.[9] Corruption is an extraordinary weapon of arms traffickers, white slave traders, smugglers, drug traffickers, and carjackers, because it serves their purposes in both direct and active, or indirect and passive ways. We could say that corruption directly serves to cover up the illegal action: allowing drug traffic and arms contraband, revealing the names of police informants, hindering antidrug raids with the purpose of picking up the drugs or the arms and delivering them elsewhere. Indirect or passive aid to corruption takes place when, for example, organized crime sets up a network of informants that detects the planned movements of the authorities or that reveals the authorities' investigations, allowing criminals to know when or where the raids will occur.

Propensity toward corruption is generated when a police officer has the discretionary power to choose between fulfilling the duties of his public office or charging for the cost of providing state services. Ordinarily, a police officer will consider two factors when deciding whether or not to aid the transgressor: (1) his personal level of decision-making power in relation to the benefit that he is granting; and (2) the level of risk to his persona or career that offering such benefit implies. (This aid might take effect through permitting the violation to occur unhindered or by reducing the fines of violating the law.) Considering these two variables, the corrupting act gains value and dimension, and becomes an issue for negotiation, transaction, or complicity.

The struggle to combat corruption should focus on two fundamental extremes: (1) increase the risk and cost of the corrupt action to the police officer; and (2) reduce the incentives for corruption by reducing the discretionary power of the officer or exerting control and surveillance mechanisms over the officer's conduct. A major obstacle in dealing with the corruption that facilitates drug trafficking, aside from the complexities of legal prosecution, undoubtedly reflects the dilemma faced by each public servant. In a country such as Mexico, that is in the midst of transition and crisis, the officer experiences a certain anxiety when trying to decide whether to fulfill his duties as a public servant or to obtain a greater remuneration for breaking his oath to compensate for meager salaries and benefits, while enduring the disrespect of high-ranking authorities. The immeasurable quantities of money in each transaction dwarf the ranks and functions of these police officers, who in the end are merely victims of circumstance.

In the last few years, according to official statistics, corruption techniques have contaminated U.S. officers as well, notably in the protection given to drug transports arriving into the United States and to the contraband of arms that benefits Mexican delinquents. Between 1995 and 1996, Mexican authorities confiscated 23,841 weapons entering through the United States, predominantly through Nogales, Sonora; Reynosa and Nuevo Laredo in Tamaulipas; Ciudad Juárez, Chihuahua; and Piedras Negras, Coahuila.[10] All these cities are located on the Mexican side along the Texas border.

However, drug and arms trafficking are not the only visible expressions of organized crime along the border that involve police forces. Another prominent and highly lucrative activity is car theft, featuring well-organized groups that steal the goods on either side of the border and transport them to the other. Evidently, the dynamic of border delinquency surpasses the ability of the state to control monitoring agencies. Not only will it be necessary to ask whether these structures, which evidently do not correspond to reality, are functioning according to regulation, but it is also necessary to ask if the flexibility, complacency, and tolerance of corruption has not infiltrated the higher echelons of authority. Sources show that corruption has penetrated the highest levels of the army in Mexico. Publicity scandals referring to the protection of drug traffickers (in Mexico) underscore the direct need to review the frailty of these state structures.[11]

Much remains to be studied, analyzed, and learned about the socioeconomic and delinquent behavior on the Mexico-U.S. border. Only then will we understand the many worlds that lie beneath the social fabric of this geographic space marked by contrasts and challenges. The diagnosis of this area will be useful to behavioral scientists because the border can be used as a laboratory to understand isolated phenomena that could appear in different communities worldwide.

Conclusion

In short, we may say that the communities on the U.S.-Mexico border belong to a unique society. Although both sides of the border have different origins and very distinct traditions, this conglomeration of human beings share a unique set of problems, full of circumstances that can only be seen and understood by living there. We find a society that thrives on the contradictions that arise from the social and economic dimensions of the border. Because of these unique characteristics—which have given both countries a chance to share culture, education, as well as many problems—the border region deserves special attention in the study of its multiple phenomena and characteristics.

It would be of great interest to this particular project to learn about the links that exist between the criminal organizations and their impact in democratic governments. It would be of utmost interest to find more examples of daily life that could enlighten the study of this phenomenon. Criminal organizations find ample opportunities and fertile ground for their activities in the border region because the lack of control mechanisms, the dynamics of the border's economy, and the flexibility of the authorities have created an atmosphere that gives way to the benefactors and beneficiaries. Behavior that is reprehensible in other latitudes has free reign in the border because of the lax morality.

Not so long ago, the involvement of government agents in these criminal activities made government agencies exclusive grounds for mafia hierarchies. In the oil sector, for example, in Tamaulipas, the immoral and delinquent relationship between the oil company and the political leadership was so prominent that its discovery in 1989 provoked not only a crisis in the oil sector, but also the loss of many electoral offices. To this day, the government party has not been able to recover these posts.

Oil union leader Joaquín Hernández Galicia, also known as La Quina, who was incarcerated at the beginning of the Salinas administration for sundry crimes, had established and maintained a true political and economic empire. The government, especially the party currently in power, still resents the consecutive electoral losses in several municipalities of Tamaulipas, caused by the withdrawal of support from Hernández Galicia's leadership and the manipulation he used to exert in previous elections.

Another equally transcendental border phenomenon, toward the Pacific, shows a different type of criminal organization, which controls common delinquency and the police forces in charge of combating common crime. The objective of these criminal organizations is to secure drug trafficking and other crimes for their own benefit. Not only do they control the police forces, but also the airports, ports, fuels, judicial agents, and the institutions in charge of preventing and prosecuting existing crime in this area.

In conclusion, we need to implement solutions that penetrate to the roots of the problem. In other words, we need effective control and oversight systems to allow a systematic and continuous inspection of the authorities' activities. Nevertheless, the strengths of the border zone are greater than the threats and problems. Little by little, the border society has started to change the criteria by which they balance, in the medium and long terms, the advantages and privileges they enjoy against their subjection to the persecution, vigilance, and control of criminal organizations. The potential and transformation of the maquiladora industry, the presence of nongovernmental organizations, and the collective conscience suggest that the development and growth of the region are signs of change. The questions left to answer are: How much longer will we have to wait until this change happens? Can the national government understand the socio-politico-economic problems of this special zone? Can it create a firm base to find the solution at all three levels of government?

Chapter 9

Mexican Drug Syndicates in California

Elias Castillo and Peter Unsinger

FOR MORE THAN three-quarters of a century, Mexican drug syndicates have been growing in power, size, and influence, fueled by their production of illicit narcotics and the smuggling and sale of those drugs into the United States. The U.S. Federal Bureau of Investigation (FBI) has described these syndicates as a serious threat to the security of the United States. This chapter examines the organization and methods used by Mexican drug syndicates to smuggle, sell narcotics, and collect and return to Mexico profits gained from the sale of drugs within the United States. The chapter concludes that Mexican drug syndicates, because of their rigorous organization, massive amount of illicitly gained money, and brutish tactics, present a significant and growing threat to the law enforcement agencies of the United States and ultimately to its democratic form of government.

Since the 1920s, a segment of Mexico's population has been involved in the production of narcotics and the smuggling of those drugs into the United States. In the earliest known pattern of this illicit activity, Mexican-Chinese grew poppies to produce opium and carried it to the United States for consumption by Chinese laborers on the West Coast.[1]

Few Americans realize that Mexico has a sizable Chinese population which has been growing since the late 1800s, when Chinese laborers were brought to the United States to work on railroad construction throughout the West. Earlier, Chinese prospectors had traveled to America to seek fortunes during California's 1849 Gold Rush. Although few of them discovered gold, all were victims of intense racism within the United States. Many fled to Mexico to escape the bigotry and were able to establish small farms and businesses there. They also brought with them the custom of smoking opium, and customers for it were plentiful on both sides of the border.

Mexican opium production was firmly established by the time opium was outlawed as a basic ingredient of early patent medicines and adventurous Americans had discovered and become addicted to its effects. Mexican-produced opium added to quantities of the drug that were subsequently smuggled into the United States from Asia and the Middle East.[2] By the late 1920s and early 1930s, however, Mexicans joined the Mexican-Chinese in growing poppies and processing the opium gum into a crude heroin that was being sold principally in the low-income urban Mexican immigrant communities of California. Marijuana was the second crop that the then small Mexican drug groups were also smuggling into the United States.[3]

In Hollywood at that time, the use of heroin was increasing among actors and musicians within the huge film and entertainment industry. Most, however, relied on the refined drug from either Asia or the Middle East. The crude "Mexican brown," so-called because of its color and its low level of purity, was not popular among that segment of society. Meanwhile, on the U.S. East Coast, heroin from the Middle East in particular was being distributed by Mafia gangs linked to outlaw groups in Sicily.

When World War II erupted, the supply of heroin from Asia and the Middle East was abruptly cut off. Mobsters in Philadelphia, aware of the crude "Mexican brown," decided to substitute it for the refined white powder they had been accustomed to receiving from Iran, Turkey, Afghanistan, and other Middle East areas. Delegates from that U.S. criminal syndicate traveled to Mexico to meet with the illicit producers of heroin and arranged for delivery of large quantities of the drug. This was a major development in the growth of Mexico's criminal drug industry. Previously, Mexican heroin production was small in relation to production in the Middle East and Asia. Users were mainly limited to a small segment of California's Mexican and black communities.

With an increasing demand for Mexican brown heroin, on both the East and

West Coasts of the United States, smugglers and dealers from Mexico, working with the Mafia mobs, created a wider demand for their low-priced heroin throughout the nation. As the war continued, the use of Mexican heroin in the United States increased, particularly in the nation's coastal urban areas. This in turn enriched the Mexican drug syndicates and allowed them to exert criminal influence throughout Mexico's poorly trained and paid law enforcement agencies, which not only were easily bribed into not interfering in their activities but actively sought payoffs in return for not interfering with the illicit drug activity.

When World War II ended, the Mafia syndicates reverted to Asia and the Middle East as their primary sources for heroin. Subsequently, the demand for Mexican brown in the United States was dramatically reduced, but the increased use of Mexican brown in the Los Angeles and San Diego areas during the war years had created a large number of low-income U.S. heroin addicts who depended on the inexpensive Mexican brown. Since, at that time, there was little emphasis by the United States on intercepting drugs along the border, it was relatively easy for the narcotic to be smuggled and delivered to Mexican syndicate dealers in the United States. They would then use cohorts, also from Mexico but living in the United States, to cut the heroin to levels that could be used by addicts. Once the dilution process was completed, the drug was ready for sale to whoever wanted to sell it on the street. The most plentiful customers were teenagers from within the low-income African-American and Mexican communities.

This pattern of smuggling and dealing was confined mainly to sales among low-income Mexican-Americans on the West Coast. In other large cities, particularly those on the East Coast, Mafia gang members, who did not have the more refined postwar Middle East or Asian heroin available to them, would travel to Mexico, pay for the drug, and then have it delivered to them in towns along the U.S.-Mexico border. Mexicali, across from Calexico, California, Tijuana, across from the busy San Diego area with its thousands of servicemen, and Ciudad Juárez, across from El Paso, Texas, became important transit points.[4]

This pattern of demand, in which addicts who could afford it used the more refined Asian and Middle East heroin while low-income addicts relied on the cruder Mexican brown, continued for twenty-five years. During those postwar years, Mexican dealers and smugglers sought to widen the use of their product, along with marijuana. Profits from both drugs were enormous, allowing the Mexican drug syndicates to further entrench themselves in Mexico's underworld and solidify their political influence.

Easing their growth was a U.S. government policy that virtually ignored the growing drug threat from Mexico and instead concentrated on narcotics being smuggled in from the Middle East and Asia. Federal drug agents made much of discovering heroin on ships in major East Coast ports, while making little effort to stop the enormous amounts of heroin and marijuana that were coming across the U.S.-Mexico border, carefully concealed in vehicles that ranged from massive tanker trucks to small family cars.[5]

Sometime during the late 1960s or early 1970s, Mexican heroin chemists discovered a new method of processing the drug into a gummy, tar-like substance that had a purity level of 50 percent, far higher than their previous production of the drug.[6] The improved processing was revolutionary for the Mexican drug syndicates. Now that the heroin was in a gummy form instead of a powder, it could literally be shaped into packets that would hold their forms; they could then be more easily stuffed in the secret compartments of vehicles or wrapped around the bodies of persons, thereby allowing them to carry from one to two kilos of the heroin.[7] The high purity levels also meant that the profit from two kilograms of Mexican goma (the street name for heroin) increased dramatically. Now, the heroin could be cut as many as six times. Thus, two kilos of heroin of 50 percent purity would produce ten kilos (nearly twenty pounds) of heroin ready for street use.[8]

During this period, French police shattered Marseilles as a major center for processing heroin destined for the United States. The French center was subsequently replaced by Culiacán, a medium-sized farm city in the Mexican state of Sinaloa. Surrounded by the rugged Sierra Madre mountains where the hot weather provided an ideal climate for the opium poppies, the region was ideal for the ever-expanding Mexican heroin industry.[9]

American drug dealers flew in daily to purchase Mexican goma as well as methamphetamines, cocaine, and huge amounts of marijuana, and then arrange for its delivery to the United States. The sale of these drugs was so blatant that two American undercover narcotics agents in the late 1970s recalled attending a lavish party provided by one of the Culiacán druglords for his American customers. Bars were set up on an immaculately trimmed lawn while buffets provided gourmet Mexican cuisine and strolling mariachis played and sang Mexican songs. Long tables, each covered by a white sheet, had been placed in the middle of the lawn. At a given signal, the sheets were suddenly pulled off, revealing heaping mounds of cocaine, amphetamines, heroin, methamphetamines, and carefully wrapped bricks of marijuana. Gang members took positions behind the tables, ready to take orders from the American customers who sniffed and tasted the narcotics before placing orders. (What was most extraordinary about the event was that major government officials, including the local police chief, were present at the event. Their presence provided proof that the syndicates were amassing not only financial power but also tremendous political clout that allowed them to operate virtually freely within the Mexican state.)[10]

This was the common method used to obtain Mexican narcotics for consumption by users other than Mexican or Mexican-American immigrants in U.S. cities: American dealers flew to Mexico and placed orders that were then delivered by the Mexican syndicates to the U.S. customers. In this manner, smuggling routes were established that wound their way across the United States from Mexicali, Ciudad Juárez, and Tijuana. The routes from those border cities stretched initially to San Diego, Los Angeles, Redwood City, Salinas, Bakersfield, Fresno, San Francisco, Dallas, Ft. Worth, Phoenix, Chicago, and Lake Tahoe. Ultimately, they would spread to include New York, Philadelphia, Boston, St. Louis, Yakima, Seattle, Tucson, Albuquerque, Des Moines, and Portland.[11]

These routes were controlled by members of the drug gangs who recruited Mexican immigrants to help in the delivery of the narcotics shipments.[12] At this point we need to emphasize that there is no evidence that Mexican-Americans have ever been deeply involved in the delivery, distribution, and preparation of Mexican narcotics or the collection of profits resulting from sale of those drugs.[13] To understand this, we must carefully distinguish between Mexican nationals, Mexican immigrants, and Mexican-Americans, three distinct groups of persons with ties to Mexico. In too many cases, the public tends to lump all three into a homogenous category when in fact they are three distinct, separate groups.

Mexican nationals are Mexican citizens who reside in Mexico and may or may not travel to the United States. Mexican immigrants are Mexican citizens who live in the United States either legally or illegally. Many members of this group frequently return to Mexico for either brief or prolonged visits. This group is also divided into recently arrived immigrants and those who have lived here for many years, establishing homes and families. The final group is the Mexican-Americans, many of whom refer to themselves as Chicanos, thus identifying themselves as having been born of Mexican ancestry in the United States. The families within this group may trace their roots back for more than eight generations in the United States.

It is from the low-income group of this segment of persons with Mexican ancestry that so-called prison gangs were spawned. Initially, the gangs were formed to protect themselves from attacks by black gangs or racist whites during the 1940s in Los Angeles. Those attacks were provoked, in many cases, by white bigots who objected to the style of dress adopted by some Mexican-American youths—the pachucos, who stood out because of their wide-brimmed hats, long coats, broad pants with narrow cuffs, and garish ties. Although it was a style of dress peculiar to only a small part of the vast Mexican-American community in east Los Angeles, it was enough to evoke the need for Mexican youths to band together in gangs, who then began battling each other for certain areas of east Los Angeles.

In the period from the mid-1970s to the mid-1980s, virtually all of these gangs turned to drug use, and generation after generation of low-income Mexican-Americans in east Los Angeles were forced to join the gangs for protection against other similar gangs seeking to expand their territories, or "turf." The violence spawned by these gangs led to numerous arrests, and members were sent to prisons, where bigotry between the blacks and Chicanos was common and led to vicious interracial wars behind bars. There was a need to organize themselves tightly into gangs that are commonly referred to as the Mexican Mafia (it appears the name was chosen because of their efforts to emulate the highly disciplined East Coast Mafia).

Despite the name, there is little connection between them and the Mexican drug gangs, who scorn them because of their lack of reliability. Whereas members of the Mexican Mafia may buy narcotics from Mexican gang members, there is little evidence that they have even come close to infiltrating the lowest levels of Mexican drug syndicate operations within the United States. The reason for their being shunned is the Mexican Mafia's disposition for open violence in settling disputes among themselves, their flashy cars and lifestyles, and penchant for

freely spending money, all of which draw attention to their group. Members of
Mexican drug gangs who operate within the United States avoid those traits at all
costs.[14]

Additionally, there is an intense dislike toward Mexican-Americans or Chicanos among many low-income Mexican immigrants and Mexican nationals. A
large number of Mexican immigrants and Mexican nationals consider Chicanos
ignorant simply because they do not speak Spanish, and they refer to them as
pochos. In their view, Chicanos have abandoned their motherland and are therefore subjects to be despised.[15]

Likewise, Chicanos dislike Mexican immigrants, though we would emphasize
again that this is a common trait among many of those in the low-income bracket
of this specific ethnic group. (This belief tends to disappear among those Chicanos or Mexican immigrants who have successfully entered the economic and social mainstream of the United States either through education or skilled training.)
Chicanos consider the immigrants ignorant, uneducated, and competitors for
low-paying jobs. This mutual dislike between Chicanos and Mexican immigrants,
again at low-income levels, is so entrenched that youth gangs composed of members from each group constantly battle each other, particularly in the low-income
Mexican communities of Los Angeles that are segmented into Mexican immigrant and Mexican-American neighborhoods. Drive-by shootings and beatings
occur daily as these gangs fight each other in that area of the city.[16]

Again, it is for these reasons that the Mexican gangs recruit their members almost solely from within Mexico's extremely large pool of urban and rural poor
(nearly 20 percent of Mexico's estimated population of 90 million is considered
living in extreme poverty, a quite substantial recruitment pool). Recruiting by the
different Mexican drug organizations is relatively easy. Jobs are not only scarce in
Mexico but are also low paying for poorly educated Mexicans. Young men and
women in this bracket are desperate to get any work and the drug gangs take advantage of this fact. However, recruitment occurs only within family members of
those who are already working within a syndicate. In this manner, there is no
question of loyalty to the syndicate since it is akin to working for one's family. Failure to carry out an assignment would be a disgrace to the family of that particular
gang member. Nor is there any trepidation about the illegality of being part of a
drug syndicate. Those who join syndicates easily shrug off that fact by pointing to

the widespread corruption within Mexico. The sentiment is: Everyone's doing it, so I'm going to do it too.

In the mountainous and isolated areas of Sinaloa, Sonora, and Michoacán, small farmers who are barely eking out an existence from nearly barren soil are easily talked into growing poppies for opium production. It is an illegal crop that will provide them a hundredfold in profits in comparison to their usual harvests of corn and beans.[17] The children of these farmers can easily be induced to join drug gangs once they are old enough. It is actually very common for young men to ask to join the group. In those areas where the organizations operate freely, there is no stigma attached to working with the gangs. The rationalization is that since no one is using heroin or smoking large amounts of marijuana in Mexico and the drugs are destined for the United States, then it is all right. In addition, as mentioned previously, there is the other rationalization that corruption is so widespread in Mexico that there is no reason not to engage in criminal activity.

New and usually young members in these rural areas may start as helpers to gang members who travel from one farm plot to another gathering raw opium or loose-cut marijuana for delivery to processing centers. Eventually, these members may move up the ladder to the point where they are helping deliver tractor-trailer loads of drugs to warehouses along the U.S.-Mexico border.

Another step up the ladder could involve gang members being sent across the border to ensure delivery of narcotics and perhaps act as couriers returning money to Mexico. Other recruits from farming areas may be given first assignments in which they become "mulas" (mules) who smuggle heroin into the United States. Still others may be sent to work in border vehicle body shops where sophisticated craftsmen devise hidden spaces in vehicles of all sizes, some so ingenious that even dogs trained by U.S. customs agents find it difficult to detect the narcotics hidden inside.

Additional sites for recruiting mules are in the border cities of Mexicali, Tijuana, and Ciudad Juárez, where hundreds of thousands of poor Mexicans gather daily to try to enter the United States illegally by evading the U.S. Border Patrol or Customs agents. It is fairly easy for members of a smuggling cell, that is, a cell whose sole job is to smuggle the narcotics into the United States and nothing more, to mingle among the would-be immigrants and hire numbers of them to carry narcotics on their bodies as they attempt to cross the border.

The pay may range from $100 to $200 to carry one or two kilos on themselves and deliver it to specific border addresses in the United States. Smugglers for the gangs may recruit as many as 100 immigrants, load them with a total of 100–200 kilos of heroin or cocaine in plastic packets, then send them across the border separately. If one of them is caught, the loss is acceptable since the other 99 mules got through. If a recruited smuggler makes it across and wants to continue working as a mule, he or she is quickly accepted.[18]

Still another area of recruitment is in farm labor camps in the United States, where Mexican immigrants live almost year around. There, an offer to make more than $100 a day from a relative already involved in a drug gang is bound to be accepted by a worker who may be willing to replace his backbreaking work with the easy pay and labor offered by a gang member.[19]

The work may range from simply being the driver of a car acting as an escort for a vehicle carrying either drugs or money. The escort's job is not to interfere but simply observe if the vehicle carrying a drug cargo is stopped by police and then to report the occurrence to a gang headquarters in the United States. Other positions may involve working as a guard at a home or building where drugs are being stored. Still another job is disposing of dismantled vehicles used to smuggle the drugs into the United States. These vehicles may range from late-model autos or trucks to run-down vehicles. The goal is to get rid of them if they cannot be reused.[20]

Among gang members there is no concern that what they are doing is wrong. Virtually all of them are poorly educated or have no education at all. The loyalty patterns are shaped solely by what is needed to ensure that the syndicates operate efficiently and profitably. Young gang members who have exhibited intelligence and loyalty are sent to the United States and rank among the most trusted. Throughout California in the 1980s, for example, the syndicates established specific routes that were to be used within the state, drop-off points for collecting money, producing or diluting narcotics, and delivering drugs. It was the responsibility of the gang members in charge to ensure that they operated in the most efficient manner. In different U.S. cities, gangs operated these centers using state-of-the-art technology. They were manned by trusted members who, as previously stated, had other relatives involved in the operation.

A glimpse of one of these centers illustrates the scope of their operations. In

Oakland, one of our sources was taken to a large, dilapidated house in that city's low-income district as part of an attempt to recruit her as a street dealer for one of the syndicates. As she entered the house she heard a muffled whirring sound coming from behind a closed door. She was led inside and was astonished to see a long table with approximately twenty to thirty nude Mexican women sitting around it. Each was wearing only a dust mask and had a blender and small, precision electronic scales in front of them. The noise she had heard was the now almost deafening noise from all the blenders operating simultaneously.[21]

The women were diluting heroin for street sales. At each workplace, there were bags of undiluted heroin on one side and bowls of diluted heroin ready for packaging on the other. The women used the scales to measure the correct amount of heroin and lactose (the diluting substance), then emptied the combination into the blender.[22] Armed guards stood at the two entrances to the room and carefully watched the women. The source's escort explained that the women were nude to keep them from hiding any of the heroin on themselves. The room, she was told, operated twenty-four hours a day with different shifts of workers. The source, who declined the offer to become a street dealer, was told that she would be given free pounds of already cut heroin to sell. In return she would share the profits with the distributor. Her escort was a Mexican immigrant who had been recruited by a gang many years before and now had responsibility for stockpiling the drug.[23]

The example illustrates the sophistication involved in only one segment or cell of a syndicate's activities in the United States. Each point and the responsibility that goes with it is under the direction of a separate gang member who usually does not know who is in charge of another segment. By using this method, each cell operates independently of the other, and in case of arrests his or her ignorance ensures that the manager or members of another cell will not be revealed. Another tactic syndicates use to keep from attracting attention to themselves is to maintain two homes—an opulent, lavish house in Mexico and a run-down home in the United States. To all outward appearances in the United States, gang members appear to be simply laborers driving broken-down vehicles that draw little attention from police. They dress simply and so do their families. But behind that simplicity is an intricate system of code words used to control deliveries of drugs, complex surveillance procedures when drugs are en route or money is being returned to Mexico, and two-way radio equipment, all aimed at staying one step ahead of law enforcement.

It is this combination of complex security procedures plus simplicity that has allowed the syndicates to escape detection in the United States and vastly expand their operations. Linked to these patterns is the reluctance to betray other gang members since most members are related to each other. The family links between gang members also increase the use of trust to oversee many narcotics operations. For example, the manager of the dilution operation is obligated to deliver the purchase price of his drugs to a point in the United States where the money is collected and counted. He simply takes his profit and delivers the remainder to the predetermined location.

Trust, then, is another important component of efficiency within the syndicates. Drug wholesalers, once established, do not have to pay at the time the drug is delivered; they can do so later after they have sold it. Likewise, if a wholesaler can induce a close friend also to peddle the drug, as in the example cited, and if that friend is successful in his venture, then he simply asks for more of the drugs from the person who delivers to him. If he has three or four friends whom he is supporting by providing them with drugs for sales, he then becomes a "major" drug dealer. Thus, what the news media call a drug ring is created. Every so often, drug enforcement agencies describe to news agencies how they have broken one of these rings. Their descriptions are accurate, however, the problem is that another drug ring, perhaps much more cautious than the first, will quickly fill the void left by the first group.[24]

The Mexican points and routes, established to ensure rapid delivery of narcotics, attracted Colombia's cocaine cartels to Mexico's drug syndicates in the early 1980s after U.S. pressure forced the Colombians to move their smuggling points from Florida to the Southwest. Both groups forged agreements in which the Colombians would deliver cocaine to Mexico and the syndicates there would use their networks to smuggle it into the United States. The agreement was so lucrative that cargo jets laden with cocaine destined for the United States began to be detected in Mexico.[25]

The lure of joining or starting up a drug ring comes, of course, from the immense profits involved, so large, in fact, that many gangs feel no need to mete out punishment if a shipment of money is occasionally seized by police. The method of transporting the money in the United States is simplicity at its best. Couriers in different U.S. cities are given large, sealed cardboard boxes filled with dollar bills, which are usually placed in the trunk of a vehicle. They are then instructed to follow a certain highway route. If for some reason they are stopped, their instructions are to deny any knowledge of the contents of the box. A courier is told to say he was paid by a stranger to deliver the box to a certain point and had no knowledge of what was in it. Any officer who stops a courier is also told by the courier that the money can be confiscated since the courier has no connection to it.[26]

If the courier is arrested and the money seized, there is little cause for concern. Police have little evidence that the courier has done anything wrong. There is usually no proof that the money was obtained from illegal activity, and it could, in fact, actually be some eccentric's life savings. If an arrest is made, the courier, usually being a first offender, is given a light sentence. To the courier, going to jail is of little concern. He will have three meals a day, a soft bed, and a warm room in which to sleep. To syndicate members, the seizure is just a small annoyance that can easily be shrugged off.[27]

A simpler method of transporting money is to stuff a battered cardboard box with money, wrap it tightly with duct tape, scrawl an address on it, and send it by bus express package service. Once the money arrives at its destination, it is picked up, and the bills, easily totaling millions of dollars each month, are counted electronically, bundled in the different denominations, and reshipped to border cities. Either couriers or bus express package service are used again to get the money into Mexico. Crossing the money into Mexico is not a problem, since Mexican customs agents rarely search vehicles entering Mexico. To ensure that the money is not seized, the Mexican customs agents are usually bribed in advance to allow the vehicle to enter Mexico freely.

When the money arrives in Mexico, it is quickly laundered and reinvested in projects that may range from hotels to stocks. The tragic reality of the illicit drug industry is that there is so much money being earned (amounting to billions of dollars annually) that there is more than enough for all gang members from the lowest to the highest. It is an enticing industry that has virtually no ceiling to it and can make millionaires out of enterprising *campesinos* who often can neither read nor write.[28]

It is also money that evokes the strongest and most brutal response from the Mexican drug cartels. If payoffs to the organization are withheld by gang members who have been provided drugs on consignment, the response from Mexico can be brutal. Narcotics agents know of cases where hit men were flown aboard private aircraft from Mexico into the United States for the purpose of killing an errant gang member. With the murder done, they returned to the airport where the waiting aircraft quickly whisked them back to Mexico. American police are simply helpless against this operation.[29]

Syndicate members know all too well that such will be their fate if they violate the rules. Yet, unlike the American East Coast mobs, no violence has erupted over disputes arising from control of specific regions within the United States. Apparently, there are enough cities, drug addicts, and potential drug addicts for everyone. Gunplay, however, has broken out within Mexico when a gang has challenged another for control of the supply of narcotics flowing into the United States.[30] Those gang members operating within the United States lead fairly stable lives and are free from such conflicts because they are the recipients of the drug. Their task is to sell it, then return the proceeds to Mexico. Within the United States, some members involved with Mexican narcotics, those in lower echelons of the syndicates, are choosing to stay in America and forego establishing a second home in Mexico. They may return to Mexico but only for visits; their permanent home is in the United States. However, by staying in America, they run a greater risk of being caught in a country where law enforcement agencies cannot be bribed as easily as they are in Mexico.[31]

Narcotics agencies believe those members who choose to remain in the United States are involved in the production of methamphetamines within the country, a fairly new development by the Mexican syndicates. Up to the early 1990s, the production of methamphetamines was largely controlled by U.S. citizens. That production has shifted in the late 1990s to Mexican nationals operating in the United States, specifically in California.

The production of methamphetamines requires heaters, large amounts of chemicals—some of them unstable—and precision-made glass laboratory flasks and tubes. Chemicals are blended and then heated to temperatures that create extremely poisonous fumes during the preparation of the drug. The production of these narcotics also requires proper ventilation and isolated areas in which dangerous by-products can be easily dumped. The result can be serious ground contamination.[32]

When U.S. citizens were at the forefront of methamphetamine production, the preparation occurred in trailer homes or garages and the output was normally between two to five pounds of the crystalline substance. Meanwhile, production of methamphetamines was growing in Mexico and it was not uncommon to have illegal labs in that country producing up to 100 pounds at a time.

A problem the drug syndicates faced was trying to smuggle the methamphetamine across the border in large quantities. Sometime during the past five years, one of the syndicates launched an innovative concept: Why not obtain the chemicals in the United States and do the "cooking" of "meth" in that country instead of producing it in Mexico and facing the task of smuggling it across the border?

A positive factor about methamphetamines is that they do not require lengthy growing times. Opium poppies, although a hardy plant that grows in hot climates, must be carefully tended to maturity before a small amount of raw opium can be obtained from the numerous but small plots in the states of Sinaloa, Sonora, Jalisco, and Michoacán. Likewise, marijuana requires careful irrigation and a lengthy growing time in which there is a high risk of having the crop spotted from the air by government aircraft and subsequently destroyed. The production of methamphetamine requires only an isolated, well-ventilated site to produce a highly profitable product within days.

The result is that methamphetamine labs controlled by Mexican drug gangs are now being raided in the San Joaquin Valley of California. This lush farming region is ideal for the production of the drug, which requires isolated areas. Many old and out-of-the-way farmhouses pepper the valley and are being rented by meth crews as sites for the illegal labs. The danger of meth labs was best demonstrated when police found four dead persons inside a southern California motel where an attempt had been made to produce the drug without adequate ventilation. The victims had died almost instantly once the chemicals started getting hot and began giving off fumes. Outdoor mountain sites have also been discovered in which the crews lugged in portable generators for the heaters and set up shop near streams which, while serving as handy dumping sites, carry the contaminant downstream and endanger wildlife.[33]

In one case, an outdoor lab was discovered only because the landowner heard the sound of generators and, believing cattle rustlers were operating on his California land, investigated the source of the noise. He discovered a fully equipped lab operating at the bottom of a slope next to a stream. Tables had been carried in to support the laboratory equipment and 50-gallon barrels of chemicals needed to produce methamphetamine were found at the site. The lab crew was never found. Government cleanup crews were needed, as they are at all methamphetamine sites, to make the site safe. When arrests have occurred at meth labs, all the suspects have been Mexican nationals. The labs are now so numerous and produce so much meth that they have quietly edged out production of the drug by U.S. citizens. The statistics are staggering: Mexican nationals accounted for 17 percent of the methamphetamine lab crews seized in California, but their operations provided 73 percent of the seizure of methampetamine in the state. Most of these highly secretive labs are being found in the California Central Valley region, the cities of Los Angeles, East Palo Alto, and Stockton, and Orange and San Bernardino counties. In 1997, California narcotics agents seized forty-two labs in the Fresno, California, area. Statewide, that number soared to 800 labs.[34]

Suspects arrested in connection with the labs have told police they were hired from street corners while seeking day labor jobs. In most cases, a pickup truck would pull up to the workers, and a Hispanic driver would ask if they wanted to work. When the answer was affirmative, he would tell a specific number of them to climb aboard. The truck would then drive off. En route, the workers would be told they would be going to an isolated work site where they would earn $500 a day, a staggering amount to workers used to earning $40 a day. Once at the site, they were shown the chemicals by an instructor who oversaw production of the drug. The workers were not given any gloves, masks, or protective clothing to guard against the dangerous fumes that can cause pneumonia because of the corrosive effect they have on lungs. The entire crew lived and slept in close proximity to the lab until the batch, which may total 100 pounds, was finished.[35]

The operation, while complex, has become simplified by the use of careful instructions and premeasured, color-coded bags of chemicals. Instructions found by agents provide step-by-step descriptions, which include statements such as "when the thermometer reaches this temperature, then add the entire contents of the blue bag into each flask."[36]

Like the development of Mexican heroin tar or goma that increased its potency but reduced its size, the strategy of moving methamphetamine labs from Mexico into the United States poses another unexpected major obstacle to the reduction of drug use in America. It is almost impossible to stop the widespread establishment of carefully hidden meth labs that produce the drug in large quantities. Police also run into a virtual stone wall in trying to find out who is behind the labs. The crews, when arrested, maintain the only person they know linked to the lab is the one who hired them from a street corner or a farm labor camp.[37]

Still another problem is that the number of lab crew leaders is growing exponentially. In the few times that agents have arrested a crew leader, they discovered that he had started by being a lab worker and had simply asked his crew leader if he could set up a lab for himself. There was no problem with the request and he was quickly supplied with all the equipment and chemicals needed for the process. The meth that he produced was quickly purchased by the original crew leader.[38]

With a near constant supply of poor Mexican national laborers in the United States and drug syndicates willing to pay them up to $500 per day for the 4–5 days of actual "cooking" involved in each drug production cycle, it appears narcotics agents face a daunting task in trying to stop the spread of meth labs. It is also probably accurate to say that many Mexican national laborers will succumb to working at the labs because of their desperate search for work.[39]

The Gerardo Delgado Garibay 1995 case, which was tried in federal court in Fresno, California,[40] provides an example of the staggering profits that can be made from the production of methamphetamines. It is also a major example of the links that drug producers and smugglers have with Mexico. It took a total of eighteen different investigations from a variety of southern California law enforcement agencies to amass the evidence needed to convict Garibay, who is now serving a life sentence in federal prison. At his peak, in 1993, Garibay had six laboratories producing as much as 2,000 pounds of methamphetamine per lab. His operation was then selling the methamphetamine at $3,500 to $4,000 per pound for a total of $48 million. He was also able to escape detection from about 1990 to his arrest in August 1994, allowing him to produce tons of methamphetamine for distribution throughout the United States. Garibay was just one independent producer of methamphetamine among an unknown number who, up to the present, have eluded police.

During Garibay's trial, agents from California's Bureau of Narcotics Enforcement and the federal Drug Enforcement Administration provided evidence of phone calls and travel to Mexico where he used his profits to purchase enormous amounts of land and other assets. However, Garibay's apprehension is rare. Narcotics enforcement agents believe there may be dozens of independent drug entrepreneurs like Garibay operating throughout the United States in addition to those linked to the powerful drug cartels of Mexico. The ability to detect illegal drug operators who use Mexico as a home base but conduct the production and sale of drugs in the United States is extremely difficult because of the tight security involved in those small drug gangs.

There is no question that the smuggling of heroin, cocaine, and marijuana into the United States and the Mexican-controlled production of methamphetamine within America's borders are major problems that threaten not only the economy of the country but its constitutional liberties. Despite massive operations, Mexico has been unable to fully eradicate the drug syndicates' operations because of government corruption, inefficiency and lack of resources, and the sheer scope of the problem. The result has been that the Mexican cartels are operating freely in the United States. It is likely that as the situation deteriorates further in Mexico, and subsequently in the United States, American citizens may be willing to accept police tactics that are on the razor's edge of being unconstitutional, such as allowing a freer hand in authorizing phone wiretaps that could threaten the right to privacy as provided by the Constitution. Other areas may involve expanding the parameters that allow police to search vehicles, again infringing upon the individual rights of a citizen. This would mean that police, instead of gathering evidence or having a justifiable reason to stop and search a vehicle, could simply stop vehicles because an officer had a hunch that a driver may be carrying narcotics. Politicians may exploit the drug problem, winning elections by voters who are fed up with drug-related crime, and introduce laws drastically restricting entry and activity by citizens of another country, Mexico for example, as an effort to bring drug crime under control.

Already, the federal government has clearly violated long-standing policies by using military resources in assignments that are the responsibility of civilian law enforcement agencies. Those acts include the use of Marines and members of other military forces to guard stretches of the U.S.-Mexico border, an assignment ill-suited to soldiers who are trained for combat and quick reaction but not the complex task of trying to determine by observation whether a person is simply an illegal alien trying to cross the border or a smuggler laden with drugs.[41]

The use of the military resulted from law enforcement agencies' agreeing that they have no choice other than to turn to the military for help against a foe that is better equipped in radio communication gear and transportation and can call on a vast pool of manpower, namely, Mexico's poor. Unless there is a dramatic reversal in the drug problem facing the United States, it is likely that within five to ten years an outraged American public, intent on stopping the cartels, may demand enforcement tactics and laws that, while unconstitutional, will go unchallenged in courts because of public sentiment that they are the only way to stop the drug problem. The effect of such laws would be minimally noticed by the nation's non-Hispanic population, but they could have a strong impact on the Hispanic population, specifically in the Southwest, which would have to bear the brunt of potentially heavy-handed police tactics that could merge antidrug activities with racism and bigotry.

Another concern is that the economy of the United States could be influenced to some degree by financial bodies in which there has been heavy investment of money by drug cartels.[42] In Mexico alone, that figure has been estimated at $2.4 billion per year.[43] Virtually all of that money would have come from drug sales in the United States. The amount has become so critical to Mexico's economy that if it were to launch an intensive and efficient crackdown on the drug syndicates, it is possible that the drug cartels could suddenly yank their billions of dollars of laundered money from large corporations and banks into which it has been invested. The result could send the Mexican economy into a chaotic tailspin and create serious repercussions in international financial markets. How prolonged the effects would be is unknown since no one, except the cartels and their financial advisors, knows exactly how much of their money has become a vital part of the economies of both the United States and Mexico.

In January 1998, FBI Director Louis Freeh testified before the U.S. Congress that not only were the Mexican drug syndicates a major threat to the corruption of public security in the United States, but that the violent acts associated with the movement of drugs and arms posed a major threat to national security.[44]

Chapter 10

Conclusion

John Bailey and Roy Godson

GOVERNABILITY, as we have used the term, refers to
the ability of a government to allocate values over its society, to
exercise ultimate authority in the context of generally accepted
rules and procedures. In the Introduction we offered a set of criteria for governability: monopoly of legal coercion, administration of justice, administrative capacity, provision of minimum
public goods, and conflict management. *Democratic* governability adds the notion of procedures and guarantees: freely contested, periodic elections, with maximum feasible participation
of the citizenry, who enjoy basic rights including freedom of
speech and of assembly. In addition to the standard procedural
notions, our approach included Guillermo O'Donnell's emphasis
on institutions that ensure the accountability of chief executives
to courts and legislatures and that provide the administrative capacity for governments to carry out basic tasks, such as collecting taxes and enforcing the law.

The chapters herein were prepared by knowledgeable academic specialists and experienced U.S. and Mexican practition-
ers. We should recognize, however, that there are obstacles to
drawing firm conclusions. First, the contributors do not always
agree among themselves. Second, there are difficulties in obtaining reliable data on criminal organizations and their effects on
the political system. Not only do criminals try to hide their activities, which is to be expected, but law enforcement authorities
operate largely in secret as well, to protect their crime-control
operations and techniques, to hide their corrupt collusion with

criminals, or because of a traditional lack of transparency and oversight. Thus research on organized crime rests on much more tentative theoretical and empirical grounds than most "orthodox" subjects of analysis, such as public opinion or elections, and we need to be cautious about framing generalizations.

The research reported here is limited and preliminary, covering a small fraction of the empirical work that remains to be done. Further, most of the contributors emphasized crime related to drug trafficking, although several included broader notions as well. Emphasis on drug trafficking is useful in the sense that such crime generates enormous incomes and is involved in the most egregious cases of corruption. It has been arguably the most difficult bone of contention between the United States and Mexico since the mid-1980s. Even so, drug trafficking is but one of many manifestations of organized crime. The contributors did not develop at length the many other forms of organized crime (e.g., alien smuggling) and their various connections with different levels and activities of government. Finally, the time frame for the studies varied considerably, with most emphasizing the period from the mid-1980s to the mid-1990s.

With these caveats noted, the findings point to the hypothesis that organized crime has represented a significant challenge to democratic governability in Mexico. This is most clearly the case with respect to problems of law enforcement. There may have been other threats to democratic procedures, as for example with criminal involvement in campaign finance, but this is less clear. With regard to the United States, the threats were focused primarily on border control agencies. Even here the degree of the threat is unclear.

In the Introduction we sketched six broad images of the criminal-political nexus in Mexico and the borderlands. In the broadest sense, and with occasionally conflicting findings, the chapters seem to point toward Image IV (fragmented-contested political-criminal linkages) as a plausible hypothesis to describe the current relationship between organized crime and democratic governability in Mexico at least until the mid-1990s. With respect to the U.S. side of the borderlands, Image V (marginal, ad hoc corruption) seems a more useful depiction than Image VI (decentralized, targeted corruption), which portrays more intrusive and extensive forms of criminal penetration of law enforcement and other political institutions.

Beginning with administrative capacity, that is, the ability of government to implement policies and programs, none of the contributors emphasizes effective central control by the formal national government bureaucratic machinery over its field operations with respect to law enforcement (as suggested by the centralized-systemic Images II and III). The contributors suggest that important law enforcement offices may have been "sold" or "rented" by national-level authorities on a sort of "franchise" basis (e.g., the plaza system that Pimentel and Arzt describe) and that lower-level officials funneled payments upward through bureaucratic channels. The law enforcement chain of command could work effectively in certain instances. But this did not necessarily imply effective central control over field operations as a matter of standard practice.

Another image conveyed (e.g., by Molina, Pimentel, Arzt) suggests that poorly paid and inadequately trained law enforcement officers lacked the support and resources needed to carry out their assigned duties. The image depicts a political system, undergoing a difficult transition, that had not made the necessary investments in training and support. The system relied instead on a kind of "self-financing" law enforcement that facilitated corruption and abuse. The picture drawn by Arzt of the attorney general's office, where she worked in the mid-1990s, suggests problems of organization, resources, and procedures that resisted reform efforts. Nor, as Benitez describes, did the involvement of the military appear to resolve problems of coordination or efficacy in law enforcement. Arzt suggests that the military appeared not to subordinate themselves to civilian law enforcement officials but rather adhered to their established chain of command. Benitez depicts a military struggling to adapt itself to a political system undergoing important change and suffering the penetration of corruption that often accompanies antidrug law enforcement.

As to the nature of the criminal organizations and their subordination to political authorities, Pimentel suggests a significant change in the balance of power: criminal organizations in the 1990s came to confront law enforcement and political authorities, under certain circumstances. Molina, Mexico's antidrug "czar" in the mid-1990s, notes the ongoing struggles among drug trafficking gangs in northern Mexico to control routes and crossing points into the United States. Further, though this is implicit, we do not get a sense from Molina's account of the northern border area that the alternation from PRI to PAN governments, as in Chihuahua or Baja California Norte, made a significant difference in combating criminal organizations.

With regard to the geographic scope of criminal activity, the contributions were either imprecise about where criminal activities were concentrated or tended to locate them in the north of the country. Curzio's chapter, which included a case study of campaign finance in the southeastern Gulf state of Tabasco, was an exception. Astorga and Molina both paint images of mobile criminal groups moving internally within northern Mexico and connected with criminal organizations in the United States and South America.

Criminal organizations, the contributors maintain, focus most aggressively on the field operations of law enforcement agencies, the police at various levels, and the army. However, we lack reliable studies on whether there has been criminal penetration of other spheres of society, such as business and banking, labor unions, the church, or the mass media. Especially important to democratic governance are the vulnerabilities of the judicial system and the effects of money laundering on elections, banking, and business. With regard to the broader political system, Curzio suggests that electoral competition and campaign finance are targets of criminal penetration, and offers the case study of Tabasco to illustrate his point. But the case itself is ambiguous. We do not know the rationale for the alleged support by a corrupt banker for the PRI campaign in that state. Was the support extorted by the party? Was it offered in exchange for anticipated benefits? Or was the support the result of cronyism, with less concern about the precise exchanges involved? In his conclusion, Astorga suggests—but does not support—a scenario in which criminal groups might join in a coalition with hardline, antireform PRIistas in order to resist a democratic opening.

Most of the authors suggest that the situation is far from stable. They convey the sense that the criminal organizations operate on a variety of levels of activity and of organization and that new organizations are formed to replace those that are disbanded by government (e.g., Molina's remarks on the restructuring of the Juárez Cartel after 1997). This has been the pattern at least since the famous "Operation Condor" of the mid-1970s.[1] The contributors also describe ways in which the Mexican government attempted to strengthen its capacity to enforce the law. The public, however, remains skeptical. Few believe these efforts have yet to make important advances in controlling organized crime in Mexico. On the other hand, one could counter that the threats from organized crime could have been worse without the government's initiatives, that the results of recent reform efforts have yet to bear fruit, and that society was not yet ready to ally with government to combat crime and corruption.

Finally, it is also worth noting what the authors do *not* report. No one suggests a connection between criminal organizations and guerrilla groups such as the Zapatista Army of National Liberation (EZLN) or the Popular Revolutionary Army (ERP). Nor are linkages drawn between criminal groups and difficult political conflicts, such as the prolonged student strike at the National University of Mexico (1999–2000), or with terrorist organizations (in any event a marginal threat in Mexico's case). These "nonfindings" help put the Mexico case in perspective. Colombia, in contrast, has suffered much more serious threats from alliances between criminal organizations, guerrilla armies, and paramilitary forces fighting for control over extensive territories. Thus, the facile use of the metaphor of the "Colombianization of Mexico" in the 1990s is mistaken and misleading.

With respect to the U.S. side of the border, impressions are mixed, but the picture seems to support Image V ("marginal corruption"). Sadler, a veteran observer of the border, suggests that the problems of corruption in the U.S. border control agencies have been more serious than generally recognized. But he does not develop or support the point. Molina is also skeptical that the volumes and values of contraband that have crossed the border do not imply broader and more systematic corruption of U.S. agencies. But, again, he offers only an impression, albeit one held by a former attorney general of the State of Chihuahua, former antidrug "czar" at the national level, and a federal senator who chaired the committee responsible for oversight of Mexico's public security.

Castillo and Unger depict a situation in California in which the larger operations of drug trafficking (i.e., smuggling and wholesale distribution) are largely contained within relatively small groups in the Mexican immigrant and Mexican-American communities, whose complexity they take pains to clarify. Though their point will rankle sensibilities among some Mexicans, there is not—at least to our knowledge—independent, scholarly research that puts other actors at the center of these operations. Their description of the fluidity of organization and ease of entry into trafficking points more toward dispersed and fragmented criminal organizations in sporadic contact with U.S. and Mexican law enforcement than to a broader and more patterned penetration of judicial branches or state and local governments. At the same time they offer rather thin support for their suggestion that drug trafficking is reaching levels that may provoke such a harsh law enforcement reaction as to endanger civil liberties in the United States. Also, they do not provide the data to back up the claim that drug money laundered through the U.S. or Mexican banking system could provoke financial instability. Finally, we simply do not have a clear picture about whether the situation in the U.S. borderlands is becoming more or less stable.

In all, the various contributions serve best to point toward interesting hypotheses, stated in the form of images. With respect to the nature of the criminal-political nexus, Image IV seems useful to characterize Mexico in the mid-to-latter 1990s. As described in the Introduction (see Table 1.1), this image depicts segmented, fragmented, and opportunistic cooperation between criminals and some government officials (principally in law enforcement) at different levels of government and on an opportunistic basis. Image IV suggests incomplete control exercised by central bureaucracies over field operations. The complexity and weak control suggest that elected or appointed officials may or may not have been linked to criminal corruption. That is, criminal-political networks could have been "built around" specific officials. The image also emphasizes the fluidity, volatility, and conflicts that occurred within and between political authorities, law enforcement forces, and criminal organizations. Thus, in contrast to a centralized, hierarchical, and coherent pattern of government control over criminal groups (as suggested in Images II and III), the findings point more toward fragmented-contested political-criminal linkages in the 1980s and 1990s.

Image V, marginal corruption, is suggestive for the U.S. borderlands during that period. As summarized in Table 1.2, the image suggests that criminal penetration of U.S. law enforcement or judicial agencies was occasional, but there were U.S. officials in the border region, acting alone or in small groups, collaborating with Mexican and U.S. criminals. However, corruption was not widespread in law enforcement or border control agencies and did not reach into the judiciary or local elected officials, at least in a systematic way.

In sum, the contributors, U.S. and Mexican alike, conclude that organized crime's involvement with the political system at various levels significantly threatened public security and democratic government in Mexico into the mid-1990s. They suggest as well that threats to U.S. law enforcement and border control agencies may have been more serious than generally recognized. The contributors were not asked to couch their studies in policy-relevant terms or to devise "solutions" to the challenges they described and attempted to explain.[2] But it is reasonable to conclude from their contributions that they did not believe there was a "quick fix" to the deep-rooted problems they were addressing. Although they either directly or indirectly placed the primary burden of responding to the threat on the political establishment, and particularly on the central government, it should not be inferred that they believe that government alone can shoulder the entire burden. There would appear to be an important role for civil society as well. Regulatory and law enforcement responses, combined with societal and cultural change, will not come easily or quickly. Optimists will trust that creative and courageous leadership on both sides of the border now have recognized the profound nature of the challenge and will promote well-designed institutional and cultural change. Others may caution that solutions to deeply ingrained problems require time, resources, political will, and persistence to show significant results.

Notes

Chapter 1: Introduction

1. Five events since 1982 put Mexico's governability to the test: (1) Mexico's virtual default on its foreign debt in August 1982 and the subsequent prolonged recession; (2) the split in the governing party in 1987 and subsequent electoral fraud in the presidential elections of 1988; (3) the Zapatista rebellion of January 1994, which projected peasant violence into a difficult regional and national political situation; (4) a series of assassinations of high-level political and religious leaders in 1993 and 1994; and (5) the peso crisis of December 1994, which brought the most severe recession since the Great Depression of the 1930s.

2. See, for example, Andres Oppenheimer, *Bordering on Chaos* (Boston: Little, Brown and Co., 1996); Sebastian Rotella, *Twilight on the Line* (New York: W. W. Norton, 1998); Oscar Martinez, *Border People* (Tucson: University of Arizona Press, 1994); Carlos Fuentes, *The Crystal Frontier* (New York: Farrar, Strauss and Giroux, 1997).

3. Rafael Perl, in "United States Foreign Narcopolicy: Shifting Focus to International Crime?" *Transnational Organized Crime* 1:1 (Spring 1995), 38, provides several general reasons for the shift to focus on international crime: a decline in public concern about drug use, a tendency to subordinate drugs to other issues, a shift from unilateral to multilateral measures, and an increased focus on drug gangs for nondrug reasons. For a view that suggests that the threat of organized crime has been exaggerated, see R. T. Naylor, "From Cold War to Crime War: The Search for a New 'National Security' Threat," ibid. 1:4 (Winter 1995), 37–56. In Mexico's case, the concern about drug trafficking as a national security matter, which appears in the Miguel de la Madrid administration (1982–1988) and is formalized in various ways in the Carlos Salinas government (1988–1994), is expanded under Ernesto Zedillo to encompass organized crime more generally, as seen in his national plan for 1995–2000.

4. Paul Buchanan, for example, notes that "primary to the current U.S. strategic vision on the hemisphere is a concern with the prevalence of narcotrafficking, arms dealing, and other trans-national criminal en-

terprise, as well as the larger socioeconomic problems that are the root causes of national instability. . . . More insidiously, from a long-term perspective, these [criminal] organizations are increasingly capable of exercising a dominant voice in national and regional politics." Paul Buchanan, "Chameleon, Tortoise, or Toad: The Changing U.S. Security Role in Contemporary Latin America," in Jorge I. Dominguez, ed., *International Security and Diplomacy: Latin American and the Caribbean in the Post-Cold War Era* (Pittsburgh: University of Pittsburgh Press, 1998), 274.

5. See Peter A. Lupsha, "Transnational Narco-Corruption and Narco Investment: A Focus on Mexico," *Transnational Organized Crime* 1:1 (Spring 1995), 84–101.

6. Shadow government interpretations are a staple of Mexican fiction. See, for example, Hector Aguilar Camin, *Morir en el golfo* (Barcelona: Circe, 1988); and Carlos Fuentes, *The Hydrahead* (New York: Farrar, Strauss and Giroux, 1978).

7. This image broadly coincides with the interpretation offered by the Instituto Mexicano de Estudios de la Criminalidad Organizada, *Todo lo que deberia saber sobre el crimen organizado en Mexico* (Mexico, D.F.: Oceano, 1998).

8. See John Bailey and Sergio Aguayo, eds., *Strategy and Security in U.S.-Mexican Relations: Beyond the Cold War* (University of California-San Diego, Center for U.S.-Mexican Studies, 1996). A third project is under way to consider the policy implications of crime and insecurity for Mexico and the United States.

9. The definition draws on Roy Godson and William J. Olson, *International Organized Crime: Emerging Threat to U.S. Security* (Washington, D.C.: National Strategy Information Center, 1993), 4; Phil Williams, "The Nature of Drug Trafficking Networks," *Current History* (April 1998), 154–59.

10. Peter A. Lupsha, "Transnational Organized Crime and the Nation-State," *Transnational Organized Crime* 2:1 (Spring 1996), 21, "prefers the capstone term, 'Transnational Organized Crime,' which not only stresses the cross-national jurisdictional and 'organized' nature of modern crime groups, but also the transnational character of their activities."

11. Jorge Fernandez Menendez, *Narcotrafico y poder* (Mexico, D.F.: Rayuela, 1999), 43–48 and passim, discusses third country–based organized crime groups operating in Mexico and the United States.

12. This notion of legitimate coercion fits in Weber's category of "legal domination." See Reinhard Bendix, *Max Weber: An Intellectual Portrait* (Garden City, N.Y.: Anchor Books, 1962), 290–97.

13. Regulatory effectiveness is a key component of administrative capacity. To what extent are market transactions regulated by public law? One might argue that gray markets or the informal economy can be functional for governability in a variety of ways, e.g., by providing employment at wages that do not meet the legal minimum or by providing shortcuts around burdensome regulations. But at some point the growth of the informal economy can undermine governability in a number of ways: e.g., tax income is lost, unsafe practices go unchecked, incentives for legitimate businesses to pay taxes and obey regulations are reduced, informal markets provide large-scale outlets to sell stolen or smuggled

merchandise. Market transactions also require notions of property, titles, and contracts enforced by public agencies in ways that are predictable. A weak regulatory regime foments criminal activity.

14. For an interesting discussion of how criminal groups can challenge and even supplant legal authorities see Elizabeth Leeds, "Cocaine and Parallel Polities in the Brazilian Urban Periphery: Constraints on Local-Level Democratization," *Latin American Research Review* 31:3 (1996), 47–83.

15. The reader will note the obvious influence here of Samuel Huntington, *Political Order in Changing Societies* (New Haven: Yale University Press, 1968), in which institutions play a central role, and of Max Weber's discussion of legitimacy formulas as cited in note 12 above.

16. Samuel Huntington, "The Modest Meaning of Democracy," in Robert Pastor, ed., *Democracy in the Americas: Stopping the Pendulum* (New York: Holmes & Meier, 1989), 11–28.

17. Guillermo O'Donnell, "Delegative Democracy," *Journal of Democracy* 5:1 (January 1994), 55–69. Cases that fit O'Donnell's notion of delegative democracy might include Argentina under Menem, Peru under Fujimori, Russia under Yeltsin, Brazil under Collor, and Mexico under Salinas.

18. Lorenzo Meyer discusses these issues in a dissent to Huntington's "modest meaning" of democracy. See Lorenzo Meyer, "Democracy from Three Latin American Perspectives," in Pastor, ed., *Democracy in the Americas*, 29–38.

19. This paragraph draws on Stephan Haggard and Robert R. Kaufman, "The Challenges of Consolidation," in Larry Diamond and Marc F. Plattner, eds., *Economic Reform and Democracy* (Baltimore and London: The Johns Hopkins University Press, 1995), 1–12.

20. A good discussion is found in Moises Naim, "Latin America: The Second Stage of Reform," in Diamond & Plattner, eds., *Economic Reform and Democracy*, 28–44.

21. Sidney Weintraub, *NAFTA at Three: A Progress Report* (Washington, D.C.: Center for Strategic and International Studies, 1997) provides a useful recent assessment of economic reforms.

22. The literature on Mexico's dual transition is extensive. Maria L. Cook et al., eds., *The Politics of Economic Restructuring: State-Society Relations and Regime Change in Mexico* (La Jolla, California: UCSD Center for U.S.-Mexican Studies, 1994) is a useful collection. For a discussion of the reform agenda in the wake of the 1997 midterm elections, see John Bailey and Arturo Valenzuela, "Mexico's New Politics: The Shape of the Future," *Journal of Democracy* 8:4 (October 1997).

23. Sergio Zermeño, *La sociedad derrotada: el desorden mexicano del fin de siglo* (Mexico, D.F.: Siglo XXI, 1996), 11 and passim.

24. Secretaría de Gobernación, *Public Security and the New Strategy against Drug-Trafficking* (Mimeograph, February 15, 1999), 1.

25. Rafael Ruiz Harrell, "Seguridad Publica: La impunidad y la ineptitud," *Reforma (Enfoque)*, March 29, 1999 (Internet edition).

26. Ibid. In 1996, only 2.46 percent of the crimes reported resulted in convictions.

27. "Alarmantes indices de criminalidad en el pais; 5,700 delitos diariamente: ALDF," *Excelsior*, April 2, 1997 (Internet).

28. Reports of armed battles between criminals and police are not infrequent. In the northwestern state of Durango, for example, drug traffickers reportedly attacked the city hall of San Dimas, then occupied the town for a week and fought off state police, retreating only when the Mexican army arrived. The mayor and a state legislator declared, "Today nobody wants to serve as chief of police or city councillor in this area because of fear of violence." Ten persons had been murdered in the town in drug-related crimes in the first two months of 1999. "Regarding the wave of assaults and robberies against persons and institutions (six armed robberies of Diconsa [a government food agency] and three kidnappings), they noted that insecurity permeates the lives of the 200,000 people in the area." "Narcotraficantes Ocuparon Durante Toda una Semana un Pueblo en Durango," *Excelsior*, February 20, 1999 (Internet edition).

29. Former Mexican Attorney General Antonio Lozano Gracia has given several estimates of the seriousness of corruption in the Federal Judicial Police. In a talk at Georgetown University on April 14, 1998, he stated that corruption affected approximately 70 percent of the officers. Tim Golden provides an extensive report on corruption in the army, "U.S. Officials Say Mexican Military Aids Drug Traffic," *New York Times*, March 26, 1998, A1, 6.

30. An important test of administrative control over police came with the arrival of the opposition-party government of Cuauhtemoc Cardenas in the Federal District in December 1998. Cardenas had campaigned on an anticrime platform and for civilian control over the police. The response was a kind of "police strike" and a marked upsurge of crime. See Julia Preston, "In Defiance of Reforms, Crime Rises in Mexico City," *New York Times*, November 17, 1998 (Internet edition). The new civilian police chief, Alejandro Gertz, subsequently struggled to gain control through a kind of emergency program. See Jose Galan, "Aplica la SSP plan de emergencia para el control de 37 mil policias," *La Jornada*, March 2, 1999 (Internet edition). For a useful policy-oriented discussion of the judiciary, see Hector Fix Fierro, ed., *A la puerta de la ley: El estado de derecho en Mexico* (Mexico City: Cal y Arena, 1994). As to criminal impunity, a recent study of the Federal District estimated that the percentage chances of delinquents actually being detained for an offense in 1997 was approximately 0.0128, or about 13 detentions for every 1,000 crimes. See Guillermo Zepeda Lecuona, "Delincuencia: Fachada reformadora y los sotanos de la impunidad," *Revista del Senado de la Republica* 4:11 (abril–junio 1998), 6.

31. Interior secretary Fernando Labastida requested a 1999 appropriation of just over 8.2 billion pesos (about U.S.$891 million at the April 1999 exchange rate), or 320 percent over the 1998 level. "Piden cuadruplicar gasto en seguridad," *Reforma*, November 15, 1998 (Internet edition).

32. This is because the electorate's main concern—as reflected in opinion surveys—is street-level insecurity, and a democratic response to public opinion might focus police and

judicial efforts against common crime, leaving larger-scale, organized crime relatively unaffected.

33. "Encuesta/Narcotrafico: Importante, no prioritario," *Reforma*, March 10, 1998 (Internet edition). A more perverse implication may be that organized criminal groups might foment common crime (or even insurrection) to deflect attention from their own activities. Or, alternatively, the larger, better-organized criminal groups might assist police in controlling street crime as part of a tacit or explicit pact of mutual support.

34. This sort of hierarchical division of labor is depicted in the case of the border by Rotella, *Twilight on the Line*.

35. See Fernandez Menendez, *Narcotrafico y poder*, 49; IMECO, *Todo lo que deberia saber*, 63–64; Sergio Aguayo, "Intelligence Services and the Transition to Democracy in Mexico," in Bailey and Aguayo Quezada, eds., *Strategy and Security in U.S.-Mexican Relations*, 145–48.

36. IMECO, *Todo lo que deberia saber*, can be read as an elaboration of Image IV.

37. To illustrate Image V, an anticorruption task force involving federal, state, and local agencies arrested three agents of the Immigration and Naturalization Service (INS). Based in Nogales, Arizona, the three were accused of accepting bribes to help smuggle some 20 tons of cocaine into Arizona. Pertinent to Image V, "Authorities said the border inspectors operated independently and apparently were unaware of each other's activities." Dennis Wagner, "Bribes Snare Border Agents," *The Arizona Republic*, February 3, 1999, 1.

38. "Crackdown on Corruption," *Washington Post*, April 5, 1999, A15, reports: "The U.S. Customs Service, faced with concerns that its inspectors are increasingly vulnerable to bribes by drug smugglers, plans to make the fight against corruption a priority for agency officials. . . . A recent Treasury Department review found no evidence of systematic corruption in the Customs Service but said 'individual acts of corruption have occurred and continue to occur.'"

39. U.S. police emphasize the role of foreign-based criminal organizations and ethnic ties among drug distribution groups within the United States. DEA Administrator Thomas Constantine recently stated, "Unlike the American organized crime leaders, organized crime figures in Mexico have at their disposal an army of personnel, an arsenal of weapons and the finest technology that money can buy. They literally run transportation and financial empires, and an insight into how they conduct their day-to-day business leads even the casual observer to the conclusion that the United States is facing a threat of unprecedented proportions and gravity." Remarks before the Senate Caucus on International Narcotics Control regarding United States and Mexico Counterdrug Efforts, Washington, D.C., February 24, 1999.

Chapter 2: The Nexus of Organized Crime and Politics in Mexico

1. I wish to express my gratitude to Peter A. Lupsha, Professor Emeritus, University of New Mexico, for the theoretical framework employed here. I would also like to thank many current and former members of the Mexican government, who do not wish to be identi-

fied, and who gave of their time and expertise to assist in this project. I have relied particularly on three sources in this chapter who have provided reliable information in the past, and are well placed in the system. To the extent possible, their information has been corroborated by others.

2. A. Curtis Wilgus and Raul D'Eca, *Latin American History* (New York: Barnes & Noble, 1963), 3.

3. Ibid., 67. To this day, many of Mexico's government agencies continue to have a "visitor-general," a sort of "inspector general," to report irregularities to the cabinet minister; but sometimes the person in this position acts more like the hatchet man for the superior.

4. Ibid., 67–73.

5. Ibid., 115.

6. Hubert Herring, *A History of Latin America* (New York: Alfred A. Knopf, 1962), 300–302.

7. Ibid., 372–73.

8. Roberto Blum, "Corruption and Complicity: Mortar of Mexico's Political System?" (Institute for Contemporary Studies, National Strategy Information Center, Hacienda San Antonio, Mexico, 1997), 8.

9. Demetrio Sodi de la Tijera, "1997, The Year of the Democratic Change," *El Universal* (Mexico City), January 3, 1997. (Unless otherwise noted, I am responsible for all translations from Spanish.)

10. Alan Riding, *Distant Neighbors* (New York: Vintage Books, 1989), 91.

11. Ibid., 95.

12. Ibid., 77.

13. Peter A. Lupsha, "Transnational Organized Crime versus the Nation-State" in *Transnational Organized Crime* 2:1 (Spring 1996), 21–48. Also see chapter appendix for a further comparison of these two models of organized crime provided by Lupsha.

14. Peter A. Lupsha and Stanley A. Pimentel, *Political-Criminal Nexus* (Washington, D.C.: Institute for Contemporary Studies, National Strategy Information Center, Hacienda San Antonio, Mexico, 1997).

15. Ibid., 8–9.

16. Ibid., 9–10.

17. Yolanda Figueroa, *El Capo del Golfo* (Mexico D. F.: Editorial Grijalbo, 1997), 71.

18. Riding, 27.

19. Luis Astorga, "Crimen Organizado y Organizacion del Crimen" (Mexico D.F.: Instituto de Investigaciones Sociales de la Universidad Nacional Autonoma de Mexico, 1998), 6–7.

20. Luis Astorga, *El Siglo de las Drogas* (Mexico D.F., Espasa-Calpe, 1996), 81.

21. Peter A. Lupsha, "Drug Lords and Narco-Corruption: The Players Change but the Game Continues," Reprinted from *War on Drugs* (Boulder: Westview Press, 1992), 179;

quoting Terrance E. Poppa, *Drug Lord: The Life and Death of a Mexican Kingpin* (New York: Pharos Books, 1990), 41–42.

22. Luis Astorga, *El Siglo*, 161.

23. Peter Lupsha, "Drug Lords," 180, quoting from *Proceso*, a Mexico City weekly magazine.

24. Ibid., 180–81, quoting from *Proceso* (August 5, 1985) and *Penthouse* magazine (December 1989).

25. Ibid., 183; quoting from Rogelio Hernandez, *Zorrilla: El Imperio del Crimen* (Mexico City: Editorial Planeta, 1989).

26. Ibid., 188.

27. Carlos Marin, "Military Intelligence Documents Entangle High Ranking Chiefs, Officers and Army Troops in Narcotics Trafficking," *Proceso*, no. 1082 (July 27, 1997), 19.

28. Figueroa, 69.

29. The commander was fired by Attorney General F. Antonio Lozano Gracia in September 1996.

30. Figueroa, 137.

31. Astorga, *El Siglo*, 166.

32. Lupsha, "Drug Lords," 182.

33. Astorga, "Crimen Organizado," 8.

34. Peter H. Smith, *Drug Trafficking in Mexico* (Washington D.C.: Institute for Contemporary Studies, National Strategy Information Center, 1996), 14–16.

35. J. Jesus Blancornelas, *Una Vez, Nada Mas* (Mexico D. F.: Editorial Oceano, 1997), 143.

36. Andres Oppenheimer, *Bordering on Chaos* (New York: Little, Brown & Co., 1996), 301.

37. Riding, 114.

38. Blum, 12.

39. Sodi de la Tijera, "Power Vacuum," *El Universal* (Mexico City), January 2, 1998.

40. This legislation was passed as the Federal Law against Organized Crime in November 1996.

41. This program was launched as the "National Crusade against Delinquency" in October 1998, including legislation establishing the Federal Preventive Police.

42. Oppenheimer, 318.

Chapter 3: Organized Crime and the Organization of Crime

1. Louis J. Freeh, Statement before the Senate Appropriations Committee, Subcommittee on Foreign Operations, Hearing on International Crime, March 12, 1996; *Federal Law against Organized Crime, Official Journal*, November 7, 1996.

2. General Records of the Department of State, Record Group 59, 812.114 Narcotics/12–22, U.S. National Archives II, College Park, Maryland; Joseph Richard Werne, "Esteban Cantú y la soberania mexicana en Baja California," in *Historia Mexicana* 117:30, (July–September 1980), 1–32.

3. Daniel D. Arreola and James R. Curtis, *The Mexican Border Cities* (Tucson: University of Arizona Press, 1993), 102.

4. Report by Dr. Bernardo Bátiz, Health Officer in Baja California, to Dr. Rafael Silva, head of Department of Public Health, Mexicali, B.C., May 18, 1931, in the Archives of the Secretariat of Health (ASS), Public Health Fund (FSP), Legal Services Section (SSJ), Box 26, File 16.

5. Letter from Dr. Rafael Silva, head of Department of Health, to Carlos Trejo y Lerdo de Tejada, Governor of the Northern District of Baja California, Mexico City, July 13, 1931, in ASS, FSP, SSJ, Box 28, File 8.

6. Confidential memorandum sent by Francisco Vázquez Pérez, head of Legal Services of Department of Health, to Dr. Rafael Silva, head of Department of Health, Mexico City, September 4, 1931, in ASS, FSP, SSJ, Box 28, File 28.

7. Report by Dr. Bernardo Bátiz B., health officer in Baja California, to Dr. Demetrio López, head of Service of Chemistry and Pharmaceuticals of the Department of Health, Mexicali, B.C., August 19, 1931, in ASS, FSP, SSJ, Box 28, File 8.

8. Alfred W. McCoy, *The Politics of Heroin: CIA Complicity in the Global Drug Trade* (Chicago: Lawrence Hill Books, 1991).

9. *Novedades*, May 14, 1962.

10. Harry J. Anslinger and William F. Tompkins, *The Traffic in Narcotics* (New York: Arno Press, 1981), 152–53; *El Diario de Culiacán*, April 1, 1949; *La Voz de Sinaloa*, November 23, 1951; *El Universal*, March 18, 1958. For a more detailed account of the relationship between Siegel and Virginia Hill and their role in drug trafficking in Mexico, see Ed Reid, *La Bella y la Mafia* (Mexico: Editorial Diana, 1973).

11. Letter to General D. Eulogio Ortiz, head of Operations of the State of Chihuahua, undated, in ASS, FSP, SSJ, Box 28, File 6.

12. Report of Juan N. Requena to the head of Department of Public Health, Mexico City, July 20, 1931, in ASS, FSP, SSJ, Box 28, File 6.

13. Letter sent by Dr. Alberto Jacqueminot, federal health officer, to General Enrique Zertuche González, Jefe de la Guarnición de la Plaza, Ciudad Juárez, Chihuahua, May 28, 1931, in ASS, FSP, SSJ, Box 28, File 6.

14. Telegram from Dr. Ulises Valdés, Secretary General of Health, to Juan N. Requena, Mexico City, June 2, 1931: Letter 25/12348 sent by Dr. Demetrio López, head of the Service of Chemistry and Pharmaceuticals, to Juan N. Requena, Mexico City, June 4, 1931, in ASS, FSP, SSJ, Box 28, File 6.

15. Confidential memorandum, Department of Public Health, Mexico City, June 16, 1931, in ASS, FSP, SSJ, Box 28, File 6.

16. Report by Juan N. Requena to the head of Department of Public Health, Mexico City, July 20, 1931, in ASS, FSP, SSJ, Box 28, File 6.

17. Ibid.

18. *El Universal Gráfico* (evening edition), December 16, 1937.

19. *La Prensa*, May 9, 1936.

20. *El Universal Gráfico* (evening edition), November 9, 17, 23, 1937; December 14, 16, 27, 1937; January 13, 26, 1938.

21. *El Universal*, February 28, 1937.

22. *Excélsior*, November 14, 1947; *El Universal*, November 16, 1947; *Ultimas Noticias*, November 17–19, 1947; December 26, 1947.

23. Luis Astorga, *El siglo de las drogas* (Mexico: Espasa-Calpe Mexicana, 1996), 68–79.

24. *La Voz de Sinaloa*, November 8, 10, 1947; *Excélsior*, November 8–12, 1947.

25. *La Voz de Sinaloa*, February 12, 1948; June 19, 1948.

26. General Records of the Department of State, "Report of the Assistant Military Attaché on the National Security Police of Mexico" (confidential no. 4543), Embassy of the United States of America, Mexico City, September 4, 1947. Record Group 59, 812.105/ 9–447, U.S. National Archives II, College Park, Maryland.

27. Elaine Shannon, *Desperados* (New York: Viking, 1988), 186–88. Operation Condor officially began in mid-January 1977; however, it began unofficially at the beginning of 1975. It was announced as "the largest raid ever on drug trafficking in Mexico (Northwest), with the participation of 10,000 soldiers." It was headed by General José Hernández Toledo of the army and Carlos Aguilar Garza, of the PGR. The general was a veteran of the Tlatelolco student massacres in 1968 and the crackdown on universities, such as UNAM, Nicolaíta in Morelia, and the University of Sonora in Hermosillo. Aguilar later had a stormy career as a drug trafficker, until his assassination in 1993. The results of the military raids include the destruction of drug plantations using nonecological chemical defoliants, the exodus of mountain-dwelling campesinos to the cities, human rights violations, and the temporary displacement of crops and traffickers to other regions of the country (see Luis Astorga, *El siglo*, 119–26).

28. "America's Habit: Drug Abuse, Drug Trafficking, and Organized Crime," President's Commission on Organized Crime, 1986, chap. 3, part 1; Mora Stephens, "Global Organized Crime," Woodrow Wilson School Policy Conference 401A, Intelligence Reform in the Post–Cold War Era, January 6, 1996.

29. *La Voz de Sinaloa*, June 11, 12, 18, 1969, July 8, 1969; *Noroeste*, March 3, 26, 1977.

30. Manuel Lazcano Ochoa, *Una vida en la vida sinaloense* (Los Mochis, Sinaloa: Talleres Gráficos de la Universidad de Occidente, 1992, 226.

31. Terrence E. Poppa, *El zar de la droga* (Mexico: Selector, 1990).

32. Ibid., 277–94.

33. Shannon, *Desperados*, 418–19.

34. *La Jornada*, September 23, 1994, March 29, 1995; *Proceso*, March 13, 1995.

35. Eduardo Valle, *El segundo disparo* (Mexico: Océano, 1995), 131.

36. *La Jornada*, January 18, 1996.

37. *La Jornada*, February 19, 1997.

38. Roy Godson, "Threats to U.S.-Mexican Border Security." Testimony before the Committee on the Judiciary, Subcommittee on Immigration and Claims, U.S. House of Representatives, April 23, 1997, 5.

39. *Reforma*, July 8, 11, 15, 1997; *El Financiero*, July 6, 1997; *Miami Herald*, September 9, 1997.

40. In the end of 1995, a little more than a month after U.S. Secretary of Defense William Perry's visit to Mexico, and his announcement (which he later denied) that the armies of both countries would work together, a plan to replace the police forces with the military was instituted in Chihuaha. More than 100 military troops were incorporated into the Federal Judicial Police (PJF) based in Chihuaha. On December 13, 1996, the head of PGR, Jorge Madrazo, named Generals Guillermo Alvarz Nara and Tito Valencia Ortiz as directors of the PJF and of the Planning Center to Combat Drugs (CENDRO), respectively. Days before, General Jesús Gutiérrez had been named to direct the National Institute to Combat Drugs (INCD). The justification was that the honor and discipline of the military would impede the dangerous relations developing between federal agents and traffickers. Francisco Molina Ruiz, head of the INCD from March to December of 1996, summed up the situation in an interview: "The Army, in an assault, captured the PGR, the INCD, the CENDRO, 23 of the 35 national airports and all of regional offices of the PGR on the Northern border." *Proceso*, January 8, 1996; June 12, 1997; August 3, 1997; *La Jornada*, December 14, 1996.

Chapter 4: Organized Crime and Political Campaign Finance in Mexico

1. Klaus Von Beyme, *La clase política en el Estado de Partidos* (Madrid: Alianza Universidad, 1995), 63ff.

2. See, e.g., Khaygam Z. Paltiel, "Financiación de partidos político," in *Enciclopedia (Blakwell) de las instituciones políticas* (1991); Michael J. Malbin, *Parties, Interest Groups and Campaign Finance Laws* (Washington, D.C.: American Enterprise Institute for Public Policy Research, 1980). In these two texts, ranging from a general article to a detailed debate in the North American case, the possibility of infiltration of organized crime in campaign financing is not contemplated.

3. The first experience with public financing of political parties was the Puerto Rican of 1957 and had as its main objective to preclude the possibility of disloyal competition from candidates supported by powerful interest groups from the sugar industry. See Manuel Barquin, "El financiamiento de los partidos políticos en México en la reforma de 1993," in *La voz de los votos: Un análisis crítico de las elecciones de 1994*, eds. German Perez, Arturo Alvarado, and Arturo Sanchez (Mexico City: Miguel Angel Porrúa-FLACSO, 1995).

4. Peter Lupsha, "Transnational Organized Crime versus the Nation State," in *Transnational Organized Crime* Vol. 2, No. 1 (Spring 1996), pp. 21–48. Quote is from pp. 23–24.

5. Even in countries where the traditional link between organized crime and the political system exists, the political-criminal nexus tends to remain invisible. See Letizia Paoli, "The Political-Criminal Nexus in Italy or Mafia and Politics in Italy" (mimeograph), 1997.

6. The first statistic is from *Information technologies for the control of money laundering* (Washington, D.C.: Office of Technology Assessment, Congress of the United States, 1995). The second (US$500 billion) is suggested by William McLucas, "Global Financial Systems

under Assault: Countering the 500 Billion Conspiracy," in *Global Organized Crime* (Washington, D.C.: CSIS, 1994), 15.

7. Robert S. Leiken, "Controlling the Global Corruption Epidemic," in *Foreign Policy,* No. 105 (December 1996–1997), 55–73.

8. Jean Marie Pontaut, "L'argent du crime," in *L'Express,* October 7, 1997, 42–45.

9. Eduardo Valle, *El segundo disparo: La narcodemocracia mexicana* (Mexico City: Océano, 1995).

10. Silvano Paternostro, "Mexico as a narcodemocracy," *World Policy Journal,* Vol. 12, No. 1 (Spring 1995), 41–47. The article was reprinted in *Trends in Organized Crime,* Vol. 1, No. 1 (Fall 1995), 33.

11. Executive Office of the President, Office of National Drug Control Policy, "United States and Mexico Counterdrug Cooperation: Report to Congress," Washington, D.C., September 1997. Also see Observatoire Geopolitique des Drogues, *Atlas Mondial des Drogues* (Paris: PUF, 1996), 84–86.

12. In the strategies and action plans proposed by Ernesto Zedillo to guarantee Mexico's national security: "To coordinate the departments and agencies under federal Public Ad ministration and those of the states of the Federation in their relations with other nations. In particular, to ensure the unity of criteria in the fight against modern threats to national security: drug trafficking, money laundering, arms-trafficking and terrorism." Poder Ejecutivo Federal, "Plan Nacional de Desarrollo 1995–2000," Mexico City, 1995, 10.

13. In his third Informe de Gobierno, Ernesto Zedillo explained the situation in the following manner: "The Government of Mexico attributes special importance to international cooperation in the fight against narco-trafficking since it is a phenomenon with global reach . . . In the multilateral environment, Mexico subscribed to the Twentieth Century Anti-narcotics Strategy in the framework of the OAS-CICAD. Likewise, Mexico promoted the calling of an extraordinary session of the General Assembly of the United Nations, in 1998, to examine and promote a global focus against narco-trafficking, which represents a grave danger for humanity at the end of the twentieth century." Poder Ejecutivo Federal, "Tercer Informe de Gobierno," Mexico City, 1997, 31.

14. *Reforma,* February 16, 1998, 1. In political terms, other governors of the state of Jalisco have also been implicated in situations somehow related to narco-trafficking. Such is the case of Guillermo Cosío Vidaurrí. See the statements of the PAN Representative, Fernando Pérez Noriega, who, incidentally, headed the Justice Commission in the Chamber of Deputies (Comisión de Justicia de la Cámara de Diputados) in the case of the ex-governor. *El Financiero,* January 11, 1996, 38.

15. For an overview of the period, see Jorge Chabat, "Seguridad nacional y narcotráfico: Vínculos reales e imaginarios," in *Política y Gobierno,* 1:1 (Mexico City: CIDE, 1994).

16. Roy Godson and W. Olson, *International Organized Crime: Emerging Threat to U.S. Security* (Washington, D.C.: National Strategy Information Center, 1993), 29.

17. Jorge Tello Peon, "El control del narcotráfico: operaciones estratégicas e intereses nacionales de México y Estados Unidos en el período posterior a la guerra fría," in Sergio

Aguayo and John Bailey, eds., *Las seguridades de México y Estados Unidos en un momento de transición* (Mexico: Siglo XXI, 1997), 169.

18. "Entrevista de Francisco Garfías, con Jorge Carpizo," *Excelsior*, March 21, 1997, 1.

19. See the investigation by José Alberto Villasana, "Caso Posadas: Las injerencias del FBI," *Reforma*, February 7, 1998, 6.

20. In the cited report on the bilateral battle against drugs, the North American Anti-Narcotics Office presented the case of Raúl Salinas in the following manner: "Hacienda has announced that it has opened 27 money laundering cases since May 1997, and the Government of Mexico presented one complaint under the 1996 money laundering law against Raúl Salinas. Unfortunately the Salinas case was dismissed, raising further concerns regarding the status of prosecutions in Mexico. In the Salinas case a federal judge ruled that the money laundering charges could not be brought against Salinas without his first being convicted for the underlying predicate offense, in this case illicit enrichment." Executive Office of the President, Office of National Drug Control Policy, "United States and Mexico Counterdrug Cooperation. Report to Congress." Washington, D.C., September 1997, 34.

21. Representing the Mexican government, Jorge Madrazo, Attorney General of the Republic (Procurador General de la República), announced, in official communique number, PGR 335/95, dated May 29, 1997, to the Ministry of Justice and Grace (Ministerio de Justicia y Gracia) of Costa Rica that Carlos Hank González was not the subject of any investigation in Mexico. The letter was the answer that the Mexican Attorney General gave to the request from Fairid Beiurute Brenes, the Attorney General of Costa Rica, which stated: "El Gobierno de la República de Costa Rica, a través de su Ministro de Justicia y Gracia, Licdo. Juan Diego Castro Fernández, ha solicitado a esta representación estatal interponer sus oficios ante su excelentísima autoridad, con el propósito de que se proporcione a la Procuraduría General de nuestro país [Costa Rica] toda la información que tramita su despacho relativa al ciudadano mexicano Carlos Hank González." See the report by Celia Garcia Flores that reproduces the fascimiles of the letters in *El Financiero*, June 14, 1997, 20–21.

22. *El Economista*, June 25, 1997.

23. Keep in mind, as a complementary detail, that Costa Rica is known as one of the money laundering paradises. André Chauvett, *La experiencia francesa y la movilización internacional en la lucha contra el lavado de dinero* (Mexico City: Servicio de cooperación técnica internacional de la Policía francesa en México, 1996), 248.

24. *El Financiero*, June 14, 1997, 1, 20. In the Costa Rican press, various accounts appeared which linked Hank with illegal activities. See the Costa Rican daily *La Nación*, June 28, 1997, 8a.

25. *Reforma*, June 17, 1997.

26. Jorge Chabat, "Seguridad nacional y narcotráfico."

27. The absence of fairness in the electoral process was the primary focus in the debate over the elections in 1994. According to top-level internal advisors at IFE, it was without a doubt "that the presidential election of August 21, 1994 was profoundly inequitable." *La Jornada*, April 8, 1995.

28. Oscar Hinojosa, "Partidos políticos, financiamiento público, privado y secreto," in Jorge Alcocer and Rodrigo Morales, coordinators, *La organización de las elecciones* (Mexico City: CIIH-Miguel Angel Porrúa, 1994), 80.

29. The change in power is producing detailed information about the support that the PRI secretly received from the government. A recent example is that in the Federal District, the PRI occupied 23 buildings that were property of the district government. In March 1997, when the polls favored Cuauhtémoc Cárdenas of the PRD, the district government established a legal institution called temporary loan, revokable after 10 years. However, in reality, the PRI has occupied the buildings for many years. *Reforma*, February 9, 1998, B-1.

30. Jaime Rivera, "Michoacán 92: La historia sin fin," in Jorge Alonso and Jorge Tamayo, *Elecciones con alternativas* (Mexico: CIIH-La Jornada, 1994), 153.

31. Instituto Federal Electoral, *Memoria del proceso electoral federal* (Mexico City: IFE, 1994), 233–48.

32. Martín Moreno, "Los dineros de PRI," *Epoca*, August 24, 1995, 10.

33. Ibid.

34. Andrés Oppenhcimcr, *México en la frontera del caos* (Mexico City: Javier Vergara, 1996). See the chapter titled "El banquete," 95–121. See also Rafael de Rodriguez Castañeda, "Borrego, 29 magnates y el Presidente de la República . . ." in *Proceso*, No. 853 (March 8, 1993), 6–9.

35. Octavio Paz, "Reestablecer la credibilidad," in *Proceso*, No. 854 (March 15, 1993), 7.

36. Author's interview with Porfirio Muñoz Ledo. Mexico, D.F., May 15, 1997.

37. Andrés Oppenheimer, *Bordering on Chaos: Guerrillas, Stockbrokers, Politicians, and Mexico's Road to Prosperity* (Toronto, Canada: Little, Brown & Co., 1996), 87–88.

38. Pedro Pérez, "Del neoliberalismo al neoclientelismo: Cambio económico y transformación política en México in Joan Alcázar and Nuria Tabanera," *Historia y presente en América Latina* (Valencia: Bancaixa, Fundación, 1996), 86.

39. A study of this electoral process can be found in Leonardo Curzio, "Las elecciones de 1995 en Tabasco o al comedia de las equivocaciones," in *El Cotidiano, UAM*, No. 60, 1995.

40. López Obrador refuses to reveal how he received the controversial boxes. In his latest book, he leaves the subject in the dark, suggesting that the boxes arrived anonymously. Andrés Manuel López Obrador, *Entre la historia y la esperanza. Corrupción y lucha democrática en Tabasco* (Mexico City: Grijalbo, 1995).

41. The complaint was also filed against former governor Manuel Gurría Ordoñez and leaders of the PRI State Directorate.

42. Those cited were: Hugo Alejandro Zuñiga Rojas (Director of Administration at CDE), Oscar Saenz Jurado (Secretary of Finance), Floricel Medina Pérez Nieto (Coordinator of the Vote Promotion Program), Angel Augusto Buendía Tirado (Coordinator of Roberto Madrazo's campaign), Feliciano Calzada Padrón (Secretary General of CDE of PRI), Carlos Alejandro Martínez Santiago (Permanent Program in Defense of the Vote), Jesús Alamilla Padrón (Administrative Coordinator of the program), and Pedro Jiménez León (Secretary of Organization and President of the CE of PRI Tabasco).

43. In other documents he appears with the name William. *El caso Tabasco* (Mexico City: Barra Nacional de Abogados, 1997), 13.

44. Procuraduría General de la República, "Boletín de Prensa número 536/96," Mexico, D.F., June 6, 1996.

45. See the report by Puig about Carlos Cabal in *Proceso*, No. 932, September 12, 1994, 6–14.

46. Roberto Madrazo, "Precisiones," *El Financiero*, June 18, 1996, 46.

47. *Proceso*, No. 971 (June 12, 1995), 21.

48. Statements of Javier Nuñez López, legal advisor of CODEHUTAB. *La Jornada*, June 14, 1995, 11.

49. *La Jornada*, June 10, 1995, 3.

50. The reason he was removed from his post was "that an investigative commission of the management agency (organismo patronal) proved that Madrazo Cadena had benefited from PRI funds during the campaign of his relative." *Proceso*, No. 982 (August 28, 1995), 30.

51. *La Jornada*, August 26, 1995, 6.

52. German Dehesa, "Gaceta del ángel," *Reforma*, June 13, 1995.

53. *Crónica*, July 16, 1996, 9.

54. *Crónica*, September 22, 1997, 12.

55. Two of the most important political concessions made to advance the negotiations on political reform were the resignation of the governor of Chiapas, Eduardo Villaseñor, and the reversal, through political negotiation, of the triumph of the Priista mayor in Huejotzingo, Puebla.

56. See Article 49 of the *Código Federal de Instituciones y Procedimientos electorales* (Mexico City: IFE, 1996).

57. See Article 41, *Constitución Política de los Estados Unidos Mexicanos.*

58. The development of the constitutional debate is outlined in José Barragan, "Democracia: financiamiento a partidos," in *Crónica Legislativa*, Organo de Información de la LVI Legislatura, Cámara de diputados, No. 14, April–May 1997, 11–20.

59. See Article 49, Part V., *Código Federal de Instituciones y Procedimientos electorales* (Mexico City: IFE, 1996).

60. IFE, *Proceso electoral federal 1997. Información básica.*

61. Statement of November 16, 1996, at the closing of the National Industrialists Convention (Convención Nacional de Industriales). El Gobierno de México, *Crónica Mensual*, No. 24, November 1996, 48.

62. Author's interview with Porfirio Muñoz Ledo, May 15, 1997.

63. *Proceso*, No. 965 (May 1, 1995).

64. *Proceso*, No. 966 (May 8, 1995).

65. Peter A. Lupsha, "Transnational Narco-corruption and Narco-investment: A focus on Mexico," at the website: http://www.pbs.org/wgbh/pages/frontline/shows/mexico/readings/lupsha.html, Spring 1995.

66. National Defense University, *Strategic Assessment 1997*, Washington, D.C., 201.

Chapter 5: Scope and Limits of an Act of Good Faith: The PAN's Experience at the Head of the Office of the Attorney General of the Republic

1. I refer to the murders of Cardinal Posadas, Luis Donaldo Colosio, and José Francisco Ruiz Massieu. During President Carlos Salinas de Gortari's six-year term, the chronological order of attorneys general was: Enrique Alvarez del Castillo, Ignacio Morales Lechuga, Dr. Jorge Carpizo, Dr. Diego Valadez, Humberto Benítez Treviño.

2. Although beyond the scope of this chapter, four extradition requests were brought against Mario Ruiz Massieu, none of which were deemed admissible on the part of the United States. Mario Ruiz Massieu committed suicide in early 2000. The U.S. Department of Justice sought to investigate him for the crime of money laundering. Additional proceedings were instituted in Mexico for drug trafficking as a result of declarations made by the ex-director of the Federal Judicial Police, Adrian Carrera.

3. Samuel González, Ernesto López Portillo, and Arturo Yáñez, *Seguridad Pública en México: problemas, perspectivas y propuestas* (Mexico City: UNAM, Serie Justicia, 1994), 17.

4. That is, a police officer would obey his superior, regardless of the legality of an order, with the understanding that he would not be held accountable. Antonio F. Lozano, *Compromisos con la Justicia, Informe de Gestión de Fernando Antonio Lozano Gracia, Procurador General de la República* (Mexico City: Epessa, S.A. de C.V., 1998), 3.

5. Carpizo encountered an institution in an advanced state of internal decomposition for which the passing of laws and regulations was not enough. Most of the changes he made focused on two areas: electoral offenses, and the creation of new areas within the structure of the PGR. As discussed below, the main result was to concentrate the operating power of the Federal Judicial Police under a single command but without real internal supervisory balances or efficient coordination of resources.

6. Speech by Ernesto Zedillo as president-elect of the Institutional Revolutionary Party in Guadalajara, Jal., July 14, 1994.

7. Antonio F. Lozano, *Compromisos con la Justicia*, 70.

8. Diego Fernández de Cevallos, interview, *Proceso*, July 9, 1995.

9. Antonio F. Lozano, *Compromisos con la Justicia*, 70.

10. A clear example was the continual references to Lozano as "the PAN Attorney General," which politicized law enforcement.

11. President Zedillo's state of the union address, September 1, 1995.

12. *Proceso*, July 16, 1995.

13. President Salinas's brother was accused on February 28, 1995 of plotting the assassination of his ex-brother-in-law, José Francisco Ruiz Massieu. As the investigation progressed he was also charged with illicit enrichment, money laundering, and even the murder of Muñoz Rocha, a key actor in the death of José Francisco Ruiz Massieu. As of late 1998 he was being held in Almoloya (a high-security prison) only for murder. The other charges were gradually rejected by the judge owing to lack of evidence on the part of the PGR.

14. "December error" refers to a mishandled devaluation of the peso that resulted in a major financial crisis. Mexico has no extradition treaty with the Irish government, so if Salinas were found guilty, any future attempt to extradite him would be very difficult. Furthermore, it has always been denied that there is any investigation under way against him.

15. *Constitución Política de los Estados Unidos Mexicanos, Colección Jurídica* (Mexico City: Esfinge, 1997).

16. Published in the *Gaceta Oficial de la Federación* on August 30, 1934. Amended most recently, according to the 52nd edition of Colección Porrúa, by decrees published on January 10 and July 22, 1994, May 13 and November 7, 1996.

17. Mexico: *Federal Code of Penal Proceedings* (CFPP), Colección Porrúa (1997), Preliminary Title.

18. CFPP, 1997, Article 2, Preliminary Title.

19. CFPP, 1997, 17.

20. González et al., *Seguridad Pública*, 100.

21. Mexico: "Organic Law of the PGR," Article 17, *Gaceta Oficial*, 1993.

22. "Regulations for the Career of Agent of the Federal Public Prosecutor's Office," *Gaceta Oficial*, May 18, 1993; González et al., *Seguridad Pública*, 100.

23. *Gaceta Oficial*, April 11, 1996. The INACIPE had been dissolved three years previously owing to differences between academics and politicians of the Institute of Juridical Research regarding its management. As of 1993, the Training Institute took over the responsibility of promoting generations of agents and public prosecutors, thus overloading its operation and efficiency.

24. As of late 1998, the average monthly wage for an MP agent was around US$850, and for Federal Judicial Police officers, around US$750.

25. *Gaceta Oficial*, May 10, 1996.

26. *Gaceta Oficial*, November 7, 1996.

27. Lozano, *Compromisas con la Justica*, 39–50, chapters 2 and 5.

28. "Organic Law of the Office of the Attorney General of the Republic," published in the *Gaceta Oficial*, May 10, 1996, and "Regulations of the Organic Law of the Office of the Attorney General of the Republic," August 27, 1996.

29. According to a published survey, 60% of those surveyed had more confidence in the military and 70% considered the judicial police to be more corrupt. *Reforma* (Mexico City), May 3, 1997. These results are not very different from the surveys carried out during Lozano's term of office.

30. For a theoretical discussion of the concept of "Rule of Law," see Guillermo O'Donnell, *Polyarchies and the (Un) Rule of Law in Latin America: The Rule of Law and the Underprivileged in Latin America*. Kellogg Institute for International Studies, Working Paper No. 254, 1998.

31. González et al., *Seguridad Pública*, chapter 4.

32. See the *Gaceta Oficial* for the Organic Law of the Office of the Attorney General of the Republic and its regulations, and the evolution of its amendments from 1985 to 1994.

33. Toward the end of the Salinas administration, the principal deputy attorney general was Mario Ruiz Massieu, who subsequently fled to the United States. The PGR initiated a fifth charge against him after an ex-subordinate of his, Commander Adrian Carrera, former head of the Federal Judicial Police, joined a plea-bargain program under the Federal Law Against Organized Crime and declared, as reported in the press, that he turned over drug trafficking money to his boss, the general deputy attorney general. Adrian Carrera faced charges of money laundering, whereas an investigation was opened against Mario Ruiz Massieu concerning drug trafficking.

34. Deputy attorney general's office "A" is in charge of the state delegations of Aguascalientes, Campeche, Durango, the Federal District, Guerrero, Morelos, Nuevo León, Sonora, State of Mexico, and Veracruz. "B" is in charge of the state delegations of Baja California Sur, Chihuahua, Colima, Guanajuato, Hidalgo, Jalisco, Oaxaca, Tabasco, Tamaulipas, Yucatán, and Zacatecas. "C" directs the state delegations of Baja California, Chiapas, Coahuila, Michoacán, Nayarit, Puebla, Querétaro, Quintana Roo, San Luis Potosí, Sinaloa, and Tlaxcala.

35. PGR, "Las 29 preguntas."

36. *Gaceta Oficial*, May 10, 1996, article 27, section I.

37. The department carried out random tests on 1,422 public servants, with the following results: 92 employees tested positive, among them some 20 agents of the Public Prosecutor's Office. One year earlier 63 positive cases had been detected, 34 of which were PJF officers. *Excelsior*, August 5, 1996.

38. The Deputy Attorney General's Office for Juridical Affairs has a General Directorate of International Legal Affairs which, in addition to coordinating with the Ministry of Foreign Affairs, is in charge of implementing international efforts and commitments to which Mexico adheres in the fight against organized crime and drug trafficking. To that end, in accordance with Article 50 of the Regulations of the Organic Law of the PGR, published in the *Gaceta Oficial* on August 27, 1996, there are currently attachés' offices at border points between Mexico and the United States. There is also a representation in Madrid, Spain, to deal with affairs in that region.

39. For example, disputes among states, or between states and the federal government. Constitución Política de los Estados Unidos Mexicanos, Articles 102 and 105.

40. As of April 30, 1997, Attorney General Jorge Madrazo dissolved the INCD and created the Special Public Prosecutor's Office for Attention to Health Crimes (FEADS). *Gaceta Oficial*, April 30, 1997. However, we refer to this Institute because under the direction of Commissioner Francisco Molina, the restructuring and transformation implemented by Madrazo had been envisaged prior to the removal of Attorney General Antonio Lozano.

41. The INCD was created following the assassination of Cardinal Posadas. Prior to this it was the Deputy Attorney General's Office against Drug Trafficking and was headed by Javier Coello Trejo, known as the "Iron Prosecutor."

42. Some of the commissioners of the INCD since its establishment have been: Jorge Carrillo Olea (June 1993–May 1994), Rene Paz Horta (May 1994–March 1996), Francisco

Molina Ruiz (March 1996–December 1996), General Jesús Gutiérrez Rebollo (December 1996–February 1997). In March 1997 Mariano Herran Salvatti took office and in May that year it changed from the Institute to the Special Public Prosecutor's Office.

43. *Gaceta Oficial*, November 7, 1996.

44. There are eleven crimes that the OCU should investigate and prosecute: terrorism, arms trafficking, drug trafficking, money laundering, aliens, body parts trafficking, kidnapping, stolen cars, chemicals precursors, trafficking of minors, and assault. See Article 2 of the Federal Law against Organized Crime.

45. According to an anonymous official, more verification mechanisms are needed. Recently a "super" agent had to be returned to Mexico after he was discovered stealing a pair of tennis shoes. This agent had passed all the exams in Mexico and the United States.

46. The application of lie-detector tests and psychological, financial, and intelligence exams on Prosecutor Mariano Herrán and the attorney general were publicized. However, according to U.S. reports, some staff members have not taken the exams, or have failed them, and continue to collaborate in FEADS. On this last point see GAO *Drug Control: U.S.-Mexican Counternarcotics Efforts Face Difficult Challenges*, June 1998 (GAO/NSIAD-98-154), 16.

47. *Excélsior* (Mexico City), December 10, 1997. President Zedillo announces constitutional amendments to confront insecurity.

48. *Gaceta Oficial*, March 26, 1993.

49. According to the Organic Law of the PGR, Article 23 states that to join and serve as an agent of the Federal Judicial Police, the following is required: full Mexican citizenship; good conduct without legal conviction or formal accusation; no abuse of psychotropic substances, narcotics, or other charges, and no alcohol abuse; and no prior suspensions or dismissals from public service.

50. Article 2 of the Regulations states that "the Federal Judicial Police is a direct auxiliary organ of the Federal Public Prosecutor's Office which acts under the latter's authority and direct command in the prosecution of federal crimes."

51. Axiological examinations attempt to probe values and beliefs. "Regulations for the Career of Federal Judicial Police Officer," Chapter 1, Article 2, *Gaceta Oficial*, March 26, 1993.

52. The creation of the National Public Safety Council in December 1995 sought to expedite this task, but its results are as yet unknown.

53. *Gaceta Oficial*, August 27, 1996. During the administrations prior to the one in question, the training course lasted four months. Lozano extended it to nine months for the first generation, then to one year four months, and finally to one year six months.

54. Constitución Política de los Estados Unidos Mexicanos, Article 16 of the Constitution, Paragraph 5.

55. Members of the army interviewed about the appointment of military officers in the PGR said: "Members of the Army will always respond to their military superior, and to no one else." *La Jornada* (Mexico City), December 8, 1996.

56. See, for example, *Servicio Universal de Noticias* (SUN), "The Military in Sonora, 10% of military-police forces contaminated by drug trafficking," January 27, 1998; SUN, "Soldiers arraigned, SEDENA," January 8, 1998; Carlos Fazio, "Mexico, the case of the narco-general," April 29, 1998, *http://www.worldcom.nl/tni/drogas*, 1–17; Gustavo Castillo, "Twelve members of the army involved with the Juárez Cartel," *La Jornada* (Mexico City), March 13, 1998.

57. The word *polla* describes the accumulation by various police agents and public prosecutors of a particular sum of money to secure an appointment as a police commander or delegate. Most often this occurs for the appointment of commanders of the Federal Judicial Police.

58. SUN, June 16, 1996.

59. *El Universal* (Mexico City), August 21, 1996. Subdelegates are in charge of supervising and controlling judicial police agents in each PGR state field office. They tend to be the first to be the most exposed for collusion with drug traffickers because it is they who coordinate raids and inspections in each state.

60. This was the case in Baja California, Tamaulipas, Sinaloa, and Sonora. For example, in the Tamaulipas delegation, a total of 25 PJF agents tested positive in the anti-doping tests carried out by the army, and they were therefore arrested. In the state of Sinaloa the total number of agents was 27, including some INCD agents. Nonetheless, the reaction of the population was one of fear that the purge would produce a rise in violence and more delinquents on the streets.

61. From October 1995 to August 1996. The GAFE were later replaced because they were corrupt. "The border is militarized," *Reforma* (Mexico City), May 15, 1996.

62. *Excelsior* (Mexico City), September 10, 1996.

63. F. Antonio Lozano, "La Seguridad Pública en América Latina," *Enciclopedia Británica*, 1996.

64. *Gaceta Oficial*, November 7, 1996.

65. *Proceso*, October 30, 1995.

66. Patricia Zugayde, "El enemigo, adentro," *El Universal* (Mexico City), September 11, 1997.

67. See the Mexico City press from January to April 1998, in which a complete account appears of the events related to officials' links to activities such as extortion, kidnapping, and drug trafficking in the state of Morelos. Another interesting example is the collusion between different actors in the so-called maxiproceedings resulting from investigations of the Juárez Cartel.

68. According to specialist Ernesto López Portillo, in a recent radio program broadcast by Radio UNAM, 1998.

69. Organized crime occurs when three or more people carry out, in an ongoing manner or repeatedly, the following offenses: terrorism, health crimes, counterfeiting, money laundering, arms trafficking, trafficking in undocumented migrants, organs, and minors, kidnapping, and vehicle hold-up or robbery.

70. The number of army personnel recently taking courses abroad is larger than that of the police. It seems that the executive has decided that this is the best solution for the moment. From 1983 to 1997, more than 3,000 army personnel were trained. *Reforma* (Mexico City), November 7, 1997.

71. Matilde Pérez, "El Ejercito no debe ser policía," *La Jornada* (Mexico City), April 14, 1996.

72. See a recent opinion poll in which people perceived the army as being less corrupt (4%) and had 60% more trust in it, as opposed to the mistrust expressed for the Federal Judicial Police. *Reforma* (Mexico City), May 3, 1997.

73. Rachel Garst, "The Guatemalan National Civilian Police: A Problematic Beginning," *WOLA* Briefing Series, Washington, D.C., 1997; Rachel Neil, "Police Reforming in Haiti: The Challenge of Demilitarizing Public Order and Establishing the Rule of Law," *WOLA*, November 1996; and "The Colombian National Police, Human Rights, and US Drug Policy," *WOLA*, Washington, D.C., May 1993.

74. This means insistence upon transparency governing the activities carried out not only by attorney general's offices, the judiciary, and the armed forces, but also by the Ministry of the Interior and state governments. In short, accountability requires bringing the actions undertaken by the State in the area of security and intelligence under public scrutiny.

Chapter 6: Containing Armed Groups, Drug Trafficking, and Organized Crime in Mexico: The Role of the Military

1. The term "military" includes the army, navy, and air force. Mexico has two military ministries: the Ministry of Defense (SEDENA), and the Ministry of the Navy—the Navy of Mexico. The army and air force are under SEDENA. In Mexico there are no general headquarters, joint chiefs, or civilian Ministry of Defense. In 1938, the National Revolutionary Party (PNR) became the Party of the Mexican Revolution (PRM), which included a military-corporate branch; in 1946 the PRM became the PRI in order to nominate a civilian for president. The military branch of the PRM disappeared in 1940.

2. Subparagraphs IV, V, VI, and VII of Article 89 of the Constitution of the United Mexican States sets out the military powers of the president, which include the appointment of all military officers and the declaration of war. See Renato de J. Bermúdez, *Compendio de derecho militar mexicano* (Mexico City: Ediciones Porrúa, 1996), 74.

3. President Gustavo Díaz Ordaz, Informe de Gobierno 1969, quoted in Luis Garfías Magaña, "El ejército mexicano actual," in *El ejército mexicano. Historia desde sus origenes hasta nuestros días* (Mexico: Secretariat of Defense, 1979), 526.

4. The legal regulations in force are the Organic Law of the Mexican Army and Air Force (December 26, 1986, version) and the Organic Law of the Mexican Navy (December 24, 1993, version).

5. On the subject of the National Guard, see Bermúdez, *Compendio de derecho militar mexicano*, 76.

6. Plan DN-III, in force since 1966, has three phases: prevention, rescue, and recovery. DN-III is in force daily between July and November (hurricane season). Politically, one of the most controversial times for implementing DN-III was during and after the earthquakes of September 19 and 20, 1985. The president did not declare martial law on that occasion, and rescue efforts were led by civilians (the mayor of Mexico City). Following the 1985 earthquakes, the National System for Civilian Protection was established under the Ministry of the Interior, to which the army, air force, and navy are subordinated. See Gen. Alvaro Vallarta Ceceña, "Plan DN-III-III-E," *Reforma* (Mexico City), October 27, 1997.

7. Alden Cunningham, "Mexico's National Security in the 1980s–1990s," in *The Modern Mexican Military: A Reassessment*, ed. David Ronfeldt (La Jolla, Calif.: Center for U.S. Mexican Studies, 1984), 175.

8. Stephen J. Wager, "The Mexican Army, 1940–1982: The Country Comes First" (Ph.D. diss., Stanford University, 1992), 216.

9. Roderic Ai Camp, *Generals in the Palacio: The Military in Modern Mexico* (New York: Oxford University Press, 1992), 84–85.

10. See José Luis Piñeyro, *Ejército y sociedad en México: pasado y presente* (Mexico City: Universidad Autonoma Metropolitana, 1985), 90–108.

11. Richard B. Craig, "La Campaña Permanente: Mexico's Antidrug Campaign," *Journal of Interamerican Studies and World Affairs* 20, no. 2 (May 1978), pp. 345–63.

12. David Ronfeldt, "The Mexican Army and Political Order since 1940," in *The Modern Mexican Military: A Reassessment*, 69–70.

13. The politicization of the army was maintained owing to the link between the objectives of the Mexican revolution, the state, and the PRI and therefore their identification with those of the army. One of the most influential generals identified the political and historical link of the army by equating "the interests of Mexico" with those of the "Mexican revolution." "If we want our action to have higher goals, if we want to fulfill our mission as protectors of Mexico, we must be true to the purposes that led to the establishment of our army. The Mexican revolution is an inexhaustible source of ideals. If we strongly adhere to them and ensure that its principles are carried out, . . . if we work in this way, our actions will be perfectly moral." Alfonso Corona del Rosal, *Moral militar y civismo* (Mexico City: Secretariat of Defense, 1991), 216–17.

14. In Mexican political opposition literature there is much evidence that the army's work supported the PRI in elections, primarily in rural areas, and also of the family and partnership ties of high-ranking officers with high-level leaders in the PRI. This is logical if one assumes that the Mexican political system is the product of the revolutionary soldiers and developed a corporatist-clientelist system.

15. "In martial institutions, there is an inalterable principle stating that orders given must be followed immediately without question; given this, subordinates must do only

what they are ordered to do by a superior. With this standard of conduct, at no level in the hierarchy is a person authorized to question whether or not an order is to be followed, since subordination requires strict compliance with a command given." Bermúdez, *Compendio de derecho militar mexicano*, 192.

16. See Military Code of Justice, Section 9, chap. 3, "Disobedience," *Código de Justicia Militar*, vol. 1 (Mexico City: Secretariat of Defense, 1984), 109–11.

17. In the 1990s, a debate began on "due obedience" and the violation of the constitution and civil laws, for example, over human rights, as will be examined further on.

18. Bermúdez, *Compendio de derecho militar mexicano*, 86.

19. Wayne A. Cornelius and Ann L. Craig, *The Mexican Political System in Transition* (La Jolla, Calif.: Center for U.S.-Mexican Studies, 1991), 94.

20. This chapter does not intend to examine the army's actions to confront the EZLN in Chiapas. See Raúl Benítez Manaut, "México. El desafío de las guerrillas," *Nueva Sociedad*, no. 130 (March–April 1994), 24–32; Stephen J. Wager and Donald E. Schulz, *The Awakening: The Zapatista Revolt and Its Implications for Civil-Military Relations and the Future of Mexico* (Carlisle Barracks, Pa.: U.S. Army War College, 1994).

21. Raúl Benítez Manaut, "Guerrilla. Civilizarse o morir," *Reforma-Enfoque* (Mexico City), January 5, 1997, 13–14.

22. "Constitution of the United Mexican States" (Mexico City: Federal Electoral Institute, 1996).

23. Ibid., 141.

24. Ernesto Zedillo, *Primer Informe de Gobierno*, Mexico City, September 1, 1995, Office of the President, 98–100.

25. Navy Captain Benjamin Pineda Gómez, *Análisis y prospectiva de los acuerdos bilaterales México-Estados Unidos de América en el ámbito naval* (Graduate thesis for the "Course on Advanced Leadership and National Security," Center for Superior Naval Studies, Secretariat of the Navy, Mexico City, 1996).

26. Since the beginning of the 1980s, authors on both sides of the border have stated that Mexico is nearing chaos. At that time, Mexico was compared to Iran. John Horton, "Mexico, the Way of Iran?" *International Journal of Intelligence and Counterintelligence* 1, no. 2, pp. 21–30; Brian Latell, "Mexico at the Crossroads: The Many Crises of the Political System," in *Hoover Monograph Series*, no. 6 (Stanford: Stanford University, 1986); Jorge G. Castañeda, *México: el futuro en juego* (Mexico City: Joaquín Mortíz-Planeta, 1987).

27. See Blanca Heredia, "Estructura política y reforma económica: el caso de México," and José Antonio Crespo, "PRI: de la hegemonía revolucionaria a la dominación democrática," in *Política y gobierno* 1, no. 1 (January–June 1994), pp. 5–46; 47–77.

28. "Mexico's Dysfunctional Neoliberalism," *North-South Focus* IV, no. 1 (Miami: University of Miami, 1995).

29. Lorenzo Meyer, *Liberalismo autoritario. Las contradicciones del sistema político mexicano* (Mexico City: Océano, 1995), 229, 231.

30. Carlos Fazio, *El tercer vínculo. De la teoría del caos a la teoría de la militarización* (Mex-

ico City: Joaquín Mortíz, 1996); Donald E. Schulz, *Between a Rock and a Hard Place: The United States, Mexico, and the Agony of National Security* (Carlisle Barracks, Pa.: U.S. Army War College, June 24, 1997).

31. Richard Craig maintains that in some states in Mexico, drug trafficking has very deeply penetrated the political elite since the 1980s, such as in Sinaloa, Durango, Chihuahua, Guerrero, Veracruz, and Oaxaca. See Richard Craig, "Mexican Narcotics Traffic: Binational Security Implications," in *The Latin American Narcotics Trade and U.S. National Security*, ed. Donald Mabry (New York: Greenwood Press, 1989), 31.

32. Stephen Morris, *Corrupción y política en el México contemporáneo* (Mexico City: Siglo XXI, 1992).

33. Fernando Escalante, "Sobre el significado político de la corrupción," *Política y gobierno* 1, no. 1.

34. *Strategic Assessment: 1997* (Washington, D.C.: National Defense University, 1997), 71.

35. Max G. Manwaring, ed., *Gray Area Phenomena: Confronting the New World Disorder* (Boulder, Colo.: Westview Press, 1993), xiv.

36. Observatoire géopolitique des drogues, *Atlas mondial des drogues* (Paris: PUF, 1996), 87–96.

37. Yuriy A. Voronin, "The Emerging Criminal State: Economic and Political Aspects of Organized Crime in Russia," in *Transnational Organized Crime* 2, no. 2–3, (Summer/ Autumn 1996).

38. Paul Vanderwood, *Disorder and Progress: Bandits, Police, and Mexican Development* (Lincoln: University of Nebraska Press, 1981), Preface.

39. Federal Executive Branch, *Plan Nacional de Desarrollo 1995–2000* (Mexico City: Secretariat of the Treasury and Public Credit, 1995), 9–10.

40. Carlos Montemayor, *Guerra en el paraíso* (México: Diana, 1991).

41. These modern guerrillas, in pursuit of socialism, first emerged in Chihuahua in 1964. See Jaime López, *Diez años de guerrillas en México* (Mexico City: Posada, 1974), for an extended discussion of the various guerilla forces.

42. Carlos Tello, *La Rebelión de las Cañadas* (Mexico City: Cal y Arena, 1995), 60–85.

43. "Declaración de la Selva Lacandona, 2 de enero de 1994," in *EZLN. Documentos y Comunicados*, vol. 1 (Mexico City: ERA, 1995), 34.

44. "Accords on the indigenous rights and culture arrived at by the EZLN and Federal Government delegations in the first part of the plenary session of the Diálogos de San Andrés Sacamch'en," in *Chiapas*, vol. 2 (Mexico City: Instituto de Investigaciones Económicas, 1996).

45. Luis Hernández Navarro, "Entre la memoria y el olvido: guerrillas, movimiento indígena y reformas legales en la hora del EZLN," in *Chiapas*, vol. 4 (Mexico City: Instituto de Investigaciones Económicas, 1997).

46. Claudia Guerrero, "Una guerra paralela," *Reforma* (Mexico City), December 8, 1997, 4-A.

47. Human Rights Watch/Americas, *Mexico. The New Year Rebellion: Violations of Hu-*

man Rights and Humanitarian Law During the Armed Revolt in Chiapas, vol. 6, no. 3, Washington, March 1, 1994.

48. The most powerful "family" of caciques in Guerrero is that of Rubén Figueroa. In this case, it is difficult to distinguish the power structure through the "families" between Guerrero and Sicily, Italy.

49. La Jornada y Reforma (Mexico City), December 24, 1997.

50. Strategic Assessment: 1997, 74–75.

51. See Paul Henze, "Organized Crime and Drug Linkages"; Charles Frost, "Drug Trafficking, Organized Crime, and Terrorism: The International Cash Connection"; and Sam Sakesian, "Defensive Responses," in Hydra of Carnage. International Linkages of Terrorism. The Witnesses Speak, ed. Uri Ra'anan et al. (Lexington, Mass.: Lexington Books, 1986).

52. Bruce M. Bagley, Myths of Militarization: The Role of the Military in the War on Drugs in the Americas (Miami: North-South Center, 1991).

53. Kate Doyle, "The Militarization of the Drug War in Mexico," Current History 92, no. 571 (February 1993).

54. Gregory F. Treverton, "Narcotics in U.S.-Mexican Relations" in Mexico and the United States: Managing the Relationship, ed. Riordan Roett (Boulder, Colo.: Westview Press, 1988), 220.

55. Samuel del Villar, "The Illicit U.S.-Mexico Drug Market: Failure of Policy and an Alternative," in Mexico and the United States, ed. Riordan Roett.

56. Jorge Chabat, "Seguridad nacional y narcotráfico: vínculos reales e imaginarios," in Política y gobierno 1, no. 1, (January-June 1994), pp. 97–123.

57. William O. Walker III, "After Camarena," in Drug Trafficking in the Americas, ed. Bruce M. Bagley and William O. Walker III (Miami: North-South Center, 1996).

58. Maria Celia Toro, "Drug Trafficking from a National Security Perspective," in Mexico: in Search of Security, ed. Sergio Aguayo and Bruce Bagley (Miami: North-South Center, 1993), 324.

59. Jorge Carrillo Olea, "El control de drogas: situación y perspectiva," La Jornada (Mexico City), October 15, 1993, 23.

60. Ibid.

61. Los Angeles Times, June 7, 1990, A-16.

62. Federal Executive Branch, El control de drogas en México. Programa Nacional 1989–1994. Evaluación y seguimiento (Mexico City: General Attorney Office, February 1993), 11.

63. El control de drogas en México. Programa Nacional 1989–1994. Evaluación y seguimiento, 155.

64. México y Estados Unidos ante el problema de las drogas. Estudio diagnóstico conjunto, Mexico City (Secretariat of Foreign Affairs, May 1997), III.

65. Ibid., 56.

66. El control de drogas en México. Programa Nacional 1989–1994. Evaluación y seguimiento,

155; and Federal Executive Branch, *Segundo Informe de Gobierno*, Mexico City, September 1, 1996, 29.

67. Ibid., Presentation.

68. Ernesto Zedillo and William Clinton, "The Declaration of the Mexican-U.S. Alliance Against Drugs," Weekly Compilation of Presidential Documents, May 12, 1997, 664–65.

69. "Declaración de San José," *Reforma* (Mexico City), May 9, 1997, international page.

70. William Perry, "Good Bridges Make Good Neighbors," in *Joint Force Quarterly* 11 (Spring 1996, Special edition "The Security of the Americas"), 41.

71. Barry R. McCaffrey, "A Former CINC Looks at Latin America," in *Joint Force Quarterly* 11 (Spring 1996, Special edition: "The Security of the Americas"), 41.

72. Schulz, *Between a Rock and a Hard Place*, 6.

73. *Reluctant Recruits: The U.S. Military and the War on Drugs* (Washington, D.C.: Washington Office on Latin America, August 1997), 19.

74. Jorge Luis Sierra, "Hechos en México. Entrenados en Estados Unidos," *Reforma* (Mexico City), November 7, 1997, 4-A.

75. Andrés Oppenheimer, *Bordering on Chaos: Guerillas, Stockbrokers, Politicians, and Mexico's Road to Prosperity* (Boston: Little, Brown and Co., 1996), 298.

76. *U.S.-Mexico Counterdrug Cooperation*, Washington, Office of National Drug Control Strategy, Report to Congress, September 1997 (Washington D.C.), 20. The U.S. Congress stipulates that the delivery of military equipment is for use exclusively in the war on drugs and explicitly prohibits its use in the army's activities against armed groups in Chiapas or Guerrero.

77. Ibid., 18.

78. *Informe de Labores 1996–1997* (Mexico City: SEDENA, September 1997), 10–11.

79. Observatoire géopolitique des drogues, *Atlas mondial des drogues. 1996* (Paris: PUF, 1997), 85–86.

80. Raúl Benítez Manaut, "Narcotráfico: desafios para el ejército," *Novedades*, Mexico City, February 26, 1997.

81. Enrique Cervántes Aguirre, Secretary of Defense, press interview, *Reforma* (Mexico City), November 12, 1997, 4-A.

82. "Entrega el ejército a 34 narcomilitares," *Reforma*, July 28, 1997, 1. Research on inmates in military prisons indicates that in the main prison, located on Military Camp No. 1, there are 402 prisoners, 53 of whom are in for "crimes against health" (drug trafficking), 29 were in the navy and were detained in April 1990 when a large scandal led to the resignation of the Secretary of the Navy. *Reforma* (Mexico City), August 1, 1997.

83. Statements made by the Secretary of the Navy, José Ramón Lorenzo Franco, *Excelsior* (Mexico City), sec. 2, 1.

84. *México y Estados Unidos ante el problema de las drogas. Estudio diagnóstico conjunto*, 121–22.

85. Oppenheimer, *Bordering on Chaos*, 301.

86. *México Social. Indicadores Seleccionados 1985–1986* (Mexico City: BANAMEX, 1987), 315.

87. *Carpeta Informativa. Sistema Nacional de Seguridad Pública*, no. 1 (Mexico City: Sistema Nacional de Seguridad Pública, October 1997), 36.

88. "Informe de la Procuraduría General de Justicia del Distrito Federal," *La Jornada* (Mexico City), December 31, 1997, 53.

89. Ibid.

90. "La violencia en México," *El Cotidiano*, no. 82 (Mexico City: UAM-Azcapotzalco, March–April 1997).

91. There have been over 20 hypotheses on the assassination of Colosio, ranging from a drug trafficking conspiracy to a single assassin—which is the one currently being accepted in the courts. Regarding Ruiz Massieu, the hypotheses state that Manuel Muñoz Rocha, a politician very close to Raúl Salinas de Gortari and linked to the Gulf Cartel, masterminded the assassination. See *Caso Ruíz Massieu. Informe sobre la primera etapa de las investigaciones y resultados*, Mexico City, PGR, November 1994.

92. *Carpeta Informativa. Sistema Nacional de Seguridad Pública*, no. 1 (Mexico City: National Public Security System, October 1997), II.

93. "Acuerdo por el que se crea la Coordinación de Seguridad Pública de la Nación," *Diario Oficial* (Mexico City), April 26, 1994. This unit was established in response to the government being called into question on numerous occasions, beginning with the outbreak of the crisis in Chiapas, but also as public insecurity increased with the assassination of Luis Donaldo Colosio on March 23, 1994, and the kidnapping of Alfredo Harp, one of the richest men in Mexico.

94. "The National Public Security System Bill," September 18, 1995. This bill includes coordination of the different levels (federal, state, municipal), units (military, PGR, state governments), and security systems to prevent inefficiency stemming from the scattering of a large number of security forces.

95. *Diario Oficial de la Federación* (Mexico City), November 7, 1996.

96. "Militarización en 29 estados," *La Jornada* (Mexico City), August 30, 1997.

97. In February 1997, following the Gutiérrez Rebollo scandal, the INCD changed its name to "Special Inspector's Office on Narcotics."

98. My compilation of statistics.

99. In approximately 300 municipalities, which are the smallest and most backwards and basically the indigenous communities, there is no municipal police.

100. *Carpeta Informativa. Sistema Nacional de Seguridad Pública*, no. 1, 31 (Mexico City: Sistema Nacional de Seguridad Pública, October 1997).

101. General Enrique Salgado, *Informe de 100 días de trabajo en la Secretaría de Seguridad Pública (SSP-DDF)*, Mexico City, September 1996.

102. *Reforma* (Mexico City), September 24, 1997.

103. Enrique Cervantes Aguirre, Secretary of Defense, press interview, *Reforma* (Mexico City) November 12, 1997, 4-A.

104. See the complete statement of the Office of the Attorney General in *El Nacional* (Mexico City), 19 November 1997. Also see the statement of General Salgado in the Assembly of Representatives of the Federal District of September 23, 1997. See *Reforma* (Mexico City), September 24, 1997.

105. *Reforma* (Mexico City), November 19, 1997.

106. The official name of the Jaguares is the Special Dissuasion Group. It was dissolved on October 17, 1997. *La Jornada* (Mexico City), October 18, 1997.

107. *Reforma* (Mexico City), sec. B, 1, October 19, 1997.

108. Even the military personnel appointed by Cuauhtemoc Cárdenas in the SSP have experience working in the SSP and other institutions in the country. Retired Lieutenant Colonel Rodolfo Debernardi was appointed to head the SSP, and nine of the ten general directors of the SSP-DDF that he appointed were retired soldiers, including a major general, five brigadier generals, and a lieutenant colonel. Reforma (Mexico City), sec. B, 2-B, December 7, 1997.

109. Luis Rubio, "La inseguridad pública y el Estado," *Reforma* (Mexico City), November 16, 1997, 11-A.

110. Ibid.

111. Fernando del Collado, "El reto de las policías. Seguridad pública, primera caída," *Enfoque-Reforma*, no. 188 (Mexico City), August 17, 1997, 13–14.

112. This is examined in detail in José Luis Piñeyro, "Las fuerzas armadas en la transición política mexicana," *Revista Mexicana de Sociología* 59, no. 1 (January–March 1997), pp. 163–189.

113. Lt. Com. Wayne G. Shear Jr., "The Drug War: Applying the Lessons of Vietnam," *Naval War College Review* (Summer 1994): 110–11.

114. See "¿Rumbo al narcoestado?" *El Financiero*, Special Report (Mexico City), August 17, 1997.

115. Gabriel García Márquez, "Apuntes para un debate nuevo sobre las drogas," *La Jornada* (Mexico City), October 15, 1993; and Gustavo de Greiff Restrepo, "Estrategias para combatir las drogas psicotrópicas. Pros y contras," in *Relaciones de México, América Latina y la Unión Europea*, ed. Patricia Galeana (Mexico City: AMEI-UNAM, 1997).

Chapter 7: The Historical Dynamics of Smuggling in the U.S.-Mexican Border Region, 1550–1998: Reflections on Markets, Cultures, and Bureaucracies

1. Gordon Gaskill, "Smuggler's Paradise," *American Magazine* 143: 4 (April 1947), 32–33, 154–56.

2. For example, see Everett S. Allen, *The Black Ships: Rumrunners of Prohibition* (Boston: Little Brown and Co., 1979); and Allen S. Everest, *Rum Across the Border: The Prohibition Era in Northern New York* (Syracuse, N.Y.: Syracuse University Press, 1978).

3. See Gannett News Service story on Captain James McGovern Jr., in the *El Paso Times*, June 9, 1998. For Allen Lawrence Pope, see David Wise and Thomas B. Ross, *The Invisible*

Government (New York: Random House, 1964), 145–56; and Thomas Powers, *The Man Who Kept the Secrets: Richard Helms and the CIA* (New York: Knopf, 1979), 103.

4. Private communication. Like most historians, I am skeptical of footnotes like this one. However, I do not wish to violate what I consider to be a confidential communication. My source (who is identified in footnote 35 below by his organization and rank) was in a position to have knowledge of what he conveyed to me and, in my judgment, was providing highly accurate information. I was able to verify most of the information he conveyed to me from several independent sources.

5. For example, see Colin M. MacLachlan, *Spain's Empire in the New World: The Role of Ideas in Institutional and Social Change* (Berkeley: University of California Press, 1988), 76–78.

6. For Pike's own account of his adventures, see *An Account of Expeditions to the Sources of the Mississippi and Through the Western Parts of Louisiana, 1810 . . .* (Philadelphia: C. & A. Conrad and Co., 1810). To describe Pike as a spy might seem something of a misnomer. There, of course, was not a U.S. military or civilian organization in the first decade of the nineteenth century that could be identified as an intelligence agency. However, President Thomas Jefferson utilized army personnel (Captains Meriweather Lewis and William Clark), for example, to carry out what could only be called an intelligence gathering and mapping operation. They simply did not utilize that terminology at the time. See also Nathan Miller, *Spying for America: The Hidden History of U.S. Intelligence* (New York: Paragon House, 1989), 66–67; and Frank J. Rafalko, ed., *American Revolution to World War II*, vol. I of *A Counterintelligence Reader* (McLean, Va.: National Counterintelligence Center, 1997), 41.

7. For an excellent description of smuggling along the U.S.-Mexico border during this era, see Jorge A. Hernández, "Trading Across the Border: National Customs Guards in Nuevo Leon," *Southwestern Historical Quarterly* 100:4 (April 1997), 433–50.

8. See Robert Ryall Miller, *Arms Across the Border: United States Aid to Juarez During the French Intervention in Mexico* (Philadelphia: American Philosophical Society, 1973), 7, 32, 38.

9. For an excellent account of Gen. Diaz's successful overthrow of the Lerdo de Tejada administration, see John Mason Hart's *Revolutionary Mexico: The Coming and Process of the Mexican Revolution* (Berkeley: University of California Press, 1987), 120–28.

10. Unfortunately, the Catarino Garza rebellion has yet to find a historian. See Daniel Cosio Villegas et al., *Historia Moderna de Mexico* vol. 4, pt. 2 (Mexico City: Editorial Hermes, 1963), 324–26.

11. Paul Vanderwood has produced a classic account of the Santa Teresa rebellion in northwestern Chihuahua. See *The Power of God Against the Guns of Government: Religious Upheaval in Mexico at the Turn of the Nineteenth Century* (Stanford: Stanford University Press, 1998). For an earlier account by a Mexican scholar, see Francisco R. Almada, *La Rebelión de Tomochi* (Chihuahua: Talleres Linotipográficos del Gobierno del Estado, 1938).

12. The Opium Exclusion Act of 1909, *Statutes at Large*, 35 (Washington: U.S. Government Printing Office, 1909), 275.

13. See the El Paso reports, March–May 1912, Federal Bureau of Investigation, Old Mexi-

can 232, Reel 2, Record Group 65 (Washington, D.C.: National Archives and Records Service). Also see Charles H. Harris III and Louis R. Sadler, *Bastion on the Border: Fort Bliss, 1854–1943* (El Paso, Tex.: U.S. Army Air Defense Artillery Center, 1994), 29–30.

14. Harris and Sadler, *Fort Bliss*, 71–84.

15. Oscar Martinez, *Border Boom Town: Ciudad Juárez Since 1848* (Austin: University of Texas Press, 1978), 64–66.

16. Walter Prescott Webb, *The Texas Rangers: A Century of Frontier Defense*, 2d ed. (Austin: University of Texas Press, 1965), 554–57.

17. Unfortunately, no worthwhile history exists of the U.S. Border Patrol. Typical studies of the Border Patrol include John Myers, *The Border Wardens* (Englewood Cliffs, N.J.: Prentice Hall, 1971).

18. See William O. Walker III, *Drug Control in the Americas* (Albuquerque: University of New Mexico Press, 1981) 11, 81–82, 99–112.

19. Donald W. Baerresen, "Economic Overview," in *Borderlands Sourcebook: A Guide to the Literature on Northern Mexico and the American Southwest*, eds. Ellwyn R. Stoddard, Richard L. Nostrand, and Jonathan P. West (Norman: University of Oklahoma Press, 1983), 122–23. Although now dated, the *Borderlands Sourcebook* remains a useful publication for students of the U.S.-Mexico border.

20. For example, see Stoddard, "Mexican Migration and Illegal Immigration," in *Borderlands Sourcebook*, 204–8. For the bracero program, see Richard B. Craig, *The Bracero Program: Interest Groups and Foreign Policy* (Austin: University of Texas Press, 1971).

21. Karl M. Schmitt, *Mexico and the United States, 1821–1973: Conflict and Coexistence* (New York: John Wiley and Sons, 1974), 219.

22. See C. Daniel Dillman, "Border Urbanization," in *Borderlands Sourcebook*, 237–40.

23. Ibid., 144–52.

24. Schmitt, *Mexico*, 218–19.

25. G. Gordon Liddy, *The Autobigraphy of G. Gordon Liddy*, 2d ed. (New York: St. Martin's Press, 1980), 133–35.

26. This is based on my personal knowledge (for example, if one wished to clear the Mexican *aduana* at a small port of entry quickly in the 1970s and 1980s, placing a couple of dollar bills inside one's passport always speeded up the process).

27. Personal observation; on a number of occasions I had lunch with Mexican customs and municipal officials, often in the company of U.S. customs officials. Regrettably, the restaurant is currently closed for reasons that are too lengthy to describe here.

28. Personal knowledge.

29. Ibid.

30. Ibid.

31. This point vis-à-vis quid pro quo was implicitly emphasized to me by a number of U.S. customs officials.

32. The Bell UH-1 was the workhorse helicopter of the U.S. Army during most of the Vietnam War. In the latter stages of the war, the so-called Huey Cobra, a variant of the UH-l,

replaced it. The helicopter referred to here was a UH-1 with a variety of electronics installed.

33. This particular anecdote was told to me by the Customs Agency Service investigator who was responsible for retrieving the helicopter from Mexico. The story was confirmed by several other U.S. government officials. Although the individual has been retired for a number of years, I have chosen not to further identify him.

34. Beyond identifying the source as a senior Texas Ranger captain (see footnote 4 above), I am unwilling to further identify the officer in question. The time frame is the late 1970s and the location of my interview was Austin, Texas. Although the precise date of the interview is known, using it would further identify the source.

35. This footnote and subsequent ones are my personal opinion. These statements are derived from approximately a quarter of a century worth of research on the U.S.-Mexican border. For the record, I served as the state of New Mexico's representative on the District Director, U.S. Customs, El Paso, advisory board for several years. In addition, during the past two decades I interviewed dozens of U.S. customs officials from Brownsville to San Diego at ranks from inspector to regional commissioner and up. In addition, I have interviewed customs brokers, Mexican *administradores de aduana* at a variety of ports, and various *presidentes municipales.* A number of senior U.S. customs officials (now retired) who no longer feel constrained about revealing problems were interviewed. A number of congressional staffers and several congressmen and two U.S. senators discussed border problems with me during this time frame. A decade ago I organized for the governor of New Mexico (the host governor) the December 1987 U.S.-Mexico Border Governors Conference, which was attended by governors of the states of California, Texas, Arizona, and New Mexico along with the governors of the six Mexican border states, the U.S. ambassador to Mexico, and the Mexican Ambassador to the United States, as well as a variety of other Mexican and U.S. diplomatic personnel.

36. See footnote 35 above. These statements are my personal opinions. They are derived from discussions with U.S. customs officials, congressional staffers, and a variety of U.S. diplomats (including several who had retired) who had Mexican responsibilities during the past quarter century.

37. For example, see Richard B. Craig, "Illegal Drug Traffic," in *Borderlands Sourcebook,* 209–13. For an analysis of the DEA takeover, see Patricia Rachal, *Federal Narcotics Enforcement: Reorganization and Reform* (Boston: Auburn House Publishing Co., 1982).

38. This statement is derived from discussions with both Mexican and U.S. law enforcement officials over an extended period of time.

39. For example, see Dillman, "Border Urbanization," in *Borderlands Sourcebook,* 238–40, 242.

40. Ibid. The growth in population of the small border town of Palomas is derived from my own research.

41. Dillman, "Border Urbanization," in *Borderlands Sourcebook,* 239–40.

42. Ibid., 239.

43. See the 1982 Universal Pictures film, *The Border,* which was filmed in El Paso.

44. This is derived from my own observation. In one notorious case, a port director who had been a port director in Alaska and knew absolutely nothing about Mexico—had never been based on the border—and spoke not a word of Spanish was assigned as the district director in Laredo, the busiest commercial port on the entire border. He was a disaster. See, for example, *The Economist*, February 28, 1998, 32.

45. For details on corruption in U.S. customs on the southern border, see an outstanding series in the *Albuquerque Journal*, October 22–24, 1995, by the journal's chief investigative reporter, Mike Gallagher.

46. See Donald Baerresen, "Economic Overview," in *Borderlands Sourcebook*, 121–24.

47. As described in the text, this anecdote is derived from my conversations with a U.S. Customs Air Support pilot (tragically now deceased) with whom I flew on a number of occasions along the U.S.-Mexico border. I was able to confirm the story from other customs investigators.

48. Unfortunately, The Popular department store of El Paso shuttered its doors in 1997, in significant part because of the peso devaluation of the 1990s.

49. This account is derived from a native Chihuahuanese who is a distinguished Mexican historian. The method described was the one utilized by the historian's mother and aunt for decades when they shopped in El Paso. I have redundant confirmation from ranking U.S. customs officials

50. Ibid.

51. This statement is supported by personal observations made over a two-decade time span, particularly along the Texas border.

52. See Baerresen, "Economic Overview," *Borderland Sourcebook*, 124; conclusions of the author.

53. For a good contemporary description of the Lopez Portillo administration and the beginning years of the de la Madrid administration, see Alan Riding, *Distant Neighbors: A Portrait of the Mexicans* (New York: Knopf, 1984), 210–22.

54. Perhaps the best description of the importance of Mexico joining GATT is found in Sidney Weintraub's *A Marriage of Convenience: Relations Between the United States and Mexico* (New York: Oxford University Press/Twentieth Century Fund, 1990), 69–93.

55. Personal conclusions.

56. Telephone interview with Mike Gallagher, *Albuquerque Journal*, July 8, 1998; personal conclusions.

57. See Tracey Eaton, Havana, Cuba, dateline as it appeared in *Albuquerque Journal*, June 17, 1988.

Chapter 8: Organized Crime and Democratic Governability at the U.S.-Mexico Border: Border Zone Dynamics

1. Alan Riding, *Distant Neighbors, A Portrait of the Mexicans* (New York: Alfred A. Knopf, 1984; reprint, New York: Vintage Books Edition, 1989), xi.

2. Serge Antoni and Daniel Ripoll, *El combate contra el crimen organizado en Francia y en la Unión Europea* (Mexico, D.F.: PGR, 1990); and Procuraduría General de la República (Attorney General's Office), *La lucha contra el crimen organizado: la experiencia de Geovanni Falcone* (Mexico, D.F.: PGR, 1995).

3. Mario Puzo, *Salvatore Guiliano. El Siciliano* (Mexico, D.F.: Editorial Grijalvo, 1984).

4. High Level Contact Group, *México y Estados Unidos ante el problema de las drogas: Estudio-diagnóstico conjunto* (Mexico and the United States with Regard to the Drug Problem: A Joint Diagnostic Study: Mexico D.F., 1997).

5. Federal Bureau of Investigation (FBI), File information (United States: FBI, 1996).

6. Policía Nacional de Colombia (Colombian National Police), File information (Bogota, Colombia: Policía Nacional de Colombia, 1996).

7. Instituto Nacional para el Combate a las Drogas (National Institute to Combat Drugs), File information (Mexico: PGR, 1996).

8. The estimate is based on DEA reports. The DEA has stated that the three most powerful criminal organizations of the past ten years—the well-known Pacific cartel (the Arellano brothers), the Juárez cartel (Amado Carrillo), and the Gulf cartel (Juan García Abrego)—engaged in intense competition to introduce cocaine to the United States. There are two sources, one documented and the other oral (both in the author's possession), stating that, on one hand, Juan García Abrego, one year before his persecution and arrest, introduced around 60 tons of cocaine to the United States, and that, on the other hand, the Arellano brothers, before the so-called "war of the cartels," introduced between 1 and 1.5 tons per week into the California area. While neither refers directly to Amado Carrillo, intense competition led DEA officials to conclude that his was an equally powerful cartel.

9. Susan Rose-Ackerman, *Corruption and Government: Causes, Consequences and Cures.* (New York: Cambridge University Press, 1999). See especially chapter 11, pp. 198–223.

10. The information concerning arms trafficking is contained in the joint diagnostic study produced by the Mexico-U.S. High Level Contact Group, *México y Estados Unidos ante el problema de las drogas* (Mexico: Grupo de Contacto de Alto Nivel, 1997), 133. It refers to chapter 5, "Tráfico Ilícito de Armas Entre los Dos Países."

11. Informal conversations with officials of the US Drug Enforcement Agency (DEA).

Chapter 9: Mexican Drug Syndicates in California

1. Drug Enforcement Administration (hereafter DEA), "The Early Years," *Drug Enforcement* (December 1980), 26–65; *Report,* Subcommittee on Narcotics Trafficking, California Senate Committee on Judiciary, July 14, 1976. Also, interviews with various narcotics agents who wish to remain anonymous.

2. DEA, "The Early Years."

3. The following paragraphs draw on DEA, "The Early Years."

4. Interviews with Bureau of Narcotics Enforcement agents in San Diego, Los Angeles, San Jose, and Sacramento, California, 1974–1988.

5. Ibid.

6. Elias Castillo, "Powerful Heroin Fuels Fears of Mexican Drug Rings," *San Jose News*, September 16, 1982, 1B; "Heroin Deaths," Associated Press, August 26, 1986 (Internet edition).

7. Interview with Henry Lopez, acting Bureau Chief, Bureau of Narcotics Enforcement, San Jose, California, May 1979.

8. Ibid.

9. DEA, "The Early Years."

10. Interview with anonymous narcotics agents, June 1980.

11. Interview with Don Meyers, Western States Information Network, Sacramento, California, June 24, 1997.

12. Remarks by Donnie Marshall, Chief of Operations, DEA, before the House Judiciary Committee, Subcommittee on Immigration and Claims, regarding Border Security and Alien Smuggling, April 23, 1997, 7; interview with members of San Diego Police border team, 1976–1980.

13. Interview with Joseph Doane, Chief, California State Bureau of Narcotics Enforcement, Sacramento, California, June 1997.

14. Interviews with California State Bureau of Narcotics Enforcement agents, San Jose, Sacramento, and Los Angeles, 1979–1986.

15. Interviews with Los Angeles Police gang squad members, Los Angeles, California, 1977–1984.

16. Ibid.

17. Peter A. Lupsha and Kip Schlegal, "The Political Economy of Drug Trafficking: The Herrera Organization (Mexico and the United States)" (Alburquerque, N.M.: Latin American Institute, University of New Mexico, 1980).

18. Interviews with U.S. DEA and California State Bureau of Narcotics Enforcement agents, Los Angeles, San Francisco, San Jose, Sacramento, and Salinas, California, and Washington, D.C., 1976–1984.

19. Ibid.

20. Ibid.

21. Interview with street source, San Jose, 1981.

22. Ibid.

23. Ibid.

24. Interview with Wil Cid, Bureau Chief, California State Bureau of Narcotics Enforcement, Fresno, California, June 13, 1997.

25. DEA, "Mexico, Status in International Drug Trafficking," *DEA Intelligence Bulletin*, April 1997, 1–3.

26. Interview with Wil Cid (see note 24 above).

27. Ibid.

28. Ibid.

29. Interviews with Los Angeles County Sheriff's narcotics detectives, 1977; remarks by Donnie Marshall, 13 (see note 12 above).

30. "Mexican Narcotics Related Killings," Associated Press, September 24, 1997.

31. Interview with California State Bureau of Narcotics Enforcement agent Joe Vasquez, Los Angeles, June 23, 1997.

32. Interview with Wil Cid (see note 24 above); also, remarks by Thomas Constantine, Administrator of the DEA, before the House Subcommittee on the Western Hemisphere House International Relations Committee regarding drug control in the Western Hemisphere, June 6, 1996, 6.

33. Interview with Wil Cid.

34. Ibid.

35. Ibid.

36. Interview with Robert Pennal, Special Agent, Clandestine Laboratory Investigations, California State Bureau of Narcotics Enforcement, Fresno, California, June 24, 1997.

37. Ibid.

38. Ibid.

39. Ibid.

40. *US v. Garibay, C.R.F. 94-5011 OWW*, U.S. District Court, Fresno, California, 1994.

41. This was an unfortunate incident of a U.S. Marine on border patrol who shot and killed a Mexican national. Reuters News Agency, June 24, 1997 (Internet edition).

42. "Investiga la PGR 22 denuncias de la SHCP por lavado; 21 más, concluidas," *La Jornada* (Mexico City), April 16, 1998; "Flood of Stories Spotlight Mexico Drug Laundering," Reuters News Agency, March 20, 1998 (Internet edition).

43. "Flood of Stories Spotlight Mexico Drug Laundering," Reuters News Agency, March 20, 1998.

44. "La mayor amenaza para EU, los narcos mexicanos: FBI," *La Jornada* (Mexico City), January 29, 1998.

Chapter 10: Conclusion

1. "Operation Condor" was a major effort by the Mexican and U.S. governments to eradicate opium poppy cultivation in the "critical triangle" of Sinaloa, Durango, and Chihuahua. "Nothing before or since has so impacted the Mexican drug scene and so pleased the United States." Richard Craig, "U.S. Narcotics Policy toward Mexico: Consequences for the Bilateral Relationship," in Guadalupe Gonzales and Marta Tienda, eds., *The Drug Connection in U.S.-Mexican Relations* (La Jolla: Center for U.S.-Mexican Studies, University of California, San Diego, 1989), 74.

2. A project directed by John Bailey and Jorge Chabat, a researcher at the Center for Economic Research and Teaching (CIDE) in Mexico City, is currently assembling policy-oriented studies on police organizations, courts, intelligence systems, interorganizational and intergovernmental behavior, public education, and public opinion about insecurity in Mexico and the borderlands with the United States.

About the Contributors

SIGRID ARZT served in the Technical Secretariat of former Attorney General Antonio Lozano (1994–1996) and as a research associate at the Center for Research and Teaching Economics (CIDE, Centro de Investigación y Docencia Económicas, A.C.) in Mexico City. In 1998 she was a visiting scholar of the Woodrow Wilson Center and at Georgetown University. Her research focuses on issues of national security in U.S.–Mexican relations. She received a Master's degree in Political Science from the University of Notre Dame and is currently a doctoral candidate in international relations at the University of Miami.

LUIS ASTORGA is a researcher at the Institute for Social Research at the National Autonomous University of Mexico (UNAM). He has written numerous articles and books on sociological and cultural aspects of drug trafficking in Mexico. Dr. Astorga received his Ph.D. in Sociology from the University of Paris in 1982.

JOHN BAILEY is Professor of Government and Director of the Mexico Project at Georgetown University, where he has taught since 1970. He has written a book and numerous articles on Mexican politics and policy making and co-edited a volume on U.S.–Mexican security issues in the post–Cold War era. He directed the Mexico Seminar at the U.S. State Department's Foreign Service Institute in 1980–91. He received a Ph.D. in Political Science from the University of Wisconsin–Madison.

RAÚL BENÍTEZ MANAUT is researcher at the Center for Multidisciplinary Research in Sciences and Humanities at the National Autonomous University of Mexico (UNAM). He was a fellow of the Latin American Program of the Woodrow Wilson International Center for Scholars in 1998 and is a member of the Peace and Security in the Americas Program. Dr. Benítez has published numerous books, essays, and articles on peace processes, geopolitics, armed forces, and Mexico's national security. He received a Ph.D. in Latin American studies from UNAM.

ELIAS CASTILLO is a journalist who now works with Linkage International Consulting. He has written extensive analyses regarding Mexican economics and politics that have appeared in outlets throughout the United States. He has won numerous journalism awards, including three Pulitzer Prize nominations. He has lectured widely on Mexico and has taught journalism courses at San Jose State University (SJSU), where he also did undergraduate and graduate work.

LEONARDO CURZIO GUTIERREZ teaches at the Faculty of Political Science at the National Autonomous University of Mexico (UNAM) and is visiting professor in the Contemporary History Program at the University of Valencia. He is author of various books and articles. In addition, he is a research associate in the Center for Multidisciplinary Research in Science and Humanities at UNAM. He holds a Ph.D. in history from the University of Valencia.

ROY GODSON is Professor of Government at Georgetown University and directs the National Strategy Information Center in Washington, D.C. He has published extensively on issues of trans-state relations, security studies, and strategic approaches to countering transnational organized crime. He has served as a consultant to the United Nations and the U.S. and other governments and is currently developing societal/cultural approaches to complement law enforcement and regulatory approaches to preventing crime and corruption. He holds a Ph.D. from Columbia University.

FRANCISCO JAVIER MOLINA RUIZ served as a Senator (National Action Party) in Mexico's Federal Congress and Chairman of the Senate's Oversight Committee on Public Security. He is former Commissioner of the National Institute for the Fight against Drugs and a member of the High Level Contact Group for Drug Enforcement. Mr. Molina received his law and M.B.A. degrees from the Autonomous University of Chihuahua.

STANLEY PIMENTEL is a former FBI Legal Attaché in the U.S. Embassy in Mexico City where he was responsible for managing the Bureau's largest overseas office. His thirty-year career with the Bureau included several tours in Latin America. Among his service awards, he received the FBI Director's Award for Outstanding Investigation. Mr. Pimentel holds a Master's degree in criminal justice from the Inter-American University in San Juan, Puerto Rico.

LOUIS SADLER is a specialist on the U.S.–Mexico border and the department head of the Department of History at New Mexico State University. Dr. Sadler is a former chairman of the New Mexico Border Commission. He has also chaired the Governor's Commission on Integrity and Accountability in Government and served for more than a decade (1978–1989) as the director of the Joint Border Research Institute at New Mexico State University. Dr. Sadler received his Ph.D. at the University of South Carolina.

PETER UNSINGER is Professor of Criminal Justice at San Jose State University. He has written numerous books and articles on arms trafficking, law enforcement, and illegal maritime immigration and has taught courses on organized crime, white collar crime, intelligence, terrorism, and management. A former police officer, Dr. Unsinger has traveled extensively in training missions to Australia, Taiwan, Brunei, Korea, and Singapore. He received his Ph.D. in political science from the University of Idaho.

Index